Their Stories, Our Stories

Their Stories, Our Stories

Women of the Bible

❖

Rose Sallberg Kam

❖

Continuum ◆ New York

1998

The Continuum Publishing Company
370 Lexington Avenue, New York, NY 10017

Printed in the United States of America

Library of Congress Cataloging-in-Publication Data

Kam, Rose.
    Their stories, our stories : women of the Bible / Rose Sallberg
Kam.
        p.   cm.
    Includes bibliographical references and index.
    ISBN 0-8264-0804-4 (alk. paper)
    1. Women in the Bible.   2. Bible—Feminist criticism.   I. Title.
BS575.K36 1995
220.9'2'082—dc20   94-42559
                                                              CIP

❖

In honor of my independence-minded mother,
Margaret Rose Sallberg (born 1909);

and

in memory of a woman of the Gospel,
Sister Nora Lowe, IBVM (1921–1993).

Let their works bring them honor.

Prov 31:31

Acknowledgments

I am indebted to my husband, Sanford Y. K. Kam, for his unfailing support; to my friend, Deborah Dashow Ruth, for her editing of early chapters; to Frank Oveis of the Continuum Publishing Group for his willingness to take on a new author; to Linda M. Maloney of the Franciscan School of Theology in Berkeley for her critique of the manuscript; and to every member of The Book Club and The Monday Night Group for her enduring interest and encouragement.

Contents

Introduction: Using This Book

Over the years I have wept and laughed, raged and rejoiced, studied and prayed with many other women who remain loyal to a biblical religion. Acutely aware of the anti-woman bias of our churches, we nevertheless refuse to be driven from our spiritual homes. Christians and Jews alike, we identify with the words of feminist writer Alice Bloch: "[B]eing Jewish is an integral part of myself; it's my inheritance, my roots."[1]

As Bloch implies, the religions that oppress us also nourish us; the traditions that bind us also set us free. These paradoxes engage us with special force when we read our scriptures. The Bible unquestionably arises from a patriarchal culture, yet for us the Bible remains a living text, and the wind of Spirit can still knock us breathless with sudden insight.

Ironically, what sometimes gives a passage new relevance is the persistence of male dominance in our own society. Bonnie S. Anderson and Judith P. Zinsser make a similar point in the introduction to their 1988–89 landmark work, *A History of Their Own: Women in Europe from Prehistory to the Present*. The central thesis of their book is "that gender has been the most important factor in shaping the lives of European women. Unlike men, who have been seen as divided by class, nation, or historical era, women have . . . been viewed first as women, a separate category." They go on to point out that many women remain in the historical record only as men's women—the daughters of Priam, the wife and daughters of Lot—and that "women's work," whether in the home or outside the home, "has traditionally been valued less and considered less important than men's work."[2] In biblical terms, women can still recognize themselves in Lev 27:3–7, for example, where their monetary "value" is set at sixty percent that of men.

Today's informed Bible readers are thoroughly aware that the findings of biologists, psychologists, and theologians render patriarchal values and attitudes unscientific, anachronistic, and incompatible with any acceptable concept of God or humanity. Yet paradoxically enough, by questioning the biblical authors' sociocultural biases and seeking fresh interpretations of biblical stories, we find that we can discover insights for our own struggles with patriarchal values.

1. In Susannah Heschel, ed., *On Being a Jewish Feminist: A Reader* (Schrocken Books, 1983), 174. Quoted in Elisabeth Schüssler Fiorenza, "The Will to Choose or Reject: Continuing Our Critical Work," chap. 10 in *Feminist Interpretation of the Bible*, ed. Letty M. Russell (Philadelphia: Westminster Press, 1985), 126.

2. New York: Harper & Row, 1988, I: xv–xvii; repeated in II: xii–xiv.

Purposes and Organization of This Book

This book seeks to help in that quest by presenting the stories of Bible women. Like us they struggled to deal with the inequities of a patriarchal world. Some of them survived by adopting the strategies of the powerless of every historical age: they connived, they manipulated others, they simply endured. But others transcended the limits imposed by their society: they achieved lives of fulfillment, beauty, and grace.

In some chapters, texts distorted in the past are therefore confronted, as in the story of Eve and woman in the Epistles of Paul. In most chapters, strong parallels emerge between today's world and that of the Bible. For example, women whose stepfamilies include other women's children often find Leah and Rachel's story to resemble their own. Women whose suffering has gone misdiagnosed by a patronizing, male-dominated medical profession identify with the woman who suffered from a long-term menstrual discharge, sought help from every sort of doctor, and exhausted her savings in the process. And many stories reveal a God who is neither male nor female, but who surpasses gender—a vastly compassionate Someone especially predisposed in favor of the poor and outcast of society, as in the story of Hagar, or that of the crippled woman cured on the Sabbath.

This book sets the scene for the stories of these women in an opening **Prologue**. The Prologue outlines developments and changes in the Hebrew concept of God, and describes the legal status of women in biblical times. The heart of the book, **Chapters** presenting women's stories, begins with the story of Eve and continues through the Bible to the stories of women of the early church. An **Epilogue** summarizes biblical passages and themes that do, in fact, affirm women. The book ends with two reference sections, a **Bibliography** and a general **Index**.

Organization Within Chapters

The storytelling chapters create an environment that allows readers not to view the author's interpretation as the only way to read a story, but to move back and forth between sections in order to build their own interpretations. Each chapter contains these sections:

Background: Highlights of current scholarship relevant to the story, especially sociocultural or literary information that illuminates problem passages.

Story as Told in (Book): The story of the woman or women as it appears in the Bible, summarized or paraphrased to keep the section to a manageable length and to avoid the necessity for extensive use of brackets to mark alterations of sexist language.

Reflection: Reconstruction of or reflections on parts of the woman's story, modeling one way to interpret the story and connect it with the lives of women of today.

Prayer: A psalm-like prayer the woman herself might have uttered, based on psalms or other biblical passages.

Connections: Questions relating the story to the life of the reader, suitable for use by individuals or by discussion groups.

For Further Reading: A list of readings in addition to Basic References. Chapters rely primarily on Basic References, listed in the first section of the Bibliography, but these readings further explore the story. They appear in sections two and three of the Bibliography.

The women who reviewed the book in manuscript form found that they focused more on **Background** and **Story** when reading an unfamiliar story, and more on **Reflection, Prayer,** and **Connections** when seeking insight into a familiar story. They also reported that even though progression occurs from one chapter to the next, chapters stand as self-contained units and can be read in any order.

Notes on Abbreviations and Terms

Instead of BC (Before Christ) and AD (Anno Domini, in the year of the Lord), this book uses BCE (Before the Common Era) and CE (Common Era). In wide use among scholars, these abbreviations take cognizance of the fact that millions of people find their roots in belief systems other than Christianity.

The abbreviation c. means *circa*—"about" or "approximately." It is used when scholars cannot pinpoint an exact date or time period.

As a rule, texts are quoted from *The Revised English Bible with the Apocrypha* (REB). When a text is quoted from another translation, it is accompanied by NAB for *New American Bible*, NIV for *New International Version*, JB for *Jerusalem Bible*, or NJB for *New Jerusalem Bible*.

Because the terms *Bible* and *Old Testament* imply the acceptance of a *New Testament*, they are not strictly correct in speaking of the Jewish scriptures (the Christian Old Testament). The Jewish scriptures are more properly called *Tanakh*, a word based on the first Hebrew letters of the major divisions: *Torah* (Law), *Nevi'im* (Prophets), and *Ketuvim* (Writings). For convenience and clarity, however, this book uses the more familiar terms throughout: *Old Testament, New Testament,* and—as including both of these divisions—*Bible.*

Prologue: Deities and Women in Biblical Times

Deities of Old Testament Times (c. 1800–400 BCE)

The Old Testament assumes a world in which most people worship multiple gods and goddesses. Although these deities can be placated by sacrifice and approached through reverent treatment of their images, they basically do not care that conflicts of interest among them result in violent upheavals of nature and reversals of human fortunes. In such a world, Hebrew worship of a single god emerges not as a natural evolution of religious thought, but as a startling innovation: it offers no comparably satisfying explanation for natural and human catastrophe. Thus it is surprising neither that the Hebrew people kept reverting to polytheistic ways, nor that they required centuries to refine their concept of a single omnipotent God.

The Old Testament also assumes a patriarchal social system—a Hebrew version of the male-oriented forms of religious and social organization that dominated the ancient Middle East. The origins of patriarchy remain unknown, but it dates at least to 4000 or 3000 BCE. Many scholars of the past fifty years have come to believe, however, that widespread worship of a female deity, lasting twenty millennia or more, preceded patriarchy in Europe and Asia. Called "goddess worship," this earlier system appears to have been accompanied by cooperative forms of social organization and by woman-based rules of descent and inheritance. That a goddess once served as the primary deity is supported both by archaeological findings and by myth and legend.[1] Traces of ancient woman-centered customs surface even in the Bible. The phrase "children of Abraham," for example, refers not to all descendants of Abraham, but only to those descended from his senior wife, Sarah. Nonetheless, by biblical times, goddesses of the Middle East usually served as consorts to male deities—typically gods of war, fire, and storm—who dominated councils or pantheons of deities. Attributes of the various divinities remained relatively constant from one culture to another, but their names differed, and each people regarded its gods as bound to the nation's land.

The earliest Hebrews accepted the existence of other deities, but ranked them as inferior to their god. Their god travelled where they did; their god required no assistance in any area, whether war, weather, or human fertility. They called their deity the "Shield" of Abraham, the "Kinsman" of Isaac, Judge, Savior, or Lord.[2] They also called their god *El* (the generic Semitic

---

1. See pp. 43–59 of Moltmann-Wendel, *A Land Flowing with Milk and Honey*, listed in section two of the Bibliography; and the works by Eisler, Gadon, Gimbutas, and Stone listed in section three.

2. Creator and ruler of the cosmos.

word for God), *El Elyon* (God Most High), or *El Shaddai*—a name variously translated as "God of the [Fruitful] Mountains" (i.e., breasts) or "God Almighty" (a god residing not in a specific mountain, but in spiritual heights). The very ambiguity of the name *El Shaddai* suggests a deity who incorporates the powers both of fiery male war gods and fruitful female fertility goddesses.

Use of the personal name *Yahweh* crystallized only after the Exodus from Egypt (c. 1290 BCE). Based on the verb *to be*, Yahweh is variously rendered "I AM," "The One Who Is," "The One Who Causes All Things to Be," and so on. Yahweh thus suggests Creator, but is ultimately so veiled in mystery as to denote only, "I shall be what I shall be."

None of these names for God implies gender, but Hebrew—like English—is a gender-specific language. Thus a male-dominant society tended to apply masculine pronouns to Yahweh, even while ascribing to Yahweh both feminine and masculine attributes. Deut 32:10–14 and Ex 19:4, for example, compare Yahweh with an eagle who nurtures her young. Moses' words in Num 11:11–12 imply that Yahweh should discipline her children: "How have I displeased you that I am burdened with this people? Am I their mother? Have I brought them into the world, and am I called on to carry them in my arms, like a nurse with a baby, to the land [you] promised. . . ?"

When the Hebrews ended their forty-year desert retreat with Yahweh and entered the land of Canaan, they found themselves surrounded, as in their past, by people who worshipped multiple gods. Many Hebrews succumbed immediately to the attractions of the "old" ways: they "forsook [Yahweh] and served the *baalim* and the *ashtaroth*" (Judg 2:13).[3] Baal, god of war, rain, and annual rebirth, was represented by a phallic symbol, a stone shaft or *massebah*. He was worshipped in "high places" and in specially dedicated temples (1 Kings 18:17–40, 2 Kings 11:18–19, Jer 2:8, Hos 13:1, Zeph 1:4). His followers were so devoted that when a Judge of Israel later tore down an altar of Baal at Yahweh's command, he did it secretly lest he incur reprisals (Judg 6:25–28). Many kings, like Jezebel's husband, Ahab, permitted or patronized Baal worship. Others "remove[d] the sacred pillar of . . . Baal" (2 Kings 3:2).

Asherah, goddess of fertility, was reverenced in the form of small terracotta images that depicted her with a tapering torso similar to a tree trunk. Worshippers also offered her food and drink at wooden pillars (*asherim*) erected "on high mountains or on hills or under every spreading tree" (Deut 12:2; see also 2 Kings 16:4, 17:10–11; Isa 65:7; Jer 2:20, 17:2–3; Ezek 6:13, 20:28; Hos 4:13–14). As late as 586 BCE, when Babylonian forces threatened Jerusalem, belief in a goddess remained a vital force:

> Then all the men . . . and the large crowd of women standing by, indeed
> all of the people . . . answered Jeremiah: "We are not going to listen to

3. *Baalim* is the plural form of the Semitic *ba'al*, meaning "lord" or "master." The Hebrew *ashtaroth* and the equivalent Canaanite *asherah* are variants of "Astarte."

what you tell us in the name of [Yahweh]. We . . . shall burn sacrifices to the queen of heaven and pour drink offerings to her as we used to do, we and our [ancestors] . . . in the towns of Judah and in the streets of Jerusalem. Then we had food in plenty and were content; no disaster touched us. But from the time we left off burning sacrifices to the queen of heaven and pouring drink offerings to her, we have been in great want, and we have fallen victims to sword and famine."

—Jer 44:15–18

It took mass exile from a hard-won homeland and the refining experience of domination by foreign powers to bring Israel to commitment to Yahweh alone. Exile and domination began in 722 BCE when the Assyrians devastated Israel, the northern section of a larger kingdom once forged by King David; it continued in 586 BCE when the Babylonians laid waste to Judah, the southern section. Subsequent conquerors included Persia in the sixth century BCE, Greece in the fourth, and Rome in 63 BCE. Whatever the religions of these civilizations, each, like Israel, was organized according to rules of dominance—society over society, and men over women, children, and slaves.

The Status of Women in Old Testament Times (c. 1800–400 BCE)

The status of Hebrew women in Old Testament times paralleled that of women in neighboring societies. Except for the blood taboo, laws and customs subordinating women derived from two economic concepts common to all ancient patriarchies: women were men's property, and legitimate male succession was a matter of prime importance.

The blood taboo seems to be older than patriarchy. It apparently arose from a belief that living creatures were literally coagulated from mothers' blood. The Old Testament records the belief that blood contains the life force (Gen 9:4; Lev 17:11), and Orthodox Judaism still defines as "born Jewish" someone whose mother is a Jew. Women themselves may initially have encouraged men's awe of the "blood of life" only females could produce. But by biblical times, men of the Middle East had attempted to control this mysterious force. They had declared menstrual blood and menstruating women taboo, less as objects of awe than as contaminants. Hebrew women (like women of neighboring cultures) found themselves quarantined as ritually "unclean" as much as a quarter of their lives: during menstruation (seven days, or as long as the flow lasted), immediately after childbirth (seven days for a boy, fourteen for a girl), and during an additional postnatal purification period of thirty-three days for a son or sixty-six for a daughter (Lev 12:1–5).

Other attitudes toward women arose from economic considerations. As material assets, women were prized for beauty and fertility. Fertility was attributed neither to the woman herself nor to any female deity, but to the God of Israel, who had to open a woman's womb to enable her to conceive. Bearing children (especially sons) became a mark of Yahweh's approval;

barrenness, a social and religious stigma. As her father's property, a girl could be sold into slavery[4] (Ex 21:7–11)—or into marriage. In fact, no verb "to marry" existed in Hebrew: a man "took" a wife—transferred possession of a woman to himself—by paying her father a bride price (Gen 34:12). A man who damaged another man's property by raping a maiden was required to pay her father the bride price and marry the woman (Ex 22:16). The words translated into English as "wife" and "husband" are not even "woman" (*ishshah*) and "man" (*ish*), but "woman" (*ishshah*) and "master" (*ba'al*).

Most Hebrew marriages seem to have been monogamous, but a prosperous man could take more than one wife, especially to ensure having sons (Gen 29:15–30). Ancient levirate laws[5] further specified that if a man died without a son, his brother or nearest male relative was to marry the widow and sire sons who would then legally continue the dead man's line. A man could refuse a levirate marriage, but a widow could not (Deut 25:5–10). Similarly, a woman could not end a marriage, but a man could present his wife with a bill of divorce if he found "something offensive in her" (Deut 24:1). "Something offensive" was usually limited to a major offense, however; and in practice, a man who lightly divorced his wife risked forfeiting the bride price he had paid for her and losing his claim on any property she had brought into the marriage. Further, the marriage contract or *ketuba* still in use among Orthodox Jews dates to the second century BCE. The *ketuba* spelled out the husband's financial obligations in case of divorce, thus granting wives a degree of protection that is not obvious from the Old Testament alone.

Aside from the possibility of divorce, a woman who engaged in sexual misconduct risked severe penalties. An unmarried woman who had sex with any man could be stoned (Deut 22:20–21). Adultery (defined as a betrothed or married woman's having sex with a man not her husband) was punishable by execution of both parties (Deut 22:22–24)—the woman as irreparably depreciated goods, and the man for having inflicted the damage. Again, in practice, there is no evidence that adulterers were ever actually executed. But the story of the woman accused of adultery found in John 8:1–11 demonstrates that the penalty remained on the books into the first century CE, and that some men were not above using it to terrorize women.

In contrast with restrictions on women's sexuality, men's availing themselves of prostitutes was tolerated. Not until about 750 BCE did the prophets regularly begin to inveigh against "harlots" (ordinary prostitutes) and "temple prostitutes" (both women and men engaged in ritual service of Canaanite deities). And even this fulminating may largely have derived from male resentment at the relative freedom a prostitute enjoyed. First, she was

---

4. Slavery implied no particular ignominy, especially when a time limit was stated, since vagaries of weather could impoverish any family and necessitate such a choice.

5. From *levir*, "husband's brother."

economically independent of men. Second, the money she earned could not be used for any religious purpose (Deut 23:18). Already defined as a religious and social outcast, she therefore had nothing more to lose: she could laugh at male authority.

In matters of inheritance, property passed through blood kinship on the man's side, with sons as the first beneficiaries. In early times, daughters had no inheritance rights at all. But thanks to a case initiated and argued in the desert by the five daughters of Zelophehad, it was ruled that daughters could inherit if a man had no son (Num 27:1–11), provided that these propertied daughters then married a man "within a family of their father's tribe" (Num 36:1–12). By late Old Testament times, widows had gained some economic protection from provisions of the *ketuba*, though they enjoyed no right of inheritance. Further, a levirate marriage might be arranged for a widow, or a son might support her. Still, multiple passages on the plight of the widow imply that her economic state was chancy, and that she might become dependent on public charity.

Throughout the ancient Middle East, woman's subordinate status extended into other areas of life as well. In legal cases, her testimony was disallowed. (Hebrews rationalized this particular restriction on the basis of Gen 18:15, "Sarah lied," all Hebrew women being, in theory, Sarah's daughters.) Hebrews sometimes vowed their lives or the lives of their children in service to Yahweh in return for a favor, and in redeeming such a vow, women were rated as being of less value than men. The price for release from a vow was fifty shekels for a man, thirty for a woman; twenty for a boy, ten for a girl; five for a male infant, and three for a female infant (Lev 27:3–7).

Nevertheless, women of Old Testament times were accorded respect, and their duties required skill and intelligence. Besides bearing children and caring for them, women procured fuel and water, took care of the tent or house, and did the milling and baking (although they did not serve male guests or, usually, eat with men). They did the spinning, weaving, and sewing; they helped men plow, sow, reap, and thresh. They also supplemented the family income by serving as wet-nurses, midwives, or child care workers; by growing and selling extra produce; or, like the "good wife" of Prov 31:10–31, by selling their sewing, weaving, and dyeing. Sons as well as daughters were required to obey their mothers in the home (Ex 20:12). Women's songs and dances remained integral to religious festivals (Ex 15:20, Judg 11:34, 1 Sam 18:6, Ps 68:24–25). And most notably of all, the stories of individual Old Testament women reveal them to be dynamic, articulate people who repeatedly tested the official limits of the law.

Deities of Hellenistic Times (c. 400 BCE–100 CE)

The Hellenistic period is so named because Greek or Hellenistic *cultural* influence extended into the Common Era, even though Rome succeeded Greece as the dominant geopolitical power. In matters of religion during

Hellenistic times, male gods continued to head national pantheons in Mediterranean nations. But goddess worship also retained great popularity. The Eleusinian mystery rites were unusual in that any Greek-speaker—male or female, slave or free, native or alien—was welcomed.

Other belief systems included worship of Cybele, the Great Mother, in Asia; devotion to Diana of Ephesus, whose multi-breasted images as a goddess of fertility have been found throughout the Mediterranean; and, in Rome, worship of Ceres or Demeter, in whose fertility mysteries women priests presided over female celebrants. Most popular of all were the rites of the goddess Isis, which arose in Egypt and spread as far as Spain, Germany, Asia Minor, and throughout North Africa. The status of Egyptian women had always remained relatively high, and while Egyptians worshipped many deities, Isis had retained her prestige and had reassimilated the attributes of other gods. In Hellenistic times her many titles included Creator, Thunder God, and Revealer of Mysteries.

Meanwhile, within the small and powerless nation of Israel, association of national identity with Yahweh worship had finally led to the rejection of all other deities. Through centuries of subjugation and reflection, Israel had refined its concept of Yahweh to that of a spiritual, all-powerful deity who was the only true god. Still, writers of this period continued to depict Yahweh in feminine as well as masculine terms. For example, the author of Job 38:8–11 describes the Creator as a woman who gives birth and later sets a child-proof gate to control her rambunctious offspring:

> Who supported the sea at its birth, when it burst in flood from the womb—when I wrapped it in a blanket of cloud and swaddled it in dense fog, when I established its bounds, set its barred doors in place, and said, "Thus far may you come but no farther; here your surging waves must halt"?[6]

Feminization of Yahweh appeared also in the concept of Wisdom.[7] Grammatically feminine in both Greek (*sophia*) and Hebrew (*hokmah*) and personified as a woman, Lady Wisdom approached the status of a second deity, even though her existence was inextricably entwined with that of Yahweh:

> When [Yahweh] set the heavens in place I [Wisdom] was there, when he girdled the ocean with the horizon, when he fixed the canopy of clouds overhead and confined the springs of the deep, when he prescribed limits for the sea. . . . I was at his side . . . .
>
> —Prov 8:27–30

6. Other passages from the periods of exile and Hellenization that depict Yahweh as feminine include Job 38:29–30; Isa 42:14,16, 46:3–5,9, 49:15–16; and Hos 11:1–4.

7. Lady Wisdom most often appears in the books of Proverbs, Ecclesiastes, and Job, as well as in two books accepted as biblical only by Catholics, Sirach and Wisdom.

> Wisdom . . . pervades and permeates all things. Like a fine mist she rises
> from the power of God, a clear effluence from the glory of the
> Almighty. . . . She is but one, yet can do all things; herself unchanging,
> she makes all things new. . . .
>
> —Wis 7:24–29

In the first century of the Common Era, Christian writers extended the
Wisdom tradition. They depicted Jesus both as a teacher of wisdom—"What
is this wisdom he has been given?" (Mk 6:2)—and, through statements of his
existence since the creation, as an incarnation of Lady Wisdom. The Pauline
tradition presents Jesus as "the power of God and the wisdom of God" (1
Cor 1:24), one who was present at creation, existing before anything came to
be (Col 1:15–17). Identification of Jesus with Wisdom is equally clear in Jn
1:1–3, despite the author's use of the grammatically masculine Greek term
logos ("word"): "In the beginning the Word already was. . . . and what God
was, the Word was. He was with God at the beginning, and through him all
things came to be; without him no created thing came into being."

According to the Gospels of Mark and Matthew, Jesus encouraged his
followers to address God with the familiar word "*Abba*." Derived from the
Aramaic word for "father," *abba* meant "dada" on the lips of an infant,
"beloved daddy" on the lips of an adult. (The image is conveyed well by the
character of the father in Jesus' parable of the Lost [Prodigal] Son, Lk
15:11–32.) In keeping with such an image, Jesus also avoided all attitudes of
dominance. He welcomed both women and men into discipleship, and he
taught his followers that whoever "wants to be first . . . must [become] last
of all and servant of all" (Mk 9:35). "Do not call any man on earth
'father,'" he said, "for you have one [*Abba*]. . . . The greatest among you
must be your servant" (Mt 23:9–12).

The challenge of the early Christians was to apply the attitudes of Jesus in
their own community, and texts and inscriptions from the first few centuries
CE imply that at first they met the challenge. By the fourth century CE, however, patterns of dominance absorbed from the outer political environment
had prevailed. Christian sects that practiced gender equality were declared
heretical, their books were denied official status, and the *Abba* of Jesus was re-
institutionalized as an authoritarian deity—a deity whom Christians perceived
far more exclusively as male than Jews had ever perceived Yahweh.

The Status of Women in Hellenistic Times (c. 400 BCE–100 CE)

In the Hellenized world of New Testament and late Old Testament times, the
position of woman varied from place to place. In Greece and Rome, the
strictest patriarchal traditions had begun to weaken by about 400 BCE—those
regarding women as property of men with no rights, no education, and no
role but childbearing. Hellenistic queens held real power in Greece, Syria,

and Egypt; many upper-class women became literate; and although a double standard endured for sexual activity, marriage contracts stated rights and obligations for both spouses. Roman women could mingle with men in the theater or at the games, and they could initiate divorce. By the first century BCE they had also long enough held the right to inherit that the wealth of some women enabled them to exert great political influence. Yet in both Greece and Rome, tension existed between men's patriarchal ideals and new social realities—a tension that caused a backlash of woman-hating literature to appear during this era.

Similar tensions existed within Hebrew society, both in the Jewish homeland and in *diaspora*—the countries where various conquerors had dispersed Jews. It is difficult to get a fix on the exact status of Jewish women during this period, because most of the documents come from late in the period, or even beyond it, from the second to fourth centuries CE. It seems clear, however, that many Jews adopted a degree of Hellenism, especially those living in diaspora in Egypt and other countries distant from Jerusalem. Women acquired wealth and education and played roles in business or politics. Marriage contracts traceable to the second century BCE have already been mentioned, and documents from the first centuries CE depict some Jewish women as initiating divorce.

At the same time, however, in another strand of Judaism, it appears that some male leaders sought to subject women to rules stricter than those of Old Testament times. For example, later writings declare that if a woman appeared in public with her face uncovered, or was seen publicly conversing with any man, her husband could divorce her without paying the settlement specified in their marriage contract. In reality, it is unlikely that such regulations (or the later practice of relegating women to a separate section of the synagogue) were enforced during New Testament and late Old Testament times. In economic life, women could not perform their work and, at the same time, refrain from speaking to men in public. City wives often pursued trades alongside their husbands. Country maidens fetched water from public wells. Country wives served men at table, sold produce from their doors, and worked the fields along with children and men. In religious life, inscriptions from synagogues of the diaspora indicate that women did, in fact, sometimes serve as elders, leaders, and synagogue presidents; and there is a notable lack of literary or architectural evidence for construction of women's galleries in synagogues of the time.

The mixed messages of the Hellenistic era also surface in the Bible. The books of Proverbs and Sirach contain many passages praising women (e.g., Prov 31:10–31; Sir 26:13–18). Both books further depict a good wife as "a gift of Yahweh" or "a crown to her husband" (Prov 12:4, 18:22, 19:14; Sir 26:1–4). Yet during this era, influenced by the misogynistic writers of Greece and Rome, Hebrew writers also begin to ridicule the nagging wife (Prov 19:13,

21:9, 25:24, and 27:15) and to warn young men that women are dangerously seductive (Prov 6:24–26; Sir 9:3–9). The most flagrant example of misogynism is Ben Sira's articulation of a Hebrew version of the Greek myth of Pandora: "Sin began with a woman, and because of her we all die" (Sir 25:16–24).

Ultimately the more restrictive strand of thought prevailed, giving birth to a famous men's prayer. A man thanked Yahweh every morning for not having made him "a Gentile, a slave, or a woman." The comparable woman's prayer? To thank God "for having made me according to thy will." As in the case of Old Testament women, however, women who appear in books written during the Hellenistic Era—Judith, Esther, the women of the New Testament—reveal themselves to be anything but repressed shadows. Judith and Esther rescue the entire Jewish people. Women of the Gospels seize upon the liberating message of Jesus and take charge of their own lives. Although slanted translations have obscured the fact, various Epistles and the Acts of the Apostles suggest that women served in every leadership function known to the infant church—deacon, apostle, eucharistic presider, prophet. And the God of the New Testament, like the God of the Old Testament, repeatedly graces women as well as men with divine favor. The Bible undeniably arises out of a patriarchal culture, and historically it has been used to justify oppression of women. But it offers women liberation as well.

For Further Reading

Anderson, Bonnie S., and Judith P. Zinsser, *A History of Their Own* (1988), I: 3–66.

Brooten, Bernadette J., *Women Leaders in the Ancient Synagogue* (1982), 5–56, 103–35.

Greeley, Andrew M., *Myths of Religion* (1989): *The Jesus Myth* (1971), 71–77, 111–26; *The Sinai Myth* (1972), 175–210; *The Mary Myth* (1977), 389–417.

Jeremias, Joachim, *Jerusalem in the Time of Jesus* (1969), 359–76.

Murphy, Cullen, "Women and the Bible," *The Atlantic Monthly* (August 1993), 63.

Nathanson, Barbara H. Geller, "Toward a Multicultural Ecumenical History of Women in the First Century/ies C.E." in *Searching the Scriptures*, ed. Elisabeth Schüssler Fiorenza (1993), 272–89.

Plaskow, Judith, "Anti-Judaism in Feminist Christian Interpretation" in *Searching the Scriptures*, ed. Elisabeth Schüssler Fiorenza (1993), 126.

Schneiders, Sandra M., *Women and the Word* (1986), 11–15, 20–56.

Setel, T. Drorah, "Prophets and Pornography: Female Sexual Imagery in Hosea" in *Feminist Interpretation of the Bible*, ed. Letty M. Russell (1985), 86–95.

Telushkin, Joseph, *Jewish Literacy* (1991), 47–48, 615–16.

Tetlow, Elizabeth M., *Women and Ministry in the New Testament* (1980), 5–29.

Women of the Old Testament

1 Eve: Woman of the Dawn

Genesis 2:1–5:5

In God's own image created

Background

Eve takes us to a dawn that lies outside human history. Stories about her belong to the literary genre of *myth*—stories set in time-out-of-mind and designed to dramatize beliefs about bedrock issues: How did the world come to be? Where do *we* come from? Who governs the universe? Why do we suffer? The themes are universal, but the conclusions reached and the details of the myths that embody them vary from one culture to another. In ancient Mesopotamia, for example—the Hebrews' earliest homeland—one creation myth held that the lower-class gods, the Igigi, grew tired of taking care of the universe for the seven great gods, the Anunnaki. The Igigi went on strike and war followed. The Anunnaki ultimately triumphed, and resolved the problem by creating humankind to do the work. They shaped the first human beings from clay mixed with the blood and spirit of the slain rebel chief.[1]

In their creation myths, the Hebrews borrowed some elements from Mesopotamia, such as the mix of clay and divine spirit in humankind. But every Hebrew creation account differs strikingly from the myths of their neighbors. The "seven day" account of Gen 1, the Adam and Eve stories of Gen 2–3, the "heavens like a tent cloth" poem of Ps 104, the "Where were you" monologue of Job 38—every one of these accounts features a solitary deity who alone creates the universe.[2] And this same God creates women and men not as slaves, but as creatures shaped in God's own image.

The stories of Eve are better known than the other biblical creation accounts, but their intent is often misread. The first Eve story—God's creating her from a rib—is intended primarily to account for the marriage relationship as the writer knew it. In Israel of his time, the tenth century BCE, woman was dependent upon man. The rib story suggests that dependence.

---

1. From the Atrahasis story. A more detailed summary can be found within the introduction to Genesis in *The New Jerome Biblical Commentary* (1990), 8.

2. Ezek 28:12-17 may allude to yet another Hebrew story of Creation and Fall, even though it is spoken of the King of Tyre. Woman is not mentioned: "In Eden, the garden of God, you were . . . / Blameless . . . / from the day you were created, / Until evil was found in you. . . . / Then I banned you from the mountain of God. . . ."

Yet even so, it also presents woman and man as made of the same substance, and woman as *ezer*, "helper" to man. "Partner" translates *ezer* better, since *ezer* is used in the Old Testament to denote an agent of equal or even superior strength: God is the only other entity to whom the Old Testament applies the word.[3]

The second Eve story, the one involving the serpent and the tree of knowledge, is meant to explain the origin of suffering. Overall, the story attributes suffering—including pain caused by the attempt of human beings of one gender to dominate the other—as arising not from the Creator's original plan but from human choice. In its specific details, the story also warns people of the writer's time to beware of fertility religions. Throughout the Middle East in Old Testament times, fertility goddesses were symbolized by the life-giving earth and by the serpent—the serpent because it lies close to the earth and renews its skin. Even while showing that such deities cause trouble, the writer demotes his snake to a mere mischief-maker. And he demonstrates his God's superiority by showing that Yahweh possesses the power to curse both the serpent and the earth.

Over time, a sense of the Eve stories *as* stories was gradually lost. Eve and Adam came to be treated as historical persons, and rigid orthodoxies were derived from the manner of their making and from their roles in the Fall. Proponents of male superiority began to justify sociocultural structures by claiming that Gen 2–3 depicts woman as inferior in several ways: she is created second, she is created *from* man, she is created *for* man, and she is the first to yield to the blandishments of the serpent. Proponents of these views do not worry about biology or logic. Never mind that in other creation stories the best is saved for last; that all *real* people come from *woman*; that "helper" in Hebrew implies no subservience; or that a truly superior being would hardly yield so easily to a suggestion from an inferior.

The tendency to take the Eve stories literally rather than poetically appears to have begun during the Hellenistic era (c. 400 BCE–100 CE). Earlier books of the Bible allude only to the Gen 1:27 account of the simultaneous creation of human beings, "God created humankind . . . male and female." Passages written during Hellenistic times include the verse from Sirach mentioned in the Prologue, "Sin began with a woman, and because of her we all die" (Sir 25:24). Other allusions appear in New Testament epistles. Paul contrasts Adam with Christ (1 Cor 15:22) and warns Christians not to yield to temptation as Eve did (2 Cor 11:3). A later writer who attributed his work to Paul (an accepted practice of the time) articulated a reading of the Fall story that is used against women to this day: "I do not permit a woman to teach or to have authority over a man; she must be silent. For Adam was

---

3. For example, Ps 46:1 ("a timely *help* in trouble"), Deut 33:26 ("rides the heavens to your *rescue*," JB), and Ps 70:5 ("My *helper*, my savior, Yahweh!" JB).

formed first, then Eve. And Adam was not the one deceived; it was the woman who was deceived and became a sinner" (1 Tim 2:12–14, NIV).

Later Christian theologians expanded upon such texts. Augustine (354–430), for example, declared woman not merely the legal inferior of man (a fact in his world), but also man's biological, mental, and spiritual inferior. Even though ordinary observation and advances in scientific and religious thought have long since discredited such ideas, it seems impossible now to eradicate the habit of taking the Eve stories literally. Under the circumstances, perhaps it is best simply to promote new readings.

Better translations could help, however. For example, the Hebrew word *adam* of Gen 1:27 and the phrase *ha'adam* that runs through Gen 2:7–22 actually imply no gender, as suggested by the English translations "man" and "the man." The word *adam* means "humankind" or "human beings"; the phrase *ha'adam* means "the human creature" or "the earth creature." The writer of the Eve stories switches to the gender-specific words *ish* (man) and *ishshah* (woman) only after Eve appears.[4] A simple change from "the man" to "the earth creature" can show that even the rib story presents gender-differentiated human beings as coming into existence at the same moment, exactly as a different writer presents the creation of humankind in Gen 1:27: "God created human beings in God's own image; in the divine image God created them; male and female God created them."

The Story of Eve as Told in Genesis

The Creation of Human Beings: *A Paraphrase of Gen 2:7, 16–25*

God forms a human creature from the dust of the ground and breathes into its nostrils the breath of life. God tells the creature, "You may eat from any tree in the garden except from the tree of the knowledge of good and evil; the day you eat from that, you are surely doomed to die." Observing that it is not good for the human creature to be alone, God proposes to make it a suitable partner. From the earth God forms all kinds of animals and birds, and brings them to the human creature to see what it will call them. The human creature names the birds and the animals, but no suitable partner is found. God then puts the human creature into a deep sleep. While it sleeps, God takes one of its ribs, closes up the flesh over the space, and builds the rib into a woman. God brings her to the man, and he rejoices: "This one at last is bone from my bones, flesh from my flesh!" That is why a man leaves his father and mother and attaches himself to his wife, and the two become one. Both the man and the woman are naked, but they feel no shame.

---

4. On the language of Gen 2–3, see especially the groundbreaking work of Phyllis Trible of the Union Theological Seminary, cited in the readings at the end of the chapter.

The Fall of Humankind: *A Paraphrase of Gen 3:1–21*

The serpent is the most cunning creature God has made. It approaches the human beings and asks the woman, "Is it true that God has forbidden you to eat from any tree in the garden?" She replies, "We may eat the fruit of any tree in the garden, except for the tree in the middle of the garden. God has forbidden us to eat the fruit of that tree or even to touch it; if we do, we shall die." "Of course you will not die," says the serpent. "God knows that, as soon as you eat it, your eyes will be opened and you will be like God, knowing both good and evil." The woman studies the tree. Its fruit looks tasty, it pleases the eye, and it is desirable for the knowledge it can give. She takes some and eats it. She also gives some to the man, and he eats. Their eyes are opened. Realizing they are naked, they stitch fig leaves into loincloths. When they hear God walking about in the garden at the time of the evening breeze, they hide among the trees. God calls to the man, "Where are you?" He replies, "I was afraid because I was naked, so I hid." God asks him, "Who told you that you were naked? Have you eaten from the tree which I forbade you to eat from?" The man replies, "It was the woman you gave to be with me who gave me fruit from the tree, and I ate it." God says to the woman, "What have you done?" She answers, "It was the serpent who deceived me into eating it."

Then God tells the serpent that because of its actions, it is cursed to crawl on its belly and eat dust all the days of its life. To the woman God says, "I shall give you great labor in childbearing; with labor you will bear children. You will desire your husband, but he will be your master." And to the man God says, "Because you have . . . eaten from the tree which I forbade you, on your account the earth will be cursed." Hereafter the earth will yield thorns and thistles, and man will win his bread only by the sweat of his brow until he dies: "Dust you are, to dust you will return." The man names his wife Eve, which means "mother of all the living." God makes coverings from skins and clothes the man and the woman.

The Children of Adam and Eve: *A Summary of Gen 4:1–5:5*

Adam and Eve have two sons—Cain, a farmer; and Abel, a herdsman. Each offers God the fruits of his work, but God favors Abel. Furiously jealous, Cain murders Abel, and is punished by God with exile. Adam and Eve have "other sons and daughters" before Adam dies at the age of 930.[5]

Reflection

It is impossible to reflect on Eve's story without reflecting, too, on Adam and God—especially God. "Creator" barely begins to list the roles God plays. In

---

5. Age spans like these symbolized the ancient belief that when human beings were closer to their origins, they lived on a grander scale.

this story of Maker and masterwork, God proves to be a fun-loving shaper who is head-over-heels in love with human beings. Playing role after role, God begins as a potter who sculpts a human creature from messy clay and breathes life into its nostrils. Next, as a director, God proposes creation of a companion creature, but builds suspense by first shaping a whole parade of animals. Then God turns anaesthetist and builder, putting the creature to sleep before shaping from its rib the promised partner. God becomes a midwife to bring Eve to birth, and finally, as genial host, God introduces woman and man. (How flattering to Eve, the drama and ingenuity given to her birth!) Much later God acts also as lofty judge and as lowly tanner and seamstress.

As for Eve and Adam, we can only imagine their wonder as they awaken. Instant bonding occurs between them as their Creator first looks on, then fades discreetly into the trees. An indeterminate time passes. Adam and Eve have a job—tending the garden—but their work is far from laborious, and they delight in their kinship with the other earth creatures. Their days resemble a "falling in love" sequence from a romantic movie, when a woman and a man find joy in a word, a glance, the smallest shared activity. For a time, Eve and Adam give no thought to the one tree God forbade to the original human creature that somehow lives on in both of them.

But eventually a lurker-in-the-wings, the serpent, emerges. The serpent could have approached either Adam or Eve, so attuned are they, but it chooses Eve. Was she more attractive? A greater challenge because of her questing intelligence? In any case, she proves a worthy adversary. Like a theologian, she analyzes the serpent's arguments; like a lawyer she enters into debate. When she acts, she acts decisively. She eats the fruit and hands some to Adam, an observer all this time. But Adam also acts; he eats the fruit. In breaking God's harmony as in having enjoyed it, Eve and Adam are one.

And in the "knowledge of evil" the serpent had promoted as so desirable, the first thing Adam and Eve learn is fear. They cannot move fast enough to hide from their Creator. Yet they do not seem to recognize how thoroughly they have shattered the harmony of the garden, how completely they have fragmented their own integrity, until they speak with God. Then their confusion of motivation emerges in rationalizations and mind tricks. Eve hears Adam, her very self, turn on God and on her: "That woman *you* gave me as a partner—*she* gave me the fruit!" And a disillusioned Eve, while managing not to blame God or man, hears herself blaming the serpent.

Everything changes. The Potter's clay is shattered, the paint of the garden-canvas begins to run. God does not so much sentence Eve and Adam as spell out for them what happened the instant they fractured the harmony of creation. From that moment, darkness contends with light in the human spirit. Eve continues to desire oneness with Adam, but he seeks self-respect through a dominance that demeans them both. The once-cherished earth creatures become exploitable objects; the soil resists human efforts to work it. The human body itself becomes a source of dis-ease: Eve and Adam reach frantically toward the concealing pelts in the Creator's hand.

As for the aftermath, the story is given to us only in fragments. We do not really need the details; we are well acquainted with the minutiae of a world where God seems absent, where things go wrong. But with what anguish must Adam and Eve first have watched disharmony extend to their children, the most beautiful things of their own shaping. One son even kills another.

Yet perhaps, even as Adam and Eve experience fatigue and grief and aging, they cling to a memory of the dawn and struggle toward renewed harmony with their Creator. Each time Eve suckles a child, perhaps she glimpses the tenderness with which God formed her. Each time she and Adam solve a problem or shape a thing of beauty, perhaps they catch a spark of God's creative elation. In the end, perhaps they even come to understand what an inexact, messy, exciting business it is, shaping resistant clay. And so might Eve have prayed:

Prayer

> Creator God, how glorious are you in all your works!
> When I study your heavens, the work of your fingers,
> the moon and the stars you have set in place,
> I wonder what we mortals are that you ever bore us in mind.
> Yet you make us little less than gods ourselves;
> you let us bring forth life and shape the way it grows;
> you spread out for us an entire world.
>
> Just as Cain holds forever his place in my heart,
> your love endures even when we stray from you.
> Even if I *could* forget a child of my womb,
> I know that you will never forget us—
> we who are born of you, Mother-Father God.
> Ah, I dance in memory of that dawn moment;
> I marvel at your tender guiding of my faltering steps.
> Let me never forget the touch of your hand,
> that loving palm where forever you hold me.[6]

Connections

1. Since the beginning, motherhood has been seen as a sharing in divine creativity. But people speak also of giving birth to an idea, an object, a

---

6. Based on Ps 8:1, 3–6 and Isa 49:15–16.

song. What activity in your life makes you feel especially connected with the continuing creativity of God?

2. The serpent, too, is part of God's "very good" world (Gen 1:31). Yet we can allow even good things to lead us astray. What are the serpents in your life?

3. A conflict of today is environmental responsibility versus the human "right" to dominate the earth. Human beings are shaped from the same clay as other creatures, says Gen 2; and the speaker of Ps 8 marvels that the Creator of such a universe should even notice humankind. What connections do you find among these ideas? What is your role in this world you have been given?

For Further Reading

Carmody, Denise Lardner, *Biblical Woman* (1989), 9–14.

Deen, Edith, *All of the Women of the Bible* (1955), 3–7.

Mollenkott, Virginia Ramey, *The Divine Feminine* (1983), 74–78.

Stone, Merlin, *When God Was a Woman* (1976), 198–223.

Trible, Phyllis, *God and the Rhetoric of Sexuality* (1978), 72–143.

Winter, Miriam Therese, *WomanWisdom* (1991), 3–14.

2 Sarah: Princess of the Promise

Genesis 11, 12, 16, 17, 18, 21, 23

". . . good reason to laugh . . ."

Background

Several Bible passages attest to the esteem accorded Sarah—the first great matriarch of Israel—in Jewish and Christian tradition. She is the only woman whose age at death is given; she is mentioned by name in Isa 51:2, Rom 4:19, Rom 9:9, and 1 Pet 3:6; and she is recalled in Paul's allegory on spiritual freedom (Gal 4:21–31). Her importance is further demonstrated by the fact that Genesis preserves two different versions—"doublets"—of several parts of her story. While multiple versions of a story sometimes confuse modern readers, the original readers enjoyed exploring the nuances such doublets introduced.

Sarah and her husband Abraham (Sarai and Abram) probably lived during the late Bronze Age, c. 2000–1550 BCE. In terms of today's maps, their story takes them on a journey of emigration from southern Iraq up to northern Syria, down to southern Israel, and on into Egypt. They were following the fifteen-hundred mile Fertile Crescent—a route that began at the mouth of the Euphrates River, extended northwest to the river country of Harran, curved south through Canaan, and angled west to the Nile Delta.

The stories of Abraham and Sarah run through fifteen chapters of Genesis, seven of the chapters mentioning Sarah. The writers of the different strands that were later braided together to form these chapters were first identified by nineteenth-century German scholars. The oldest stories come from the Yahwist or "J," so named because he usually calls God *Yahweh* (*Jahweh* in German). Probably working in Jerusalem at the court of David or Solomon c. 1000 BCE, J tells a vivid, earthy story. He presents human beings warts and all, neither condemning nor excusing their faults.[1] For example, J tells a story in which Abraham flatly lies, claiming that Sarah is his sister out of fear that men will otherwise kill him in order to possess her (Gen 12). J also depicts Sarah as treating her slave Hagar so badly that Hagar runs away (Gen 16). And J's drama-loving God sends the aged Abraham and Sarah three angelic visitors who create suspense by dallying over a meal before they deliver God's promise of a son (Gen 18).

---

1. J's women, especially, spring so vividly to life that Richard Elliott Friedman wonders whether J might have been a woman (*Who Wrote the Bible?*, pages 85–86).

Intertwined with these stories by J are versions of the same events by the Elohist ("E") and the Priestly writer ("P"). (E calls God *Elohim*, a majestic plural connoting "God of gods." In stories of the patriarchs and matriarchs, P calls God *El Shaddai*.) The Elohist worked in the northern part of the country about two centuries after J. His primary concern is theology, and he often provides a rationale for otherwise questionable behavior. For example, when he tells the story of Abraham's lie, he asserts that Sarah actually is Abraham's half-sister (Gen 20).[2] In his version of the Hagar story, Sarah demands that Abraham expel Hagar and her son by Abraham, but E justifies Sarah's cruelty as safeguarding the position of her son, Isaac, as God's chosen heir (Gen 21). The Priestly writer, who worked as late as the fourth century BCE, was concerned mostly with legalities and ritual. P's God, for example, promises Isaac to Abraham in the course of a legal discussion about the pact that accompanies God's promise of lands and descendants (Gen 17).

Other parts of the Sarah and Abraham saga are preserved in the work of only one of these writers. The Yahwist is unique in stressing terebinth trees, associated in the Old Testament with goddess worship. According to J, God first promises Abraham the land of Canaan under a sacred terebinth tree at Shechem (Gen 12:6–7). Later, angelic messengers promise Sarah a son at the terebinths of Hebron (Gen 18:1–15). The terebinth was a long-lived tree similar to an oak, valued for the shade of its spreading branches and the turpentine derived from its sap. Canaanites called the terebinth near Shechem the "Diviners' Oak." They called the Shechem area the "navel of the land" (Judg 9:37, JB) because it lay between two mountains perceived as joining heaven and earth, divinity and humanity. Erecting altars to the goddess under spreading trees was later banned in Israel. But considering that "Sarai" (princess) was a name customarily given to devotees of the goddess Ningal, consort of the moon god Sin then worshipped in Mesopotamia, some researchers see in J's terebinth shrines a trace of Sarah's personal dedication to the goddess, while recognizing El Shaddai as her husband's god.[3]

Unique to the Elohist is a story in which God tests Abraham by asking him to sacrifice his and Sarah's son, Isaac. Infants were burned to appease the god Molech in Canaan and in parts of North Africa, and Abraham and Sarah may have witnessed such rituals. Later, when some of their own descendants sacrificed children in misguided attempts to gain divine favor, the story of the testing of Abraham served as the basis for prohibiting child sacrifice and substituting an animal. (Condemnations of "passing children

2. It is remotely possible that Sarah *was* Abraham's half-sister, since Genesis never names Sarah's father (an unusual omission). Later on, marriage of half-siblings was discouraged (2 Sam 13:1–14) and then banned (Lev 18:9,11; 20:17).

3. In works outside the scope of this book, Savina J. Teubal, in particular, develops the concept of a lost tradition of the matriarchs: *Sarah the Priestess* (Athens, Ohio: Swallow Press, 1984) and *Hagar the Egyptian* (San Francisco: Harper & Row, 1990).

through the fire" appear in Lev 20:5, Deut 18:10, and 2 Kings 16:3, 17:31, 23:10.) Jewish legend further dramatizes abhorrence of child sacrifice in a tale that Sarah died of shock on learning that Abraham had even considered sacrificing Isaac.

The Priestly writer is responsible for tagging events with the ages traditionally ascribed to the characters at that point. Carried literally from episode to episode, the ages do not work out. But taken symbolically, the advanced ages ascribed to Sarah and Abraham dramatize God's power over biology. It is also P who introduces a basic law of Israel, the requirement that males undergo circumcision. Even though Canaanites and Egyptians had practiced circumcision since about 2300 BCE, it was only in Israel, where the ritual signified the people's covenant with Yahweh, that circumcision developed into a symbol of national identity. Finally, P is the one who reports the legal details of the purchase of Sarah's tomb. For him, clear title to one small plot symbolized Israel's future entitlement to the entire land. Solidifying the claim, Genesis goes on to report that Abraham, Isaac, Rebekah, Leah, and Jacob are later buried in Sarah's tomb (Gen 25:9, 35:27–29, 49:29–33, 50:13). The site remains a place of pilgrimage to this day.

The Story of Sarah as Told in Genesis

The Journeys of Abram and Sarai: *A Summary of Gen 11:30–12:20*

Terah, his son Abram, Abram's wife Sarai, and Terah's grandson Lot migrate from Ur in southern Mesopotamia to Harran in the distant north. Some years later, God directs Abram to migrate southwest to Canaan with Sarai and Lot. Within Canaan, they journey south to the Negeb by stages. At "the sanctuary of Shechem, the terebinth tree of Moreh," God promises the land of Canaan to Abram's descendants. But famine drives the family to the granaries of Egypt. Abram worries lest the Egyptians be so taken with Sarai's beauty that they will kill him to have her. "Tell them you are my sister," he says, "so that all may go well with me . . . and my life [may] be spared on your account." In Egypt, Pharaoh indeed takes Sarai into his harem, rewarding her supposed brother with sheep, cattle, donkeys, camels, and slaves. But God inflicts plagues on Pharaoh's household on "account of . . . Sarai." Shocked at having accidentally taken another man's wife, Pharaoh summons Abram, scolds him for lying, and evicts him from Egypt. But Pharaoh also grants him safe conduct home with Sarai and all that he owns.

Sarai, Hagar, and God's Promise: *A Summary of Gen 16:1–17:18*

Years later, Abram and Sarai are still childless. Sarai gives Abram her slave girl, Hagar, to bear a child who will legally be considered Sarai's son. Once Hagar becomes pregnant, however, she scorns her mistress. Sarai retaliates by mistreating her, and Hagar runs away. Only at God's command does Hagar return to bear her son, Ishmael. During Ishmael's early childhood, El

Shaddai establishes a covenant with Abram and Sarai. As a sign of the pact, God requires all males of the household to be circumcised. God also changes Abram's and Sarai's names to Abraham and Sarah.[4] Abraham pleads that his son Ishmael be specially favored, but God asserts that the covenant will pass only through Sarah: "I shall bless her and she will be the mother of nations. . . . Sarah will bear you a son, and you are to call him Isaac."

God Sends Angels to Promise Sarah a Son, and Isaac Is Born: *A Summary of Gen 18:1–15, 21:1–8*

El Shaddai appears to Abraham by the terebinths of Mamre, as he sits in the doorway of his tent in the heat of the day. Looking up, Abraham sees three men, whom he hurries to meet. Bowing low, he invites them to visit. He asks Sarah to bake bread; he orders his servants to bring the men water for washing and to prepare a meal of fresh veal. Abraham serves the meal. After dinner the visitors ask where Sarah is, and Abraham replies that she is in the tent. One of them says, "About this time next year I shall come back to you, and your wife Sarah will have a son." Now Abraham and Sarah are very old, and Sarah is well past the age of childbearing. Listening at the tent flap, Sarah laughs. God asks [through one of the visitors] why Sarah laughed. "Is anything impossible for [me]? In due season, at this time next year, I shall come back to you, and Sarah will have a son." Because she is frightened, Sarah denies having laughed, but God says to her, "You did laugh." As God promised, Sarah conceives and bears a son to Abraham in their old age. Abraham names the boy Isaac ("laughter") and circumcises him when he is eight days old. Sarah says, "God has given me good reason to laugh, and everyone who hears will laugh with me." The boy grows and is weaned, and on the day of his weaning Abraham gives a great feast.[5]

God Tests Abraham: *A Summary of Gen 22:1–13*

A few years later God tests Abraham by directing him to sacrifice his favored son, Isaac, on Mount Moriah. While Abraham and Isaac are traveling to Moriah, Isaac asks about a sheep for the sacrifice. Abraham tells him that God will provide one. Abraham builds an altar, arranges the wood, binds Isaac, and has already lifted his knife when an angel intervenes: "Do not raise your hand against the boy; do not touch him. Now I know that you are a godfearing man." Abraham sacrifices instead a ram he finds nearby.

---

4. The new names are dialectal variants of the former. Both sets mean "exalted father" and "princess."

5. Gen 21 goes on to report Sarah's annoyance at seeing Ishmael playing with Isaac at the party (see chapter 3), and to record E's version of Hagar's and Ishmael's expulsion.

Abraham Mourns Sarah: *A Summary of Gen 23:1–19*

Sarah dies at the age of 127 in Kiriath-arba (Hebron) in Canaan. Abraham weeps for her. When at last he rises from his mourning, he approaches the Hittites: "I am an alien and a settler among you," he says. "Make over to me some ground among you for a burial place, that I may bury my dead." After considerable haggling over the price of some land at Machpelah, east of Hebron, the contract is concluded. Abraham buries Sarah in a cave on the plot.

Reflection

As their story begins, we find Abraham and Sarah enroute from Ur to Harran. Their entourage moves at a leisurely pace, since it includes many dependents—relatives, servants, slaves, the children of these people, and unattached young men hired to tend the cattle, sheep, and donkeys. Bead trappings adorn both the people and the animals they ride. For protection from dust and sun, everyone wears heavy leather sandals and loose woolen robes dyed in brilliant combinations of yellow, red, and blue. A headdress and a veil partially obscure Sarah's face. She may be olive-skinned with dark hair and eyes, or, exhibiting the striking coloration that sometimes appears among her people, she may possess a lighter complexion, auburn hair, and blue eyes. Her baggage includes earrings of beaten gold as well as oils, perfumes, and additional jewelry to enhance her beauty.

The caravan halts for weeks at a time between major relocations. Supervising the manufacture, care, pitching, and striking of the tents devolves upon Sarah—tasks so important that one of them is enshrined in the root meaning of the Hebrew verb "to journey," which is "to pull up tent stakes." To thrive on so strenuous and challenging a life, Sarah must surely be a healthy, good-humored, capable woman.

In the evening, once people and animals have eaten and the camp has quieted, perhaps she and Abraham gaze up at the stars, talking softly. Under the vast dome of the sky, do they sometimes speculate on the Power that guards them on their way? Do they ever notice a central irony of their lives— the fact that Sarah's "curse" of childlessness may well have enhanced her stamina and the sustaining of her remarkable beauty? Whether or not they become so philosophical, they clearly develop a comfortable, supportive partnership. Later on, when Abraham worries about his personal safety, Sarah readily agrees to pose as his sister. When Sarah grows desperate for a son, Abraham accepts her plan that he father a child by her slave girl.

Even Abraham's God seems to esteem Sarah. El Shaddai inflicts plagues on Pharaoh and his household not to punish Abraham for lying, but to protect Sarah from assault. Later, when changing her name from Sarai to Sarah, God promises to make her a "mother of nations" from whom "kings . . . will spring" (Gen 17:16). The covenant rests not with all descendants of

Abraham, but only with those who can call Sarah mother. Sarah, however, seems guarded about El Shaddai—an unpredictable deity who orders them to move here and there, insists that they change their names, and even promises an old woman a child. Sarah bursts into laughter at the very thought. How can a womb past menopause yield new life?

Besides, she has already dealt with the situation. Seeing the yearning of Abraham and feeling a nearly physical ache as her own barrenness settles into permanence, she has opted for an unusual but legal solution: selecting a slave to bear a child for her. Hagar the Egyptian seemed a perfect choice. Had she not been special to Sarah, more a daughter than a slave, ever since Sarah acquired her? And has not Ishmael, the son born to Abraham and Hagar on Sarah's knees, proved a handsome, healthy lad? Yet how arrogant Hagar has grown about her fecundity, how derisive about Sarah's barrenness. In spite of Ishmael's legal status, Sarah cannot consider him anyone's son but Hagar's.

And now this enigmatic God of Abraham's, speaking through the lips of a mysterious visitor, soberly promises Sarah a son of her own! When she laughs, and then in fright denies having laughed, El Shaddai for the first time addresses her directly: "Sarah, you did laugh." She begins to think that maybe, just maybe, El Shaddai can renew a womb. Certainty comes in the unmistakable signs of pregnancy. And when she bears her son, she throws back her head in full-throated peals of joy, gladly accepting for him the name El Shaddai assigned—"Isaac," meaning "laughter." For the first time, she *enjoys* this God of surprises.

For the next three years, as Sarah nurses Isaac and guides his discovery of the world, she barely notices Ishmael. There is now no question of Abraham's making the son of a slave his major heir; all custom militates against it. And yet . . . Abraham loves Ishmael; he has begged El Shaddai specially to bless him. Meanness begins to corrode Sarah's spirit; she makes Hagar's life miserable through constant ridicule and assignment of the dirtiest tasks. Finally Hagar threatens to run away, and, with ill grace, Sarah modifies her petty behavior. But at the party celebrating Isaac's weaning, Sarah sees the two half-brothers playing together, and unreasoning protectiveness erupts within her once again. Repressing every vestige of affection, even denying Hagar and Ishmael the dignity of names, she harasses Abraham to banish "that slave and her son." In the end, to placate a partner he cannot bear to see distressed, Abraham expels not only Hagar but also his own son to the perils of the wilderness.

❖ ❖

In choosing a woman to bear a child for her, Sarah becomes sister to any woman seeking to adopt the child of a pregnant girl devoid of personal resources. In abusing another woman and her child in order to combat an imagined threat to her own, Sarah becomes sister to any woman who pickets her child's school to prevent a child with AIDS from being admitted. In trading on her husband's love, Sarah becomes sister to all who manipulate loved ones to achieve their own ends.

Does Sarah ever notice that both she and Hagar are victims of the patriarchal system? Does she ever notice that both of them have so completely absorbed their world's obsession with sons as to make victims of each other? Just as Sarah exploits Hagar's fertility to meet her own needs, so Hagar uses it to demoralize Sarah. How different the outcome might have been, had they noticed how much they shared. But as events develop, Sarah appears to suppress all thought of Hagar and Ishmael the moment they disappear from sight. She focuses instead on Isaac—a son who so deeply returns her love that his grief at her death becomes legendary (Gen 24:67).

At some point Sarah learns how she nearly lost Isaac when he journeyed to Moriah with his father. Abraham certainly does not tell her beforehand, for had a woman of Sarah's will opposed him, even El Shaddai would have been hard pressed to set him on the road. But once Sarah ponders the story and absorbs its implications, perhaps she recalls how Isaac came to her in the first place; perhaps she remembers exactly Who has repeatedly demonstrated mastery of the surprise ending. Late in life, perhaps she prays:

Prayer

How long and winding has been my path to you, El Shaddai—
its length and complexity partly your own doing.
Sometimes, God of my husband,
you seemed to ask more than a heart could bear;
sometimes you carried your jokes too far.

True, the signs of your might were ever present;
but I did not see you in the channeling of the rain,
the clearing of paths for the thunderbolts.
Only now do I truly believe
it is you who clothe the wasteland in vivid green,
you whose womb gives birth to the hoar frost in the sky.

Once, in pain, I laughed at your extravagant word,
but you smiled and renewed me anyway.
You made of me a terebinth, flourishing into ripe old age.
I know you now, God of the Unexpected!
Your blessings exceed the bounty of the lasting hills.
You lift my head high; you fill me, always,
with the reviving gift of laughter.[6]

6. Based on Ps 92:10–14 and Job 38:25–29.

Connections

1. In Sarah's and Hagar's world, a woman's ultimate value depended on her ability to produce a son. How do you value women? How do you define your own worth?

2. God speaks to Abraham and Sarah both directly and through angelic messengers. How does God speak to you? Who are God's messengers in your life?

3. Sarah imposes her will on Hagar, Ishmael, and Abraham, with no regard for their feelings. Abraham takes Isaac to Moriah without revealing the truth to him or to Sarah. Do you ever trample others in obsessive pursuit of your own goals?

For Further Reading

Deen, Edith, *All of the Women of the Bible* (1955), 8–15.

Exum, J. Cheryl, "Mothers in Israel" in *Feminist Interpretation of the Bible* (1985), ed. Letty M. Russell, 76–77.

Friedman, Richard Elliott, *Who Wrote the Bible?* (1987), 33–206.

Gadon, Elinor W., *The Once and Future Goddess* (1989), 171.

Kirk, Martha Ann, "A Story of Sarah," *God of Our Mothers* (1985), audio-tape.

Nunnally-Cox, Janice, *Foremothers* (1981), 8–9.

Sleevi, Mary Lou, *Women of the Word* (1989), 20–25.

Weems, Renita J., *Just a Sister Away* (1988), 1–21.

Winter, Miriam Therese, *WomanWisdom* (1991), 15–30, 103–5.

3   Hagar: Vindicated Slave

Genesis 16, 17, 21, 25

"... do not be afraid; God has heard ..."

Background

The story of Hagar, a slave woman, is embedded in the stories of the barren Sarah and her husband, Abraham. In accordance with legal customs of her culture, Sarah gives Hagar to Abraham to bear a child in Sarah's name. The transaction changes Hagar's status to that of Abraham's concubine (subordinate wife) and removes her from Sarah's control. Hagar herself possesses no rights in the matter, and, legally, the child to be born "on the knees of" Sarah will become Sarah's child.

Genesis provides two versions of events that result from Sarah's selection of Hagar as surrogate mother. Scholars believe that both versions are based on a single event that occurred during the childhood of her son, Ishmael; but the differences in detail and emphasis have long provided rich fare for interpretation and application of Hagar's story. In the Yahwist's version (Gen 16), the pregnant Hagar runs away to escape Sarah's abuse. This proud Hagar is a worthy ancestor of the Arab peoples. She possesses enough initiative to choose her own future. In a later version by the Elohist (Gen 21), Sarah instigates all events, and Hagar this time emerges as a downtrodden slave who, with her child, may justifiably be driven away in order to safeguard the covenant El Shaddai has promised to *Sarah's* descendants. However, E's Hagar ultimately achieves something J's does not—her freedom.[1]

In Mesopotamia, the homeland of Abraham and Sarah, the code of Hammurabi expressly forbade expelling a slave woman who had been taken as a concubine. If the woman showed disrespect to her former mistress, however, she could be returned to the status of a slave. Thus when Sarah contends, in effect, that Hagar has grown "uppity," her claim may reflect what she *wants* to see. When Sarah argues her case with Abraham, she ends with a demand expressed in the legal language of Mesopotamia: "May God see justice done between you and me." Abraham responds with a legal formula that restores ownership of Hagar to Sarah: "Your slave [woman] is in your hands." Like the code of Hammurabi, Hebrew custom (later codified into law) protected the rights of a concubine, but permitted sale or dismissal of a slave:

---

1. For an interesting discussion of the Elohist's Hagar story as an Exodus in reverse—an Egyptian's escape from oppression in Canaan—see Phyllis Trible, *Texts of Terror* (1984), 20–29.

If [a female slave] proves unpleasing to her master . . ., he must let her be redeemed; he has treated her unfairly. . . . If he takes another woman, he must not deprive the first of meat, clothes, and conjugal rights; if he does not provide her with these three things, she is to go free without payment.
—Ex 21:8,10–11

Abraham and Sarah are thus within their rights in treating Hagar as property, and even in dismissing her. But by sending her to a perilous wilderness instead of genuinely freeing her, they violate the spirit of the laws and customs of their time.

Genesis goes on to report that Hagar and her son Ishmael manage to survive—with God's help. Physically distanced from the household and traditions of Abraham, they occupy lands on the northern edge of the Sinai desert, south of Abraham's home near Beer-sheba in Canaan. Hagar and Ishmael show psychological distancing, as well, when she chooses for him an Egyptian wife rather than a woman of Abraham's clan. Even so, Ishmael returns to help his half-brother Isaac bury Abraham.

Just before the report of Abraham's death, Gen 25 makes a puzzling allusion to Abraham's "sons by his concubines." Who are these children and women? Gen 25:1–2 reports his taking another *wife* after the death of Sarah—Keturah, who bears him six sons. In 1 Chr 1:32, however, the only other Bible passage that mentions Keturah, she is called his *concubine*. It may therefore be Keturah and her sons, and Hagar and her son, who are meant by "sons by his concubines."

In any case, the only sons of Abraham who matter to Arabs and Jews are Ishmael, the son of his concubine Hagar; and Isaac, the son of his wife Sarah. Tradition honors both as founders of nations. Ishmael's twelve sons, revered as the progenitors of all Arab peoples, parallel the twelve tribes of Israel who later descend from Isaac. (Ishmael's sons are listed in Gen 25:13–16 and in 1 Chr 1:29–31.) Jews thus recognize the descendants of Ishmael as relatives, but as kin who constitute a lesser branch of the family. Even though the conflict between Arab and Jewish descendants of Abraham—a conflict that began during Abraham's lifetime—continues to this day, many points of pilgrimage in modern Israel affirm the tradition of relatedness. A case in point is the tomb of Sarah in Machpelah (Hebron). The walls that surround it enclose both a Moslem mosque and a Jewish synagogue.

The Story of Hagar as Told in Genesis

Hagar Runs Away but Returns: *A Summary of Gen 16:1–15* [2]

Abram's wife Sarai has borne him no children, but she has an Egyptian slave woman named Hagar. One day Sarai says to Abram, "Take my slave [woman]; perhaps through her I shall have a son." Abram heeds Sarai's

2. The story of Hagar's running away is told by the Yahwist, J.

wishes, and she gives him her slave woman as a subordinate wife. Abram has sex with Hagar and she conceives. When she knows that she is pregnant, she begins to look down on her mistress. Sarai complains to Abram: "I am being wronged; you must do something about it. It was I who gave my slave [woman] into your arms, but since she has known that she is pregnant, she has despised me. May [God] see justice done between you and me." Abram replies, "Your slave [woman] is in your hands; deal with her as you please." Sarai mistreats Hagar until she runs away.

By a spring in the wilderness, an angel of God speaks to Hagar. "Hagar, Sarai's slave [woman], where have you come from and where are you going?" She answers, "I am running away from Sarai my mistress." The angel directs Hagar to return to her mistress and submit to ill treatment at her hands. "You are with child and will bear a son." She is to name him Ishmael—"El (God) heard"—because God heard of her ill treatment. The angel says that God will make her descendants too many to be counted, but the son himself "will be like the wild ass; his hand will be against everyone and everyone's hand against him; and he will live at odds with all his kin."

Hagar calls the one who spoke to her El Roi—"God of Living Vision"— for she asks, "Have I indeed seen God and still live after that vision?"[3] Hagar returns and bears Abram a son, whom he names Ishmael.

The Covenant through Isaac: *A Summary of Gen 17*

As a sign of El Shaddai's covenant with Abram's family, God requires that all males of Abram's household be circumcised, including young Ishmael. God also changes Abram's and Sarai's names to Abraham and Sarah, and promises that Sarah will bear a son who is to be named Isaac. When Abraham pleads that Ishmael be shown special favor, El Shaddai says that the covenant can continue only through the as yet unborn son of Sarah. But for Abraham's sake, Ishmael will also found a great nation.

Hagar Is Rejected: *A Summary of Gen 21:2–21*[4]

Sarah conceives, and at the time foretold, she bears a son to Abraham. Abraham names him Isaac. The boy grows and is weaned, and on the day of his weaning Abraham gives a great feast.[5] Sarah sees Hagar's son Ishmael playing with Isaac and says to Abraham, "Drive out this slave [woman] and her son! I will not have this slave's son sharing the inheritance with my son

---

3. The belief that one cannot see God and live also appears in Gen 32:30, Ex 19:21 and 33:20, and Judg 6:22–23.

4. This version, the expulsion of Hagar, is told by the Elohist, E.

5. Mother's milk to some degree provided immunization from early childhood illnesses. Weaning occurred at about age three, when a child's survival seemed assured.

Isaac." Abraham is distressed but God tells him, "Do not be upset for the boy and your slave [woman]. Do as Sarah says, because it is through Isaac's line that your name will be perpetuated. I shall make a nation of the slave [woman's] son because he also is your child."

Early the next morning Abraham takes some food and a full water skin to Hagar, sets Ishmael on her shoulder, and sends them away. Hagar wanders about in the wilderness of Beer-sheba until the water in the skin is depleted. Then she thrusts the child under a bush and sits down some way off, about the distance of a bowshot. "How can I watch the child die?" she says, and sits there weeping bitterly. At this point an angel calls down from heaven, "What is the matter, Hagar? Do not be afraid: God has heard the child crying where you laid him. Go, lift the child and hold him in your arms, because I shall make of him a great nation." Then God opens her eyes and she sees a well full of water. She fills the water skin and gives the child a drink. God is with Ishmael as he grows up in the wilderness of Paran. He becomes a skilled hunter and plunderer, and his mother gets him a wife from Egypt.

Abraham's Old Age and Death: *A Summary of Gen 25:5–10*

During his lifetime Abraham assigns all that he possesses to Isaac. He makes gifts to his sons by his concubines and sends them eastwards, out of Isaac's way. Abraham dies at the great age of 175. His sons Isaac and Ishmael bury him in the cave at Machpelah with his wife Sarah.

Reflection

Just as "wage slavery" is a fact of life today, literal slavery was a fact to Abraham, Sarah, and Hagar. Though "Hagar the Egyptian" may have been a black-skinned African, in her day slavery had nothing to do with skin color and everything to do with economics and politics. Even as an employed woman of today may stand little more than a paycheck away from a homeless woman, so a mistress stood little more than a few good crops away from her slave. When a crisis arose in family finances, anyone (especially a daughter) could be sold into slavery. In war, anyone (especially a woman) could become a victor's trophy. Whether free or enslaved, a woman addressed her man as "master." Whether or not a woman knew the language or liked the climate, free woman and slave woman alike followed her man wherever he led.

Yet if all women lived a somewhat precarious existence, a slave encountered risks at every turn. If her master chose to warm his bed with her, she had better acquiesce. If her mistress disliked her, she would be wise to bear the abuse. If she gave her master a son, she could still never achieve the status of the man's freeborn wife. Success meant studying her master and mistress so carefully, making herself so valuable, that they would not sell her into a worse existence.

Previous to Hagar's experience in Sarah's household, she may have met Sarah in Pharaoh's harem. Later, in sheer relief at escaping a bad situation, Pharaoh himself may have chosen Hagar for Sarah as a personal gift—his healthiest, most intelligent, most beautiful slave woman. Since the semi-nomadic Hebrews were said to treat their slaves like members of the family, Hagar may well have considered herself lucky. But however it happened, Hagar becomes Sarah's slave. For Sarah later to choose her as surrogate mother, the bond they forge over time must surely include affection and respect.

Yet when Hagar's status changes—when she becomes no longer the property of Sarah but the concubine of Abraham (his *pregnant* concubine)—her self-concept also changes. All of her suppressed outrage at belonging to *anyone*, at being forced to place even her sexuality at another's disposal, boils to the surface. No matter how warm a relationship she and Sarah formerly enjoyed, she cannot help strutting to show off her growing belly; she cannot help taunting her sterile mistress with her own youth and vitality. But pettiness evokes pettiness, and Sarah holds the greater power. She makes life miserable for Hagar.

Hagar, saddened by her lack of power to change the situation, chooses the drastic solution of plunging into the wilderness. But she has underestimated the dangers. The heat, the aridity, the lack of readily available food weaken her resolve. Dazed by the pounding sun, she collapses near a well. Yet her heart continues to cry out, and a voice responds. It is the voice of a deity who knows that she will swallow her pride only for the sake of a life she values more than her own; it is the voice of a deity able to promise that she will bear a great son—*if* she returns and shoulders the inequities of her situation. Overlooking the fact that the voice speaks also of future conflict, Hagar hugs to herself the promise of greatness, certain that it refers to her son's future as Abraham's heir.

When Hagar's son is born, she asks Abraham to call him Ishmael, honoring the God who heard her in her need. Abraham adores the boy, and Hagar basks in the reflection of Ishmael's status. But then El Shaddai shows special regard for Abraham and Sarah by opening Sarah's womb. How can Ishmael achieve greatness if Sarah produces a son of her own flesh as Abraham's proper heir? "Was I mistaken," Hagar wonders, "in thinking my El Roi the equal of El Shaddai or even the same god?" Hagar possesses no answers, yet for a time events themselves soothe her spirit. So long as Isaac feeds at Sarah's breast, Abraham continues to dote on Ishmael. Still, Hagar can no longer completely ignore El Roi's mention of conflict.

When at last the blow falls and Hagar and Ishmael are dismissed to the wilderness, she reacts with weary resignation. Even when Abraham begs her to understand; even when he adopts a woman's role and brings her food and water, she feels nothing but bleak despair. This time, Hagar knows the desert. Defeat plagues her from the first, and with the last of the water, the last of her hope trickles into the sand. Awaiting death, she tucks Ishmael into the shade of a bush.

But the boy's cries penetrate God's hearing, and El Roi reveals to Hagar's glazed vision a refreshing well. Whatever the deity's proper name, God has not, after all, abandoned her or her son. In fact, from the boy's first drink of that living water, he seems specially favored. As he grows, he develops into a self-sufficient young archer whose prowess reawakens Hagar's own toughness and inspires within her new concepts of greatness. Together, she and Ishmael create a life in the wilderness. Together they observe not Abraham's laws, but the customs of Hagar's people. At length, Hagar returns to Egypt to select for Ishmael a resourceful desert wife.

❖ ❖

In her lack of home and lands and wealth, Hagar is obviously less favored than Sarah. Like a woman of today newly escaped from a dangerous household, does Hagar ever look back, almost with longing, to the security of bondage? On the other hand, does Hagar ever realize that Sarah also suffers? Hagar and Ishmael are indeed cast out from the covenant of El Shaddai, and their very lives are threatened by the perils of the desert. But even within the supposed safety of the patriarchal hearth, Sarah nearly loses her own son to the demands of El Shaddai.

Eventually, Sarah learns to enjoy El Shaddai as a God of surprises. Hagar may rather have perceived her desert deity as one who soared on eagle's wings. In those early desert years, perhaps she prayed:

Prayer

El Roi, be gracious to me, for you are my refuge;
I huddle in the shadow of your wings.
I call to you, God of Living Vision,
fulfill your promise in me and my son!
Send us protection, unfailing and sure,
even as we lie prostrate among scorpions.
Lift us up and set us high upon a rock;
be to us a tower of strength against all harm.
Rescue us from deadly pestilence; shelter us
from the searing torments of noonday.
Though a thousand others fall, hold us untouched;
be for us a secure place of dwelling.
Listen to my prayer, El Roi,
as I call to you with fainting heart.
In this barren end of earth,

charge your angels always to guard us.
For we sing of you daily: El Roi is our refuge;
in the God of Vision we place our trust.[6]

Connections

1. From an abusive situation, the only place Hagar can escape *to* is a dangerous wilderness. Even if you have never faced a situation as extreme as Hagar's, how do shades of her dilemma touch your life, or the lives of women you know?

2. Shackled to past dreams, Hagar is at first unable to adjust to the desert. When you must make a major change in your life, are you tempted to look back in nostalgia, romanticizing a condition that was, at least, familiar?

3. Much as Abraham loved Ishmael, he seems to have used Hagar and then dismissed her from his mind. When have you cultivated someone for your own purposes?

For Further Reading

Deen, Edith, *All of the Women of the Bible* (1955), 12–13.

Exum, J. Cheryl, "Mothers in Israel" in *Feminist Interpretation of the Bible* (1985), ed. Letty M. Russell, 76–77.

Kirk, Martha Ann, "A Story of Hagar," *God of Our Mothers* (1985), audiotape.

Nunnally-Cox, Janice, *Foremothers* (1981), 8–9.

Pui-lan, Kwok, "Racism and Ethnocentrism in Feminist Biblical Interpretation" in *Searching the Scriptures* (1993), ed. Elisabeth Schüssler Fiorenza, 105–6.

Sleevi, Mary Lou, *Women of the Word* (1989), 26–30.

Trible, Phyllis J., *Texts of Terror* (1984), 8–35.

Weems, Renita J., *Just a Sister Away* (1988), 1–21.

Winter, Miriam Therese, *WomanWisdom* (1991), 36–43.

---

6. Based on Ps 57:1–4, 61:1–4, and 91:1–15.

4 The Wife and Daughters of Lot: Women Lost

Genesis 13, 18, 19

"Do not look back. . . ."

Background

Genesis entwines the stories of Lot and his family with those of Lot's uncle, Abraham (Abram). The stories report how Lot came to settle in Sodom, what occurs one evening when Lot welcomes two angels into his home, how Lot's wife is transformed into a pillar of salt during the destruction of Sodom, and how Lot's daughters perpetuate their clan. The teller of the stories is the drama-loving Yahwist (J), who bases them on tales already embellished with folklore by his time. For example, whatever the actual manner of death of Lot's wife, storytellers had long found the pillar-of-salt legend more satisfying, even though the tale may have originally arisen to explain an unusual rock formation.

The episode explaining how Lot came to establish himself in Sodom demonstrates Lot's greediness. When he and Abraham agree to separate because one region can no longer support their herds, Lot violates the custom of deference for one's elders by immediately claiming for himself the best land, the rich plains near Sodom. Later on, when Lot has become a citizen of Sodom (a status most likely achieved by marrying a local woman), God decides to annihilate the city for the wickedness of its inhabitants. Only because of Abraham, Lot's uncle, does God send two angels (in human guise) to rescue Lot and his family.

When Lot encounters the angels in Sodom, a nobler side of his nature at first emerges. He insists upon taking "the men" into his own home, even though the rules of hospitality then oblige him to protect them. He even bakes bread for them, a task usually within a wife's province. Later that evening, however, Lot shows that he has absorbed at least one value of Sodom—its view of women as disposable commodities. The men of Sodom pound on Lot's door, demanding that he release the strangers to them for sexual abuse. Lot offers his virgin daughters instead. Only through the intervention of the angels are the daughters (and Lot himself) saved.

In the story of the destruction of Sodom, Lot and his family are characterized as people preoccupied with limited personal concerns. Lot's wife, disobeying the angel's injunction not to look back, forfeits her life for one last glimpse of home. Lot himself, placing little trust in God's promise to protect the village of Zoar from harm, takes his two daughters and flees to a cave in the hills. Finally the daughters, believing themselves to be the sole survivors of their people, seduce their own father in order to ensure clan continuity. (They succeed in that their sons, Moab and Ben-ammi, are said to father two Semitic peoples, the Moabites and the Ammonites.)

The seduction story probably originated as a Canaanite story about a different Lot, but Hebrew storytellers adopted it for a variety of reasons. The name coincidence, for example, offered them a way to acknowledge a distant kinship with the Moabite and Ammonite peoples of the region. The incident also re-dramatized a key theme of the Hebrew Flood story: the arising of new life out of destruction. (In this vein, early Jewish commentators praised Lot's daughters as admirable matriarchs who, against all odds, fulfilled the female role of perpetuating human life.) Finally, by the time the Yahwist recorded the story, in an era during which incest had long been excoriated and the Moabites and Ammonites had proved to be troublesome enemies, the story enabled the Yahwist to deride Israel's foes by assigning them incestuous origins.

As for the location of Sodom or how it met its destruction, little is known. Remains of urban areas in existence around the appropriate time suggest that Sodom was located near or under what is now the southern third of the Dead Sea. The area still boasts salt-encrusted formations that are vaguely human in shape; one of these may have given rise to the legend about Lot's wife. The story that Sodom was destroyed in a rain of fire and brimstone (sulfur) probably represents recall of an actual cataclysm. Because the region is rich in a volatile mixture of oil, asphalt, and sulfur, an earthquake could have caused these substances to ignite and then to explode into a consuming firestorm.

In any case, "Sodom" became synonymous with "wickedness." Both the Bible and non-biblical Jewish legends report that the inhabitants of Sodom violated the ancient laws of hospitality in every manner imaginable, living out their contempt of God, women, and strangers. They are said to have beaten, robbed, and starved visitors so cruelly that instances of sexual abuse serve mainly as dramatic symbols of their general level of depravity. Biblical mention of Sodom occurs in Deut 29:33, Isa 1:9 and 3:9, Am 4:11, Mt 10:15, Rom 9:29, 2 Pet 2:6–9, and verse 7 of the one-chapter epistle of Jude. Additional allusions in Ezekiel and Luke capture the tenor of all of the biblical references:

> Sodom . . . had the pride that goes with food in plenty, comfort, and ease, yet [its people] never helped the poor in their need. They grew haughty and committed what was abominable in my sight. . . .
> —Ezek 16:49–50

> In the days of Lot, they ate and drank, they bought and sold, they planted and built; but on the day that Lot left Sodom, fire and sulfur rained from the sky and made an end of them all. . . . Remember Lot's wife.
> —Lk 17:28–29, 32

The Story of the Wife and Daughters of Lot as Told in Genesis

Lot Is Established in Sodom: *A Summary of Gen 13:2–12 and 18:16–33*

Returning from a sojourn in Egypt, Abraham and Lot discover that one area cannot support all their sheep, cattle, people, and tents. Quarrels keep breaking out among their herders. The uncle and nephew agree to separate, and Abraham gives Lot first choice of lands. Lot immediately selects the well-watered plains near the city of Sodom, an area as rich as the Garden of Eden. Abraham settles near Hebron. Later, when Lot has established a home in Sodom, three angels visit Abraham and Sarah and promise them a son in a year's time. As Abraham strolls in the direction of Sodom with the departing angels, the one who speaks as God reveals a plan to destroy Sodom and Gomorrah if the other two verify that the people commit "monstrous sins." Knowing that Lot lives in Sodom, Abraham persuades God not to destroy the towns if so few as ten good people live there. The angels apparently do not find ten, for the plan proceeds.

Lot Offers His Daughters to the Men of Sodom: *A Summary of Gen 19:1–11*

Two angels arrive in Sodom in the evening to find Lot sitting by the city gate. He rises to meet them, bows low, and urges them to spend the night with him. "You can continue your journey in the morning." "No," they answer, "we shall spend the night in the street." But Lot is so insistent that they finally accompany him home. He bakes unleavened bread and serves them a meal. Before the visitors lie down to sleep, the men of Sodom, "both young and old, everyone without exception," surround the house. They call to Lot, "Where are the men who came to you tonight? Bring them out to us so that we may have intercourse with them." Lot goes out, closing the door behind him, and begs his fellow citizens to do nothing so wicked. "Look," he says, "I have two daughters, virgins both of them; let me bring them out to you and you can do what you like with them. But do nothing to these men, because they have come under the shelter of my roof." The men of Sodom deride Lot as an alien who now presumes to judge them. "Out of our way!" they shout, and crowd in upon him. When they are close to breaking down the door, the visitors reach out, pull Lot into the house, and shut the door. Then they dazzle the vision of the attackers so that they cannot even find the entrance.

God Destroys Sodom and Gomorrah: *A Summary of Gen 19:12–29*

The angels say to Lot, "Have you anyone here, sons-in-law, sons, or daughters, or anyone else belonging to you in this city? Get them out of this place, because we are going to destroy it." Lot goes out and urges his sons-in-law[1]

---

1. The Yahwist appears to base this part of his story on a different folktale, one in which Lot has two more daughters, who are married.

to leave because God is about to destroy the city, but they do not take him seriously. At dawn the angels urge Lot, "Quick, take your wife and your two daughters who are here, or you will be destroyed when the city is punished." When he delays, they grab his hand and the hands of his wife and daughters, and lead them to safety outside the city.

Outside Sodom, one angel urges the family, "Flee for your lives! Do not look back or stop anywhere in the plain. Flee to the hills or you will be destroyed." Lot argues with the angels. "No, sirs! You have shown your servant favor, but I cannot escape to the hills; I shall be overtaken by the disaster and die." He pleads to be allowed to stop in the small village of Zoar, "near enough for me to get to quickly." The angel grants Lot's request and promises not to overthrow Zoar, but urges the family to move quickly. At sunrise, as they enter Zoar, God rains fire and brimstone upon Sodom and Gomorrah. The cities, the plains, and all growing things are destroyed. But Lot's wife looks back, and she turns into a pillar of salt.

Early the next morning, Abraham goes to the place where he had stood with the angels. As he looks over the wide extent of the plain, he sees thick smoke "rising from the earth like smoke from a kiln. Thus it was, when God destroyed the cities of the plain, that God took thought for Abraham by rescuing Lot and his family from total destruction."

Lot's Daughters Secure Their Future: *A Summary of Gen 19:30–38*

Because Lot is afraid to stay in Zoar, he goes up from there and settles with his two daughters in a cave in the hill country. The older daughter says to the younger, "Our father is old and there is not a man in the country to come to us in the usual way. Come now, let us ply our father with wine and then lie with him and in this way preserve the family through our father." That night they stupefy Lot with wine so that he does not know his older daughter lies with him. The next day the older daughter proposes to the younger that they repeat the pattern. "Let us ply him with wine again tonight; then you go in and lie with him. So we shall preserve the family through our father." The daughters again stupefy Lot with wine, and he does not realize that his younger daughter lies with him. In this way both women become pregnant by their father. The older bears a son whom she calls Moab; he becomes "the ancestor of the present-day Moabites." The younger bears a son whom she calls Ben-ammi; he becomes "the ancestor of the present-day Ammonites."

Reflection

Even though the wife and daughters of Lot play key roles in these stories, their lack of names makes it difficult to focus on them. They seem to exist only in terms of their relationship to Lot. Moreover, while the daughters feature both in the story of the violent men of Sodom and in the cave-seduction story, their mother is granted only one sentence: "Lot's wife looked back, and she turned into a pillar of salt."

In fact, the entire Sodom story is compressed. Events begin one evening and end the following dawn. In the evening, the angels are compelled to take over their own defense. At dawn, they must impel Lot and his family toward safety by dragging them off by the hand. With the possible exception of the angels, no player in the drama invites much sympathy—neither Lot, his wife or daughters, nor God. And yet the women suffer the greatest losses. It is the single backward glance of Lot's nameless wife rather than the petty protests of Lot that meets with instant retribution. It is Lot's unidentified daughters who, in return for a desperate ploy to ensure family survival, acquire a scandalous reputation.

Though attempting to deduce a woman's nature from the character of the people around her is laden with pitfalls, many interpreters presume that Lot's wife grew up in Sodom and subscribed to the corrupt values of its inhabitants. Even though we are given no evidence that she approved Lot's greed or incited him to even greater avarice, this tradition maintains that she so idolized material goods as to trade her life willingly for one last look.

If such a view were correct, it would imply other assumptions as well. For example, we could easily imagine Lot's wife as a woman who would refuse to cook dinner for strangers brought in from the streets. We could assume that she would have been materialistic and preoccupied with the family image. We could imagine that, like her sons-in-law, she would have considered the prediction of catastrophe at best a tasteless joke. And, like the painter Rubens, we could certainly imagine her begging the angels for time to load a string of donkeys with all the comforts of home.

Such assumptions, however, judge Lot's wife "guilty" on the slimmest of circumstantial evidence. In the actual context of Genesis, her fate reads as little more than a curious anecdote—an aside in a cycle of stories orchestrated to contrast two men: the wise and just Abraham, who speaks intimately with God; and the weak and grasping Lot, whose life is spared only for his uncle's sake.

❖ ❖

Still, whatever the writer may have intended by even including Lot's wife and daughters, the women merit compassion. Lot's wife is reminiscent of anyone who cannot move forward: anyone obsessively mired in empty behaviors and the pursuit of transitory goals, anyone whose emotional or spiritual life remains locked "on hold." Her daughters seem simply to be victims, pawns of the only social values they know. That they should feel compelled to resort to incest as a means of bearing children evokes a sense of their profound desperation. Much like women who are raised from infancy in dependence on public aid, and who later find themselves locked into the trap of dependence on a patronizing bureaucracy, Lot's daughters could discern no other route to security or personal worth.

The stories report that Lot's daughters are, at least, left with their lives. But even this mercy is granted by a God whose terrifying power causes them to shudder every time they gaze upon the reeking furnace they once called home. Seared forever by the flames of Sodom, they may nonetheless have turned to that same El Shaddai—the only deity they knew—for further rescue:

Prayer

God Almighty, look upon our misery!
Is there any agony like ours,
any torment like the torture we have borne
since the day of your blazing wrath?
You came upon us like a whirlwind,
your fire searing our very bones.
How long will you permit this torment?
How long must we suffer anguish in our souls?
We are bowed down and utterly prostrate;
all day long we go about as if in mourning.
We burn with fever, tears scald our cheeks.
Scorched in spirit, we groan in desolation.

Show us, God of Fire,
a path of escape from the ashes of the past.
Lead us from the caves of darkness;
lift our faces to your sun.
Create us anew that we may flourish before you
like the spreading terebinth,
dressed in your unfailing strength.
El Shaddai, we bring our plea before you.
Hurry to aid us, God Most High![2]

Connections

1. How do these stories relate to your experience of God? Is your God a vengeful destroyer or enforcer of minor rules? Do you believe that God impulsively inflicts punishments disproportionate to the offense?

2. If Lot's wife had two more daughters, who were married, she may have glanced back to see whether they had changed their minds, and followed. Or her backward glance could have been sheer reflex. How do you read the story?

---

2. Based on Lam 1:12–16 and Ps 38:6–9, 21–22.

3. Lot's society considered women fulfilled only through childbearing. Considering the women you know, both mothers and those who will never bear a child, what other routes to woman's fulfillment do you perceive?

4. When Lot's wife looked back, she became frozen in that posture. We too can become mired in the past: petrified by fear or anger, frozen in resentment or hate. How do you avoid becoming locked in issues of your past?

For Further Reading

Deen, Edith, *All of the Women of the Bible* (1955), 17–20.

Nunnally-Cox, Janice, *Foremothers* (1981), 9–12.

Weems, Renita J., *Just a Sister Away* (1988), 129–40.

Winter, Miriam Therese, *WomanWisdom* (1991), 95–102.

Yamasaki, April, *Remember Lot's Wife* (1991), 9–12.

5   Rebekah: Manipulative Matriarch

Genesis 24:1–25:33 and 26:34–28:5

"Now, my son, listen to me."

Background

After Sarah, Rebekah is honored as the greatest matriarch of Israel. Her story is told by the Yahwist, who neither condemns nor praises Rebekah's behavior. Yet the Yahwist somehow manages to convey admiration both for her youthful energy and for her mature command of the art of intrigue.

The story of the young Rebekah reflects ancient Middle Eastern marriage customs. An emissary of the groom's father chooses the potential bride and negotiates terms with her family. In Rebekah's case, it is Abraham who sends an emissary to upper Mesopotamia (today's northeastern Syria) to choose a bride for his son, Isaac, from among Abraham's relatives. Because Abraham's emissary is described as "the servant who had been longest in his service" (Gen 24:2), this chapter assumes that he is Eliezer, Abraham's beloved, long-term steward (Gen 15:1–3).

Almost the moment Eliezer arrives at a well outside the village, he meets Rebekah and selects her as Isaac's prospective wife. His choice hinges upon her willingness to water his camels. Given the nature of ancient wells, such an offer represented not mere courtesy, but also the strength and spirit to perform backbreaking work. A watering trough for animals stood above ground, but the spring feeding a well could be reached only by descending a flight of broad stone steps circling deep below ground. Yet Rebekah, carrying a heavy water jar, repeats the climb until all ten camels are satisfied. Eliezer quickly establishes that this spirited girl is of Abraham's clan and negotiates the marriage with her mother and her brother, Laban. (The implication is that her father, Bethuel, is dead.) With a small entourage, Eliezer and Rebekah set out for Canaan the very next morning.

A young woman like Rebekah, acquainted only with river country, must have greeted enthusiastically each shift of scenery—desert, mountains, valleys, plains—on the five-hundred-mile journey from Aram-naharaim in Mesopotamia to Beer-lahai-roi in Canaan. The Yahwist, however, jumps to the end of the journey. At Beer-lahai-roi, a wilderness area verging on the Negeb, Rebekah meets and marries Isaac. The Yahwist then leaps ahead another twenty years, to a time when the struggling of twins in

Rebekah's womb leads her to bypass any man, and seek personal guidance from God.

When Rebekah came to term, she would have given birth, like other women of her time, in her own tent—a commodious dwelling woven of dark goat hair, with curtains separating various areas and woven mats serving as rugs, seats, and beds. As the wife of a wealthy man, she would have been assisted by slave women and a midwife as she squatted, in the last stages of labor, on cushioned stones above a space hollowed out for the newborn. As the babies emerged, Rebekah's attendants would have cut the umbilical cords, washed the infants, rubbed them with cleansing salt and oils, and swaddled them in strips of clean woolen cloth.

The Yahwist briefly describes and names the infants—Esau and Jacob—and jumps ahead again, to a time when the rivalry begun in Rebekah's womb erupts into serious conflict. This conflict centers on the birthright traditionally due a firstborn son (in this case Esau) and on a father's deathbed blessing. The firstborn was considered sacred to God, a status entitling him to later headship of the clan and a double share in his father's estate. Any blessing was a solemn matter. Like a curse, a blessing was believed to hold such power that the words, once uttered, could neither be negated nor diverted from their course. A father's final blessing (usually a confirmation of the status of the firstborn) was considered especially potent.

Jacob manages simply to buy his brother Esau's birthright. But to obtain Isaac's final blessing, he requires the help of his mother, Rebekah. Her devious plan succeeds, but arouses the murderous rage of Esau. We last observe Rebekah in the act of arranging Jacob's flight to safety in her own homeland. Perhaps fifty-five or sixty years old at this point, she may have lived another decade or so. We are told only that when Jacob returns to Canaan twenty years later, she has for some time been buried in the tomb of Sarah at Machpelah (Gen 49:31).

Tradition honors both of Rebekah's sons as forefathers of Semitic peoples. Esau is considered the progenitor of the Edomites, and Jacob the father of "the twelve tribes of Israel." The lifelong rivalry of the brothers is viewed as foreshadowing the long-term conflict between Edomites and Israelites chronicled in various places in the Old Testament. In the New Testament, Paul cites the ascendancy of the younger son to make the point that God's choices need not conform to human expectations (Rom 9:10–13).

One story about Isaac and Rebekah—a duplicate of the story in which Abraham asks Sarah to pose as his sister—is omitted below. Scholars consider it an adaptation of the earlier story, designed to dramatize the parallel importance of Isaac and Rebekah with Abraham and Sarah as founding parents of the people of Israel.

The Story of Rebekah as Told in Genesis

Abraham's Servant Chooses Rebekah for Isaac: *A Summary of Gen 24:1–60*

After Sarah dies, Abraham seeks a wife for his forty-year-old son, Isaac, by sending his trusted servant Eliezer to find a suitable woman in northwestern Mesopotamia where his brother Nahor had settled. When Eliezer arrives in Aram-naharaim, he stops at a well. He prays that the girl who gives water both to him and to his camels may be the one El Shaddai intends for Isaac. A "very beautiful" girl arrives immediately. She lowers her jar to her hand to let Eliezer drink, empties the jar into the trough, and hurries to draw water for all ten camels. Eliezer thanks her by giving her a gold nose-ring and two heavy gold bracelets. Only then does he learn that her name is Rebekah and that she is the great-niece of Abraham. While Eliezer thanks El Shaddai for leading him directly to Abraham's relatives, Rebekah rushes home. At the gleam of her jewelry, her brother Laban runs back to the well to fetch Eliezer.

Eliezer immediately delivers the marriage proposal, dwelling on Abraham's prosperity, the covenant by which El Shaddai has promised Abraham and Sarah wealth in lands and descendants, and the sign by which God chose Rebekah as Isaac's bride. Laban responds that Rebekah shall become Isaac's wife, as Eliezer's God has decreed. The bargain is sealed with gifts to the entire family. In the morning, Rebekah's family suggests a ten-day farewell party, but Eliezer wants to leave immediately. The decision is left to Rebekah. She says, "I will go," and the family sends her off with a blessing.

Rebekah Marries Isaac: *A Summary of Gen 24:61–67*

Rebekah and her maids mount their camels and depart for Canaan with Eliezer and his men. Isaac, meanwhile, has moved as far as Beer-lahai-roi in the Negeb. One evening he goes out into the open country hoping to meet the caravan, and sees camels approaching. When Rebekah sees Isaac, she dismounts from her camel and asks Eliezer, "Who is that man walking across the open country toward us?" He responds, "It is my master." She covers herself with her veil while Eliezer tells Isaac all that has happened. Then Isaac conducts Rebekah into his tent. So she becomes his wife, and Isaac loves her, and is consoled for the death of his mother, Sarah.

Rebekah Rears Twins: *A Summary of Gen 25:19–33 and 26:34–28:5*

Rebekah remains childless for twenty years, until Isaac pleads with El Shaddai on her behalf, and she conceives twins. Growing alarmed at the way they jostle each other in her womb, she goes to a sanctuary to seek an oracle (a word of divine guidance). God tells her that two peoples are quarreling within her, and that the older shall one day serve the younger. When Rebekah gives birth, the first child is reddish in coloring, his whole body like a hairy mantle, so he is named Esau (meaning unknown; possibly "hairy").

Since the second son emerges gripping the heel of the first, he is named Jacob ("heel-clutcher" or "supplanter"). Esau grows up to become a skilled hunter and outdoorsman, while Jacob, a shepherd, lives quietly among the tents. Isaac favors Esau; Rebekah dotes on Jacob. One day Esau comes in from the country so ravenous that he casually trades his rights as firstborn to Jacob in exchange for a pot of stew.

At age forty, Esau takes two Hittite wives, Judith and Basemath. His marrying outside the clan grieves his parents bitterly, but he remains Isaac's favorite. Later, when Isaac is old and nearly blind, he promises to give Esau the blessing due him as firstborn as soon as Esau can return with Isaac's favorite dish of fresh game. Rebekah overhears the conversation. She directs Jacob to bring her two young kids to cook so that he can pose as Esau and usurp the blessing. Jacob protests that Esau is hairy, while his own skin is smooth. What if Isaac penetrates the ruse and curses him? Promising to take any such curse upon herself, Rebekah solves the problem by dressing Jacob in Esau's clothes and fashioning for him a goatskin neckpiece and pair of gauntlets. Jacob then serves Isaac Rebekah's dish, saying, "I am Esau." The voice puzzles Isaac. He feels Jacob's hands, sniffs his garments, and asks, "Are you really my son Esau?" Jacob says, "Yes, I am," and Isaac blesses him as if he were the firstborn.

Jacob has barely left Isaac's tent when Esau arrives. Isaac laments that he cannot undo the blessing; he has already made Jacob Esau's superior. Weeping in bitter outrage, Esau vows to kill Jacob as soon as Isaac dies. But Rebekah again overhears. Calling Jacob, she says, "Now, my son, listen to me. Be off at once to my brother Laban . . . until your brother's anger cools. When it has died down . . . I will send and fetch you back." To justify Jacob's departure, Rebekah tells Isaac she is so weary of Hittite women "like those who live here" that her life will not be worth living unless Jacob selects a wife from among their own relatives. Adopting the idea as his own, Isaac sends Jacob off to Mesopotamia to Laban, Rebekah's brother.

Reflection

Imagine the sun sinking toward the horizon, and a scene overflowing with dusty camels, shadow-streaked sand, sparkling water, and the occasional flash of golden jewelry from a traveler's bag. A beautiful girl, carrying a clay water jar, approaches a well. To decades of movie-goers, the scene is freighted with romance. Yet as suffragist Elizabeth Cady Stanton wryly observes, girls with pitchers on their heads always seem more romantic than women with power in their hands.[1]

It is doubtful that Eliezer realizes he has chosen both: an alluring young maiden and a woman who will become, by middle age, formidable in driving

1. The *Women's Bible,* Part I (1895), 46.

home her will. Yet he surely notices that the young Rebekah positively vibrates with energy and intellectual curiosity. Not only does she run to the family tents, not the least exhausted from watering ten thirsty camels; she also leaps at the opportunity to explore new lands. In fact, as the camels plod away, it is difficult to imagine Rebekah gazing tearfully over her shoulder, but easy to imagine her prodding her camel to greater speed.

Isaac, meanwhile, paces outside his tents and anxiously scans the horizon for a glimpse of his betrothed. And from the moment Rebekah slides from her camel, modestly veiling her face until he actually takes her as his wife, Isaac loves her. Whether or not Rebekah ever returns Isaac's love with equal intensity, she is wise enough to please him so thoroughly that he never seeks another wife. In fact, for twenty years he seems barely to notice that she has not yet begun to bear the children promised him by El Shaddai. Finally, however, when Isaac is sixty and Rebekah thirty-five or forty, he does pray for a son; and El Shaddai grants Rebekah not just one son, but twins whose energy reflects her own even from the womb.

From birth, Rebekah favors her second son, Jacob. More intellectual than his brother, Jacob prefers—when not tending the herds—to spend his time "among the tents" with Rebekah. Having stressed, in their talks, the importance of alertness to opportunities for advancement, Rebekah exults when Jacob buys Esau's birthright for a mere pot of stew. She views the transaction as signaling the onset of that divinely sanctioned ascendancy of Jacob foretold to her alone. But how is Jacob to gain the blessing needed to confirm the birthright? Isaac continues to dote on Esau, despite Esau's virtual disregard for family tradition—a disregard dramatized not only by his trading a birthright for a single meal, but also by his choice of Hittite wives.

Overhearing Isaac's promise to bless Esau as the firstborn may have dashed the hopes of a lesser woman, but his words spell opportunity to Rebekah. Perhaps she has noticed that her nearly blind husband tends to distrust his failing vision and sometimes even his hearing, relying instead upon the senses that retain greater acuity—smell and touch. And perhaps she thinks that the transparently honest Isaac may prove defenseless against a brazen lie—as in one son's flatly claiming to be the other. In any case, she propels Jacob into action, fulfills her own tasks for the deception, and then hovers tensely outside the flap of Isaac's tent until her talented offspring has carried it off.

Unfortunately, Rebekah's story does not end at this point. It is no fairy tale, and she is no queen mother who spends her retirement basking in the glory of a son's splendid reign. Instead she listens in horror as Esau vows to kill Jacob the minute their father dies. She who instigated the coup is driven to conceive a second plan—this time not merely to gain wealth and status for Jacob, but to save his life.

❖ ❖

As much as forty years removed from the innocuous water girl, Rebekah has matured into an accomplished manipulator of the customs of her time. While Isaac may follow any current that arises, Rebekah charts a course and bends the elements to her will. Achieving gains for Jacob does, however, exact of Rebekah the price of a life embroiled in conflict. Surely she kills whatever trust Esau and Isaac once reposed in her. Surely Esau's wives bitterly resent her connivance in depriving Esau of his rightful position. And surely, as the brief trip she envisioned for Jacob grows into decades of absence, her loneliness deepens into an abyss of emptiness.

Like Rebekah, how many people today, having employed deception in order to further their hopes for a favored child, live in the midst of conflict or the threat of violence? How many people today, as a result of their own stage-managing attempts to play God, deprive themselves of the love of those with whom they live? On the other hand, how many people today, for emulating Rebekah's boldness in worthier causes, also suffer conflict as a result?

In Rebekah's case, one senses that even if she could have foreseen the consequences of her actions, she would have changed nothing. Driven by her own character and convinced that her vision met with divine approval, she would still have seized the initiative. Even so, perhaps sometimes she paused, as she had paused in her pregnancy, to seek God. And perhaps the very process of prayer enabled her to shed her pride and acknowledge her need for comfort:

Prayer

El Shaddai, you know me, discerning my thoughts from afar;
for you fashioned me, you knit me together in my mother's womb.
You trace my journeying and my abiding;
you know in advance every word I speak.
Yet examine me again, O God, and guide me;
wash the confusion from my heart.
I have done what I considered right,
yet my reward is strife and rage.
I seek your aid, O God, as one who knows a mother's concerns.
Do you not daily assign the morning star its place
and shake the night stars from the sky?
Is not the sea your child, burst in flood from your womb?
Do you not wrap your earth in blankets of cloud and swaddle it in fog?
Hug me to your breasts, mothering God;
tell me what to do, that my tents may ripple again with laughter.
Even as my children once ran to me, so do I turn to you.
Set me on the path to harmony; lead me in the ways of peace.[2]

2. Based on Job 38:8–13 and Ps 139:1–17, 23–24.

Connections

1. Isaac and Rebekah were not the sole practitioners of favoritism; it still thrives in many a household, classroom, and place of work. Do you sometimes foster rivalry by unthinkingly playing favorites?

2. Like Rebekah, many people feel impelled to manipulate or control others, as if they needed to help God out. How are your motives and desires revealed in your behavior? Do you genuinely trust in God's providence?

3. Like anyone else, Rebekah encompasses a mixture of qualities. She is courageous, energetic, and inventive, but she can also be rash, arrogant, and deceitful. Which "Rebekahs" do you need to invite into your life?

For Further Reading

Deen, Edith, *All of the Women of the Bible* (1955), 21–27.

Exum, J. Cheryl, "Mothers in Israel" in *Feminist Interpretation of the Bible* (1985), ed. Letty M. Russell, 78.

Friedman, Richard Elliott, *Who Wrote the Bible?* (1987), 33–34.

Great People of the Bible and How They Lived (1974), 48–53.

Nunnally-Cox, Janice, *Foremothers* (1981), 12–15.

Okure, Teresa, "Women in the Bible" in *With Passion and Compassion* (1988), ed. Virginia Fabella and Mercy Amba Oduyoye, 53.

Stanton, Elizabeth Cady, *The Woman's Bible*, Part I (1895), 46.

Winter, Miriam Therese, *WomanWisdom* (1991), 44–56.

6 Leah and Rachel: Sisters in Conflict

Genesis 29–33, 35

"Give me sons, or I shall die!"

[handwritten: Zionist Jews? land Promised]

Background

Narratives of the great matriarchs of Israel continue, in the stories of Leah and Rachel. Sisters who spring to life in tales told primarily by the Yahwist, they are the daughters of Laban—Rebekah's brother, Jacob's uncle. Leah is the older, Rachel the younger. Both fall in love with Jacob when he travels five hundred miles from Canaan to find a wife in the river country of upper Mesopotamia (today's northeastern Syria). Leah is described as being "*rak*-eyed," *rak* meaning either "dull, lacking lustre," or "gentle, lovely." Rachel, in contrast, is described as so "beautiful in both face and figure" that Jacob offers Laban seven years of work to buy her as his wife.

Laban, however, has a hidden agenda. The seven years pass, and on the first evening of the week-long wedding feast, Laban takes advantage of the custom that sends a bride to her husband heavily veiled, in silence and in darkness. He sends Leah—not Rachel—to Jacob's bed. Only at the end of the celebration, after extracting the promise of another seven years' work, does Laban allow Jacob to marry Rachel as well. The story moves immediately from the wedding to the sisters' competition to bear sons. They and their slaves Zilpah and Bilhah (as surrogate mothers) bear Jacob twelve sons in all. Leah is fertile immediately, but Rachel is barren for years before she bears Joseph. Much later, she dies giving birth to Benjamin. Over the years, the sisters' childbearing rivalry grows so obsessive that on one occasion Leah *buys* Jacob's marital services from the preferred Rachel. Leah pays Rachel in mandrakes—a herb bearing plum-like yellow fruit and featuring a forked root that roughly resembles a human body. Merely gazing upon mandrake root was believed to make a woman fertile.

Three writers—the Yahwist (J), the Elohist (E), and the Priestly source (P)—contribute to several convoluted stories about the reasons for and the journey of Jacob's family to Canaan. Even after a total of twenty years' residence in Mesopotamia, Jacob's position remains ambiguous. So long as he continues to work for Laban as a dependent, he lacks full membership in the local legal community. His wives and children also remain legal dependents of their "father's house." Understandably, Jacob yearns to return to Canaan where, as successor to Abraham and Isaac, he will be a man of stature. The fact that Laban owes much of his wealth to Jacob's unpaid development of his flocks complicates matters. Still, Laban agrees to release Jacob and to pay him the token wage of all sheep born black and all goats born striped or speckled. (At the time, most sheep were uniformly white, and most goats solidly black or brown.) But the number of unusually colored animals rises dramatically, and Jacob's wealth increases at Laban's expense. Tensions escalate until Jacob, his family, and his herds must leave in stealth.

As the caravan departs, Jacob is unaware that Rachel has stolen her father's household gods or *teraphim*—mask-faced objects believed to speak words of divine guidance and guaranteeing the leadership position and property claims of their possessor. Had Laban died sonless, Jacob would have inherited these gods, but under the circumstances, neither Jacob nor Rachel possesses any claim to them. Laban pursues the caravan, but Rachel manipulates his ritual avoidance of a menstruating woman, and he never finds the gods. By the time the entourage reaches Canaan, Jacob may know of the theft, for he demands that all gods brought from Mesopotamia be buried. Shortly thereafter, Rachel dies in childbirth. The memorial pillar Jacob sets upon her grave remains a well-known landmark five hundred years later (1 Sam 10:2). Leah lives for many more years. She is buried in the tomb of Sarah at Machpelah (Gen 49:31).

The natural and surrogate sons of Leah and Rachel are revered as the fathers of the "twelve tribes of Israel," but aside from Genesis, Ruth is the only book of the Bible to mention both Leah and Rachel by name. There they are praised as "the two who built up the family of Israel" (Ruth 4:11). Even though it was Rachel, not her child, who died in sorrow, the prophet Jeremiah later used Rachel as a personification of the land of Israel, grieving for its conquered and exiled children (Jer 31:15). Later still, the evangelist Matthew adapted Jeremiah by using Rachel to personify the grieving mothers of Bethlehem, whose babies were killed at Herod's command (Mt 2:18).

The Story of Leah and Rachel as Told in Genesis

Jacob Meets Rachel: *A Summary of Gen 29:1–13*

Near Aram-naharaim, Jacob arrives at a well that is protected from debris by a heavy stone lid. Shepherds gathered nearby tell Jacob that his kinswoman Rachel is expected any minute. He urges them to water their sheep and depart, but they explain that custom forbids them to remove the stone until all of the shepherds are assembled. During this conversation, Rachel arrives with her father's flock. Jacob rushes forward, rolls the stone off the well, and waters Laban's sheep. Giving Rachel a cousinly kiss, he is moved to tears. She runs home to report the arrival of their kinsman to her father, Laban. Laban, in turn, hurries to welcome Jacob to his home.

Jacob Marries Leah and Rachel: *A Summary of Gen 29:14–30*

After Jacob has stayed with Laban a month, Laban asks him what wages he would like. Now Laban has two daughters. The older, Leah, is "[*rak*]-eyed," and the younger, Rachel, is "beautiful in both face and figure." Jacob is in love with Rachel, so he tells Laban, "For your younger daughter Rachel I would work seven years." The bargain is struck. At the end of seven years—years that pass for Jacob like a few days because of his love—Jacob asks for Rachel. On the first evening of the wedding feast, however, Laban sends Leah to Jacob. Jacob sleeps with her, only to discover her identity in the morning. He protests to Laban, "It was for Rachel I worked. Why have you played this trick on me?" Laban replies that it goes against custom in his country to marry off a younger sister before the older, but that if Jacob will go through with the seven days' feast for Leah, he can have Rachel as well—in exchange for another seven years' work. Jacob agrees. A week later he also takes Rachel as wife, loving her "rather than Leah."

Leah and Rachel Compete in Childbearing: *A Summary of Gen 29:31–30:24*

Seeing that Leah is unloved, God grants her a son, Reuben. Leah rejoices, thinking that "now my husband will love me." She bears three more sons, Simeon, Levi, and Judah, believing that now "my husband will surely be attached to me." Rachel, meanwhile, grows jealous of Leah and complains to Jacob, "Give me sons, or I shall die!" He retorts, "Can I take the place of God, who has denied you children?" Rachel takes matters into her own hands by giving Jacob her slave woman Bilhah "so that she may bear sons to be laid upon my knees, and through her I too may build up a family." Naming Bilhah's sons Dan and Naphtali, she exults, "God has given judgment for me! I have devised a fine trick against my sister, and it has succeeded!" Leah in turn gives Jacob her slave woman Zilpah, who bears Gad and Asher. This time Leah comments, "Women will call me happy." One day Rachel grants Leah access to Jacob in exchange for some mandrakes. After this incident, Leah conceives and bears two more sons, Issachar and Zebulun. "God has rewarded me," she says. "Now my husband will honor me like a princess." Later she bears a daughter, Dinah. Finally God takes thought of Rachel and grants her a son. She names him Joseph and prays that God might give her another son.

Jacob, Leah, and Rachel Depart for Canaan: *A Summary of Gen 30:25–31:24*

After his years of unpaid labor, Jacob arranges to be paid for further work in all sheep and goats born with odd coloration. The number of strangely colored animals burgeons immensely, and Laban and his sons grow resentful. They think that Jacob is somehow using deceit to rob them. Jacob notices their feelings. Meeting secretly with his wives in the countryside, he broaches the idea of moving to his native land. Leah and Rachel are happy to leave. They feel that their father has treated them like aliens, for instead of giving them the bride price to which custom entitles them, he has used Jacob's labor for his own benefit. "All the wealth which God has saved from our father's clutches," they say, "is surely ours and our children's." While Laban is away for the annual sheep-shearing festival, Jacob slips away with his family, servants, and herds. Rachel, meanwhile, steals her father's household gods. By the time Laban returns home and discovers the theft, Jacob has a week's lead.

Rachel Deceives Laban: *A Summary of Gen 31:25–33:20 and 35:1–15*

On overtaking the caravan, Laban accuses Jacob of carrying off his daughters like captives of war, and demands to know why Jacob has also stolen his gods. Unaware of Rachel's actions, Jacob asserts, "Whoever is found in possession of your gods shall die for it." At his urging, Laban searches the tents of Jacob, Leah, and the two slave women, but finds nothing. Rachel, meanwhile, conceals the gods in her camel bag and settles herself on top of the bag. When Laban enters her tent, she asks him not to take it amiss that she cannot rise in his presence, for she is menstruating. Carefully searching the rest of the tent, Laban finds nothing. Jacob and Laban end by swearing peace, and Jacob's entourage travels on to the border of Canaan. One night Jacob wrestles with a supernatural being. For surviving the encounter, he is renamed Israel, "he who strives with God." After a tense but peaceful meeting with Jacob's estranged brother Esau, the caravan moves inland. At the terebinth of Shechem, Jacob collects all the foreign gods his people hold in their possession, and buries them. They then move on to Bethel, where Jacob ritually rededicates his household to El Shaddai.

Rachel Dies in Childbirth: *A Summary of Gen 35:16–20*

With the caravan once more on the road, Rachel goes into labor. Her pains are severe. The midwife tells her, "Do not be afraid, for this is another son for you." With her last breath she names her son Ben-oni ("son of sorrow"), but Jacob calls him Benjamin ("son of the right hand" or "son of good fortune"). Rachel dies and is buried at the roadside. Over her grave Jacob sets up a sacred pillar which becomes a famous landmark.

Reflection

The love, hate, jealousy, and strife that complicate this family saga rival the convolutions of any television miniseries. Yet the plot lines involving the women spring from a single source—Jacob's adoration of Rachel, a love so exclusive that it arouses in Leah and Rachel an impassioned rivalry.

When Jacob first arrives in Aram-naharaim, he finds himself standing at the very place where his grandfather's steward first came upon his own mother, Rebekah. Though grimy and sun-scorched, he is primed for romance: he tries to rid the scene of onlookers even before he has a clue to Rachel's incandescent beauty. When she arrives, he is dazzled. With a superhuman rush of adrenaline, he heaves aside the massive well-stone and waters Laban's sheep. Merely giving Rachel a kiss of greeting overwhelms him, and this immediate love proves to be no passing infatuation. He works fourteen years for Rachel (years that seem to him "a few days"), and becomes the first of his people ever to erect a memorial pillar to a woman.

So blazing a love acts as a negative catalyst, however, in the lives of Leah and Rachel. Sparks of resentment may first have been ignited long since, in the sisters' childhood—the adventurous Rachel forever annoyed at hearing that she ought to come in from the fields and learn to keep house; the plain Leah sick to death of halfhearted compliments on her lovely eyes. When the rivalry bursts to flame in the marriage, both women suffer: Leah, for she is fertile but unloved; Rachel, for she is loved but barren.

Despite Jacob's obvious preference for Rachel, Leah's obsession with him must have awakened early, for she willingly poses as her sister in the wedding tent. Her complicity in Laban's ruse apparently backfires, however, arousing in Jacob not love but scorn—or, at the least, indifference. In the end, Leah abandons her quest for love and settles for the more attainable goal of respect: "my husband will honor me like a princess" (Gen 30:20). The loved Rachel, meanwhile, feels equally reproached. She must listen, day after day, to the cooing of Leah's babies, evidence of her sister's fruitfulness. Despairing of her own value, she proclaims that she will die if she has no son. Then, when she does bear a son, she very humanly prays for another. Ironically, when this prayer too is answered, she dies giving birth. Yet Rachel at least lives to see her first son grow into boyhood, while Leah never gains the love for which she yearns.

❖ ❖

Other family conflicts simmer as well. Jacob's success in swelling his own flocks provokes wrath among his male in-laws; Laban's failure to give his daughters their bride price kindles in them a smoldering resentment. At last Jacob consults his wives about making a change. While both Leah and Rachel prove willing to move to Canaan, merely leaving Laban's household does not satisfy Rachel. Taking the law into her own hands, she avenges years of perceived mistreatment by stealing her father's gods. (One can imagine Leah, this one time, cheering her sister on.) Rachel's later manipulation of the blood taboo to conceal the gods is ingenious, but her vengeful triumph is short-lived. Journey's end brings heartbreak to both sisters. Rachel dies in the agonizing birth of Benjamin, and Leah will soon mourn the rape of her daughter Dinah (chapter 7).

Genesis reports nothing about the childhood of Rachel's second son, Benjamin, nor any details of Leah's later years. Perhaps Leah demonstrates a love she never knew she felt for Rachel by raising Benjamin as her own. As the uncontested senior wife of Jacob, she undoubtedly gains renown as a woman of substance. But it seems unlikely that Jacob ever turns to her in love, even though his loss of his beloved and her loss of a lifelong companion could have led them to turn to one another. Instead, the stories of Genesis that follow strongly suggest that Jacob compounds his loss and Leah's isolation by focusing his immense capacity for love on Joseph, Rachel's firstborn.

❖ ❖

Scholars question the factuality of some details of the sisters' story. Since Leah means "cow" and Rachel means "ewe," a few even dismiss the sisters as the later fleshing-out of symbolic totems for cattle-grazing "Leah" tribes and sheep-herding "Rachel" tribes. Through the stories of the Yahwist, however, these women *live*. Tough and vibrant, they translate easily to our own century. Leah is sister to any woman obsessed with a partner who barely acknowledges her existence. Rachel is but a heartbeat away from women whose ignorance or poverty denies them access to medical care, rendering childbirth a life-threatening enterprise. Both sisters live on in women whose extended stepfamilies include other women's children. And both reappear in women who, by their lack of subservience, confound those who would keep them in their place.

Like Sarah and Rebekah before them, Leah and Rachel discover that they possess power despite the system. And they use it with verve. Given their audacity, one can imagine them refusing to mince words even in prayer. Perhaps, beginning in the early years of their marriage and lasting until late in Leah's life, there arose among Leah and Rachel and El Shaddai an ongoing dialogue, a sort of antiphonal chorus:

Prayer

Leah: El Shaddai, I am sick of living;
I speak out in the bitterness of my soul.
Let me know the charge against me!
Why do you let your servant Jacob scorn me,
when I am equally the work of your hands?
Have you eyes of flesh? Are you as blind as he is?
You know that I am guiltless; in your great power,
grant me Jacob's love!

El Shaddai: Listen to me, wife of Jacob:
I have upheld you from your mother's womb,
and until you grow old, I will carry you.
Can you dismiss the wonder of a child of your womb,
forget the joy of an infant at your breast?
Even so, I will never forget you.
I have shaped you; I uphold you.
And when your hair is filled with white,
I will carry you still.

Rachel: El Shaddai, your hands molded me like clay;
will you now turn aside and let me die disgraced?
Would you shamefully reduce me to less than dust?

Though I am upright, you force me to hang my head;
I am steeped in shame and affliction.
With life so fleeting, can you not grant me a happy moment?
Before I depart to that land of gloom lit by no ray of light,
deliver me from this living death:
grant me a son!

El Shaddai: Remember that I am God; there is no other like me.
It is I who determine what is to be.
My purpose stands; I shall accomplish all I please.
For I speak and I bring it to pass;
What I have planned for you, I shall carry out.

Leah: Sustaining God, after all these years
my heart is no longer proud, nor are my eyes haughty.
You have poured me out like milk and curdled me like cheese,
torn in shreds my woman's heart and patched it together again.
Like a mother weaning her child,
you have pushed me into standing on my own;
you have broken me of seeking what cannot be.
No longer do I busy myself with things beyond my power.
In no one man, but only in you do I now rest,
calm and quiet as a child at play in her mother's tent.[1]

Connections

1. Like Leah and Rachel, some women perceive other women as the "competition." Have you ever experienced being shunted aside, like Leah, for someone younger or more attractive? On the basis of equally superficial criteria, do you yourself ever "write off" other women?

2. Both Leah and Rachel seek what the other possesses. Do you overlook the riches you already possess, pining instead for sources of fulfillment not available to you?

3. Which of Leah's qualities would you like to invite into your life? Which qualities of Rachel?

For Further Reading

Deen, Edith, *All of the Women of the Bible* (1955), 28–36.

Exum, J. Cheryl, "Mothers in Israel," in *Feminist Interpretation of the Bible* (1985), ed. Letty M. Russell, 79–80.

Nunnally-Cox, Janice, *Foremothers* (1981), 15–20.

Winter, Miriam Therese, *WomanWisdom* (1991), 57–73, 106–12.

1. Based on Job 10:1–22; Isa 46:3–11; and Ps 131:1–2.

7 Dinah, Daughter of Leah: Woman Abused

Genesis 33:18—34:31

"He took her . . . and violated her."

Background

The story of Dinah, daughter of Leah and Jacob, is inserted into Genesis just before the story of the death of Rachel in childbirth. It seems actually to occur later, however, when Jacob is a man past his prime and the family has settled permanently in Canaan. Dinah is a young woman who is raped by Shechem, the son of Hamor, prince of the Hivites who occupy the city of Shechem. At that time, the rape of a virgin constituted an economic crime against her father, who could never arrange an advantageous marriage for a "defiled" daughter. In later Hebrew law, which codified long-standing custom, a rapist was required to marry the girl—with future divorce prohibited—and to compensate the girl's father by paying him fifty pieces of silver (Deut 22:28–29).

In Dinah's story, the men of her family do not demand the substantial bride price Shechem's people anticipate. Instead they ask only that the Hivite men undergo circumcision in order to intermarry with the clan of Jacob (Israel), so that both groups may share in each other's wealth. Shechem and his father, Hamor, accept the deceptively lenient terms, and Dinah is handed over immediately. The other men of the city also accept, and the circumcisions proceed. The end of the story follows rapidly. While the Hivite men are incapacitated with pain, two of Dinah's brothers slaughter all of them and haul Dinah home. Her other ten brothers follow up, looting the town and the countryside.

At its core, this is a family revenge story. Told by the Yahwist, it offers a rationale for the later decline of the tribes of Simeon and Levi, since Simeon and Levi mastermind the plot against the Hivites, and that plot creates ill will for Israel. As the story now stands, however, the Yahwist's narrative is intertwined with elements from a more peaceful tradition about Israel's occupation of Shechem. Written by the Elohist, these strands depict Jacob as buying land and negotiating a trade agreement to be confirmed by intermarriage. In order to blend these different stories, the editor who entwines them attempts to downplay the rape by repeatedly asserting that Shechem loves Dinah.

In the composite story our Bibles contain, Dinah herself—certainly her pain—all but disappears. She becomes an object of negotiation, a political pawn. Translators of the past have further diminished Dinah's experience by titling the chapter "The 'Seduction' of Dinah." The core story shows no such confusion. The Hebrew verb *'inna* means to assault sexually, and connotes moral and social degradation as well. Contemporary translators work to convey the full meaning by rendering *'inna* as "lay with by force" (NAB) or "raped and so dishonored" (JB).

Shechem the city also figures in this story, as it does in stories from Judges and Kings, and the story of Jesus and the Samaritan woman at Jacob's well in the Gospel of John. Egyptian texts and archaeological findings at the site show that ancient Shechem was an important urban center, complete with a multiroom palace and temple complex. Situated forty miles north of Jerusalem in the pass between Mt. Ebal and Mt. Gerizim, it dominated a trade route connecting northern and southern Canaan, and commanded authority over fertile fields to the east. Canaanites considered the location sacred, "the navel of the land" (Judg 9:37) where mountains linked heaven with earth, deities with human beings. Findings from the approximate time of Jacob suggest that the inhabitants of Shechem ritually sacrificed the ass—in Hebrew, *hamor*. Thus the names of the Hivite son and father in the story of Dinah may symbolize the city itself: Shechem the city, son of Hamor the ass (the city's sacred animal). The tell, or mound, of ancient Shechem survives beside the modern village of Balata. Jacob's well lay about a quarter mile southeast of ancient Shechem, near a road forking up toward Galilee. Its shaft cut through the chalk of the valley floor, and a woman fetching water descended seventy-five to one hundred feet, depending on the water level at the time.

The Story of Dinah as Told in Genesis

A Summary of Gen 33:18–34:31

Having journeyed from Aram-naharaim in Mesopotamia, Jacob and his family reach Shechem in Canaan. They pitch their tents east of town. Jacob buys the piece of land from the sons of Hamor the Hivite, the local prince, for a hundred sheep. One day Dinah, the daughter of Leah and Jacob, goes out to visit the women of the district. Shechem, son of Hamor, sees her. He takes her by force and rapes her. But Shechem feels deeply attached to Dinah; he loves her and seeks to win her affection. He tells Hamor, "You must get me this girl as my wife."

When Jacob learns that his daughter has been dishonored, his sons are away, tending the herds in the open country. Although Hamor comes to discuss the matter, Jacob holds his peace until his sons come home. They are inflamed at the news. Hamor tells them that his son, Shechem, is in love with the girl, and begs them to let him marry her. He proposes that the two groups intermarry freely. "If you settle among us," he argues, "the country is open before you; make your home in it; move about freely, and acquire land of your own." Shechem, too, tries to win their favor. "Fix the bride-price and the gift as high as you like," he says; "only, give me the girl in marriage."

Jacob's sons reply that they cannot hand over their sister because they look upon lack of circumcision as a disgrace. If, however, every Hivite man agrees to be circumcised, they will intermingle and become one people with the Hivites. If the Hivite men refuse circumcision, "we shall take the girl and go." Hamor finds the terms acceptable, and Shechem agrees because Dinah has captured his heart. The men of Shechem also agree, and undergo circumcision. Two days later, while their pain remains intense, two of Jacob's sons—Simeon and Levi, full brothers to Dinah—arm themselves with swords and boldly enter the town. They kill every male, including Hamor and Shechem, and take Dinah from Shechem's house. Jacob's other sons seize donkeys, sheep, and cattle both inside the town and outside in the open country. They step over the dead bodies to loot the houses, and they carry off the women and children.

Jacob complains to Simeon and Levi, "You have brought trouble on me; you have brought my name into bad odor among the people of [this] country. . . . My numbers are few; if they combine against me and attack, I shall be destroyed, I and my household with me." They retort, "Is our sister to be treated as a common whore?"

Reflection

Genesis reports only that Dinah "went out to visit women of the district" and that Shechem "took her, lay with her, and violated her." As the ancient editor interwove the stories, it is only *after* the rape that Shechem seeks "to win her affection." In the rest of the story, we hear much about property, cattle, and trading, but nothing more of Dinah until her brothers remove her from Shechem's house. Not only is Dinah assaulted physically; she is also abused politically and economically. She stands in the middle as a bargaining chip while her rapist joins his kinsmen and hers in reducing her to an item of trade—or to an excuse for premeditated murder.

Imagine how Dinah herself might have perceived the double blow of sexual assault and marriage to her assailant. . . .

❖ ❖

A girl of thirteen or fourteen runs laughing through a sunlit field, her arms thrust into the air in sheer exuberance. She is all but one with the birds cartwheeling above her, for she is intoxicated with the city of Shechem and the sophisticated women of Canaan. Accustomed to her own family's flexible tents of woven goat hair, she loves the solid houses of Canaan—the spacious grace of their interior courtyards, the privacy of their small outer rooms. Then too, raised amid gangling older brothers, she has hungered to join girls her age in experimenting with rouge and kohl; she has yearned for the opinion of women other than her mother on the latest rage in jewelry and dress. Today, at last, she has spent hours with girls of Shechem, experimenting with hair styles and erupting into the giggles. Spinning to look back at the city, Dinah drops to the ground to admire its massive embankments, its sun-dappled walls of stone and brick.

But she is not alone. A figure rises from behind a small ridge—the handsome, popular Shechem. Her shy smile of greeting has barely begun to form when it dies, for before she has grasped his intention, he has shoved her onto her back, pinned her down, and raped her. When he rolls aside, releasing her, Dinah hears only the whimper of an injured animal. Some time passes before she recognizes its voice as her own. Deep in shock and shame, she stumbles home to her mother Leah.

For days she huddles in a curtained corner of Leah's tent, while Leah and Jacob, awaiting the return of her brothers, debate her future in whispers. She bathes obsessively yet never feels clean. She is terrified to venture even to her father's well. She stares in horror at the gifts that keep arriving: delicate hair pins and finely wrought combs, brightly polished metal mirrors and vials of perfume. They come from that man whose glazed, sweating face is burned forever into her memory—the man her parents say she must service the rest of her life.

❖ ❖

In this story God is mute, and Leah's reactions go unrecorded. Jacob—the wily son of the Rebekah stories and the impetuous lover of the Rachel stories—emerges as a peevish old man who cannot form a single firm opinion. Nor do the atrocities of Dinah's brothers help Dinah. If anything, her grief and unmerited guilt intensify at every glimpse of a Hivite ornament dangling from a relative's tent pole; her heart plummets every time she comes face to face with an enslaved girl of Shechem.

In our world, where girls and women are still raped and abandoned in ditches and fields, the parallels with Dinah are obvious. Studies released in the 1990s report that one-third of American women are sexually abused as children and that one-third will be raped in their lifetimes. More than half of all rapes occur when the victim is seventeen or younger; and in the years that follow, rape victims are more likely than non-victims to use drugs, suffer depression, or ponder suicide.[1]

If Dinah's story remains that of many American women, Shechem's remains that of many men. Shechem's lack of empathy for Dinah as a person matches the mental distortions of rapists, especially date-rapists. Dr. Gene Abel, professor of psychiatry at Emory University, tells the story of a man repeatedly charged with rape, who claimed he had never raped a woman: Any woman who spoke to him or allowed him into her apartment wanted sex, no matter what she said. How would he know a woman was unwilling? "If she fought me the whole time we were having sex." This man was blind to the lack of logic in his thinking.[2] Similarly, trial lawyers continue to make rape a matter of women's friendliness and manner of dress, not men's criminal behavior.

1. "Data Vastly Understate Rape," *The Sacramento Bee*, 24 April 1992, A30.
2. David Gelman and others, "The Mind of the Rapist," *Newsweek*, 23 July 1990, 50.

Women respond to these realities by cloaking their lives in caution. They sleep with windows locked whatever the weather, they avoid dark streets and parking lots, they suppress a smile lest it be construed as invitation. They have little other choice so long as society fails to recognize the simple truth that even outright enticement does not excuse assault, any more than verbal provocation excuses murder. Women cannot cure the distorted thinking that leads to rape. But they can and do fight for prosecution of rapists. They support the victims of rape, and they help their children understand that even so apparently harmless a pastime as telling "bimbo" jokes promotes the attitudes that shape and encourage the victimization of women.

To a woman, they can empathize with Dinah. And they can pray with her and other women the words of the psalmist's suffering servant:

Prayer

My God, my God, why have you abandoned me?
When I call, you do not answer;
all who see me deride me as an object of shame.
Yet you drew me from the womb,
you entrusted me to my mother's breasts:
from my mother's womb you have been my God.
How can you now stand silent?
I am in trouble and there is no one to help!
My heart clenches; my throat tastes like baked clay.
Villains encircle me, binding me body and soul
with their actions and their words.
My body is made a commodity, my spirit trampled to death.
Be with me, my Strength; save my life
so that I may praise the God
who never despises the injured or hides from them,
but answers when they call.
Be with me, O God, for I am in trouble![3]

Connections

1. Imagine Dinah's subsequent life. What taunts and whispers follow her? What thoughts torment her? Does she recover emotionally? Does she marry?

2. Consider the men of Dinah's story, Hivites and Israelites alike. How do all of them participate in the abuse of Dinah?

3. Based on Ps 22.

3. "Be careful; hurry home," mothers tell their daughters. What can you do to help create an environment where girls need not walk in constant awareness of danger?

For Further Reading

Deen, Edith, *All of the Women of the Bible* (1955), 37–40.

Nunnally-Cox, Janice, *Foremothers* (1981), 20–22.

Salholz, Eloise, and others, "Women Under Assault," *Newsweek*, 16 July 1990, 23–24.

(Jacob = Israel great trials

Leave revenge to God

(terrible slaughter of innocent
people)

Brothers wrongly thought
being set apont made
them better _

Her
Brothers were Simeon + Levi

Jacob asked for removal of
all pagan or foreign gods.

8 Tamar, Daughter-in-Law of Judah: Intrepid Outsider

Genesis 38:1–30

"She is more in the right than I am. . . ."

Background

Because the story of Tamar and Judah contains "unsavory" elements, it is seldom—if ever—read in worship services. Yet the Yahwist author celebrates Tamar, and so do Jewish and Christian tradition. She is honored in Jewish tradition in a marriage blessing that appears in the Book of Ruth: "[M]ay your family be like the family of Perez, whom Tamar bore to Judah" (4:12). In a similar Christian honor roll, Matthew lists Tamar by name in his genealogy of the ancestors of Jesus (Mt 1:3).

Tamar lived somewhat later than Dinah, at a time when clans were beginning to coalesce around the twelve sons of Jacob (Israel). Judah, Jacob's fourth son, had chosen to live among a Canaanite people, and this story reflects that milieu. One key plot element is the casual Canaanite acceptance of temple prostitutes. Distinct from ordinary prostitutes and associated with the worship of Asherah and Baal, such women functioned much like priestesses. They included unmarried virgins, but also married, well-to-do women who offered themselves to strangers a single time in order to fulfill a religious vow. Canaanites respected these women for the tribute they paid the deities responsible for fertility and for life itself.

Tamar's story also reflects an important Hebrew custom, that of levirate marriage—the obligation of a close male relative to marry a childless widow and sire sons in the dead man's name. This custom prevented the extinction of a man's family line, preserved his estate within the clan, and rescued the widow from destitution. But men sometimes refused to honor the levirate customs. In such cases, the widow was directed to complain to the town elders. If the elders' moral pressure failed to sway the man, she was directed to confront him in front of his peers, "pull his sandal off his foot, spit in his face, and declare: 'Thus we requite the man who will not build up his brother's family'" (Deut 25:9–10). This procedure shamed the man and his entire family, but it was still the widow who was left childless and financially insecure.

The story of Tamar begins with Judah's marriage to a Canaanite woman, Bathshua, who bears him three sons—Er, Onan, and Shelah. When Er reaches marriageable age, Judah selects Tamar (assumed to be Canaanite from the origin of her name) as his wife. When Er unexpectedly dies of unknown causes, he is said to have been killed by God for unspecified "wickedness." Following the levirate law, Judah gives Tamar as wife to Onan. But Onan is unwilling to father children in his brother's name, and in the act of intercourse with Tamar, repeatedly spills his semen on the ground. His name gives us the word *onanism*, used today to mean either masturbation or the *coitus interruptus* he practiced. When Onan dies, it is said that God killed him for willful violation of the levirate law.

With two sons dead, Judah treats Tamar as a jinx. He delays in giving her to Shelah, his third and last son. Tamar seems to fear that Judah means permanently to evict her from his family, but she chooses not to shame him as Hebrew custom allows. Instead, after the death of Judah's wife, Tamar disguises herself as a Canaanite cult prostitute and offers herself to Judah. Although her intent is to become pregnant, she knows that she risks capital punishment for promiscuity if she succeeds. She therefore prudently obtains evidence to identify Judah as the father. When local gossip informs Judah that Tamar is pregnant, she still belongs legally to Judah's household, and it is therefore he who must pronounce legal sentence upon her. But when Tamar satisfies Judah of his paternity, he revokes the sentence and accepts the twins she bears as his sons. In Gen 49:8–12, the dying Jacob blesses Judah as the son from whose line kings of Israel shall spring—an unlikely outcome but for Tamar's ploy, with two of Judah's sons dead and the third unmarried. Indeed, one of Tamar's sons founds the line that later produces the great King David.

The Story of Tamar as Told in Genesis

Tamar Enters Judah's Family: *A Summary of Gen 38:1–11*

Judah pitches his tents in southern Canaan in the company of an Adullamite named Hirah. Judah marries a Canaanite woman, Bathshua, who bears him three sons. She names them Er, Onan, and Shelah. As a wife for his oldest son, Er, Judah selects a woman named Tamar. But Er is wicked in God's sight, and God takes away his life. Judah then directs Onan to do his duty and raise up offspring for his brother. Onan takes Tamar as his wife, but because he knows that any offspring will not count as his own, he spills his seed on the ground whenever he lies with Tamar. What Onan does is wicked in God's sight, and God takes away his life also. Fearing that Shelah may die like his brothers, Judah says to his daughter-in-law Tamar, "Remain as a widow in your father's house until my son Shelah grows up." So Tamar returns and lives in her father's house.

Tamar Claims Her Rights: *A Summary of Gen 38:12–30*

Time passes and Shelah grows up, but Judah does not give Tamar to him as wife. Judah's wife Bathshua dies, and when Judah has finished mourning, he and his friend Hirah go up to Timnath in the southern hill country for the annual sheep-shearing festival. When Tamar hears where her father-in-law is going, she removes her widow's clothing, veils her face like a cult prostitute, and sits down where the road forks on the way to Timnath. Seeing Tamar, Judah takes her for a temple prostitute. He stops at the roadside and says, "Let me lie with you." She asks what payment he offers, and he promises to send her a young goat from his flock. She agrees, provided that he gives her as pledge the staff he carries and the legal seal he wears on a cord around his neck. He hands over the seal and the staff and lies with her, and she becomes pregnant. She returns home, removes her veil, and puts on her widow's garments again.

Judah later sends his friend Hirah to deliver the goat and reclaim his seal and staff, but Hirah cannot find the woman. When Hirah asks the men of the locality where to find the prostitute who works at the fork in the road, they answer, "There has been no temple prostitute here." Hirah goes back to Judah and reports that the people of the area know nothing about the woman. Embarrassed, Judah dismisses the matter. "Let her keep the pledge, or we shall be a laughingstock. After all, I did send the kid, even though you could not find her." About three months later, Judah hears that his daughter-in-law Tamar has "played the prostitute and gotten herself pregnant." "Bring her out," he orders, "so that she may be burnt." But as she is being brought out, she sends word to him: "The father of my child is the man to whom these things belong. . . . See if you recognize whose they are, this seal, the pattern of the cord, and the staff." Judah identifies them and says, "She is more in the right than I am, because I did not give her to my son Shelah." He does not have intercourse with her again.

When Tamar's time comes, she is found to have twins in her womb. While she is in labor, one of them puts out a hand. The midwife fastens a scarlet thread around the wrist, saying, "This one appeared first." No sooner has the infant drawn back its hand than his brother breaks out, so he is named Perez, "breaking out." Soon afterwards the infant with the thread on his wrist is born, and he is named Zerah, "scarlet."

Reflection

With its focus on bearing sons, Tamar's story is distinctly patriarchal. But she makes the achievement of motherhood a highly personal project. A German novelist, Thomas Mann, was fascinated by Tamar. In his massive tetralogy, *Joseph and His Brothers*, he speculates that she sat enrapt at the feet of the aged Jacob, and recognized in Jacob's stories a God who, unlike any Canaanite deity, established a personal relationship with people. This God was even known to ignore human custom and show preference for younger sons. Perhaps, therefore, the God of Israel might favor Jacob's fourth son, Judah, into whose family she had married.

Whether or not Mann is right, and Tamar thus became excited about a potential role for herself in ensuring a future for Judah's line, we can easily imagine her hearing and enjoying tales about the enterprising women of Judah's family—his great-grandmother Sarah, his grandmother Rebekah, his mother Leah. Their example, combined with the denial of marital rights promised to her, seems more than adequate to spur to action a woman who is no pale wallflower.

Tamar's very name, meaning "date palm," suggests the lushness and vigor that may first have led Judah to choose her as daughter-in-law. But one son's weak health and another's scorn for tradition prevent Tamar from conceiving. Still, it is only when it appears that Judah and his third son mean to abandon her that Tamar chooses an unconventional method for achieving motherhood. Drawing upon the customs of her own milieu, she devises a plan that may work, though it endangers her life. She seems to defer implementation of her plan not out of fear, but only in order to spare the feelings of her Canaanite mother-in-law, Bathshua.

When Bathshua dies, Judah attends a sheep-shearing, an annual event notorious for its carnival-like relaxation of normal standards of behavior. Seizing her opportunity, Tamar sits veiled at the roadside, confident of two things: that Judah will succumb to temptation, and that he will not want to know the identity of the woman he uses. Against all odds, Tamar becomes pregnant from the encounter. Three months later, she finds herself facing allegations of promiscuity. Even on the verge of execution, however, she avoids embarrassing Judah. Instead she sends him his property privately, allowing him either to admit his paternity or to hold his tongue and—legally—let her burn. Fortunately, Tamar is a good judge of character. Under Judah's protection, she bears not one son, but two. It is a nice balance, the twins, as it were, replacing the two dead sons of Judah and husbands of Tamar.

As the account ends, Tamar remains a member of Judah's household as the mother of his sons, but Judah never takes Tamar as his legal wife by having further intercourse with her. And, since she has already borne children by Judah, his remaining son cannot marry her. Her status represents an odd mix of legitimacy and illegitimacy. Her story is striking, too, for its lack of divine intervention. Instead of guaranteeing in a "proper" way the future existence of King David, the God of Jacob and Judah takes no action at all. The implication is that God blesses the actions of the intrepid Tamar, who manipulates the religious, social, and legal customs of her world in order to forge the future.

❖ ❖

Tamar's story may seem too entrenched in ancient customs to relate to the lives of women today. Yet in the United States, women who are single— whether by choice, death of a husband, or divorce—are far more likely than their male counterparts to live below the poverty level. An ex-wife or a widow rarely collects more than half the pension her spouse would have received, and a mid-life divorcee with grown children may actually find it necessary to return "home" to live with aging parents.[1] As recently as 1989 the U.S. Census Bureau reported that even women who held jobs earned only sixty-eight percent of what men earned for equivalent work.[2] As in Tamar's case, the "good life" implicitly promised by American society is not delivered on a platter. Like Tamar, many women must devise plans that enable them to shape their own futures. In the darkness of making such plans, they might, with Tamar, pray for aid:

Prayer

God of Jacob and Judah, listen to my pleading,
for I bring before you a cause that is just.
You have watched me by night and tested my heart;
you have watched me by day and found in me no wrong.
A path lies before me, so dangerous and dark
that its shadows shroud me with terror.
Be with me, God of justice, as I proceed;
guard me in the shelter of your wings.
I know that success will close the hearts of those around me;
they will swarm upon me with vicious intent.
O God, witness the rightness of my claim!
Keep me safe; bear me toward the life I seek—
the future you yourself have planned
for the people you have named your own.[3]

Connections   *Traditions*

1. White nineteenth-century missionaries were shocked by the religious and sexual practices of Native Americans. What was similar about the reaction of Israelites to Canaanites—the people who already occupied the Promised Land?

2. Tamar risks her life by acting instead of waiting for someone else to fulfill the rights promised by her society. Do you waste time moaning about the inadequacies of "the system" when you could be taking action on your own behalf?   *Make risks*

1. Janice Castro, "Caution: Hazardous Work," *Time* (Fall 1990 Special Issue), 79.

2. Kenneth Eskey, "Women's Paychecks Growing, but Men's Income Still Higher," *The Sacramento Union*, 27 September 1990, A1, A11.

3. Based on Ps 17.

3. Tamar is tenacious, yet she is also unfailingly considerate of Judah and Bathshua. What might she say about the difference between aggressive and assertive behavior? *Clever – planned*

4. Before she reaches her goal, Tamar is twice widowed and nearly executed. What painful experiences have led to the degree of fulfillment you now experience?

For Further Reading

Deen, Edith, *All of the Women of the Bible* (1955), 41–44.

Devens-Green, Carol, "Native American Women, Missionaries, and Scripture" in *Searching the Scriptures* (1993), ed. Elisabeth Schüssler Fiorenza, 130–39.

Nunnally-Cox, Janice, *Foremothers* (1981), 22–25.

Schaberg, Jane, *The Illegitimacy of Jesus* (1990), 22–24.

9 The Women Around Moses: Deliverers of Israel

Dec. 16

Exodus 1, 2, 4, 15, 18; Numbers 12, 20

". . . and Miriam sang . . ."

The Women Around Moses in order of appearance:
> *Shiphrah and Puah*: Egyptian midwives
> *Jochebed and Miriam*: The mother and sister of Moses
> *Daughter of Pharaoh*: The foster mother of Moses
> *Zipporah of Midian*: The first wife of Moses

Background

The figure of Moses dominates the books of Exodus, Leviticus, Numbers, and Deuteronomy. Moses speaks to Yahweh face-to-face. Moses acts as judge, prophet, and lawgiver. Moses frees his people from bondage in Egypt and leads them to the threshold of the promised land. Yet Moses would never have survived to lead the Exodus were it not for six women—women whose stories are all but forgotten today.

The Exodus occurs in Egypt c. 1290 BCE, about four hundred years after the time of Jacob, Leah, and Rachel. In Jacob's old age, his son Joseph is appointed governor of Egypt because he anticipates and outlines a plan for surviving a great famine. At the time, the Egyptians welcome Joseph's relatives into Egypt and help them prosper. By the time of Moses, however, Joseph has been forgotten, and his people work as forced laborers in Pharaoh's new city on the Nile delta. Fearing an uprising, Pharaoh attempts to subdue the Hebrews and to reduce their numbers by ordering male Hebrew babies thrown into the Nile River at birth.

Thus Moses should have died in infancy. But five women thwart Pharaoh's will, and he begins life set adrift on the Nile in a basket.[1] Two Egyptian midwives, Shiphrah and Puah, ignore the law and deliver Hebrew baby boys. Moses' mother, Jochebed, subverts the law by hiding her child for three months before placing him in the river. Moses' sister, Miriam, abets this illegal action by standing guard[2]; and Pharaoh's own daughter flouts his

---

1. Similar stories are told of other ancient gods and heroes, including Horus, son of the Egyptian goddess Isis; and a Mesopotamian king, Sargon of Akkad (c. 2242 BCE).

2. Moses' mother and sister are given no names in the infancy story, but they are called Jochebed and Miriam in Ex 6:20; Num 26:59; and 1 Chr 5:29.

decree by rescuing a child she recognizes as Hebrew. Because of these women, Moses not only survives to adulthood, but enjoys a privileged life.

Then Moses witnesses the brutal beating of a Hebrew slave, and kills the Egyptian responsible. For safety he flees to Midian, east of the Red Sea's Gulf of Aqaba. Among the Midianites (a people also said to be descended from Abraham), Moses meets and marries Zipporah—the sixth woman who will save his life. Later on, after Yahweh has ordered Moses to return to Egypt to rescue his people, Yahweh inexplicably attempts to kill him. Zipporah saves Moses' life by quickly cutting off their son's foreskin and touching it to Moses' penis.[3] It is a strange story, and no satisfying explanation has been found. Some scholars speculate that the story adapts a non-Hebrew folk tale of the time, in which a demon is fooled by the blood of someone other than its intended victim. Others read it as a literary device, a foreshadowing of the blood on the door posts that later alerts God's angel to spare Hebrew lives. Still others consider the episode a reminder that Moses cannot carry out his mission without renewing his own awareness of his people's covenant with God—a covenant symbolized by male circumcision.

After this strange incident, Moses goes on to deliver the Hebrews from bondage, a story dramatized in chapters 5 through 15 of Exodus. He leads them into "the wilderness"—not the rolling sand dunes of *Lawrence of Arabia*, but a vast expanse of rocky, arid land dotted with an occasional oasis. For many years of their wanderings, the Hebrews constitute a quarrelsome rabble. They become unified only during a long encampment at the foot of Mount Sinai, where they experience a series of profoundly moving events initiated by Yahweh, the God of Moses. These events mold them into the Israelites—a people conceived as God's very own. Forever after, memories of Sinai lie at the heart of their most enduring traditions.

During these experiences, Moses' sister, Miriam, and his brother, Aaron, serve together with him as prophets and leaders. As the prophet Micah writes in about the eighth century BCE, "I set you free from the land of slavery, I sent Moses, Aaron, and Miriam to lead you" (6:4). By the fifth century BCE, however, religious leaders were to shift the focus almost entirely to Moses, even labeling a poetic victory song originally attributed to Miriam "The Song of Moses" (Ex 15).

Also during the wilderness journey, Moses takes a second wife—a Cushite woman, an Ethiopian or African. The basic story comes from the Yahwist, the earliest biblical writer. Simply assuming the acceptability of a man's taking multiple wives, he highlights Miriam and Aaron's complaint that Moses should not have chosen a non-Israelite. This core story suggests that God accepts all people, even when human beings do not. But the final assemblers of Numbers inserted into this core several elements from versions

---

3. Ex 4:25 literally reads "feet"—a euphemism (inoffensive substitute) for penis.

of the same event by the Priestly and Elohist sources. In the composite story that thus appears in our Bibles, the emphasis shifts to Miriam and Aaron's challenge of Moses' leadership, and to Yahweh's punishment of the female complainant alone. Denial of Miriam's importance colors the remaining wilderness stories as well, for after this event she disappears from the texts except for a brief mention of her death.

Stories of the Women Around Moses as Told in Exodus and Numbers

Stories of the Women Who Rescue the Infant Moses

Shiphrah and Puah: *A Summary of Ex 1:15–22*

Pharaoh, king of Egypt, issues instructions to Shiphrah and Puah, Egyptian midwives to the Hebrews, directing them to check each infant at birth. "If it is a boy, kill him; if it is a girl, however, let her live." But the midwives, not heeding the king's words, allow male children to live. When Pharaoh has the midwives interrogated, they claim that Hebrew women are not like Egyptian women, but "go into labor and give birth before the midwife arrives." Because the midwives fear God, God makes them prosper and gives them families of their own. Meanwhile Pharaoh, seeing the Hebrew people increasing in number and strength, issues an order to all Egyptians: every new-born Hebrew boy is to be thrown into the Nile, and the girls allowed to live.

Jochebed, Miriam, and the Daughter of Pharaoh: *A Summary of Ex 2:2–10*

Jochebed, wife of Amram, bears a fine son and hides him for three months. When concealment is no longer possible, she makes a rush basket watertight with pitch, places the baby in the basket, and sets it among the reeds in the Nile. She stations the boy's sister Miriam nearby to see what happens. Pharaoh's daughter comes down to bathe in the river, while her attendants walk along the bank. She notices the basket and sends one of her slave girls to get it. When she opens it, the baby is crying, and she is moved with pity. "This must be one of the Hebrew children," she says. Miriam approaches Pharaoh's daughter and asks, "Shall I go and fetch you one of the Hebrew women to act as a wet-nurse for the child?" Pharaoh's daughter tells her to do so, and Miriam calls the baby's mother. Pharaoh's daughter says to her, "Take the child, nurse him for me, and I shall pay you for it." So Jochebed nurses her own son at her breast. When he is old enough, she brings him to Pharaoh's daughter. She adopts him and calls him Moses, "because," she says, "I drew him out of the water."[4]

---

4. "Moses" means "is born," as in the Egyptian name Tutmose. It can also be read as a pun on the Hebrew word, *mashah*, "to draw out."

Stories of Zipporah and Miriam

Zipporah and Moses: *A Summary of Ex 2:11–21 and 18:3–4*

When Moses has grown to manhood, he strikes and kills a brutal Egyptian overseer in a fit of rage. The crime is discovered, and Pharaoh seeks Moses to put him to death. Moses flees to Midian, east of the Gulf of Aqaba. One day, as he sits by a well, the seven daughters of the priest Jethro come to draw water. As usual they suffer harassment from a group of male shepherds, but this time Moses champions them. They rush home to tell their father about the "Egyptian" who rescued them, and even drew water for their sheep. "Then where is he?" Jethro asks. "Why did you leave him there? Go and invite him to eat with us." Moses takes up residence with Jethro's family and marries his daughter Zipporah, who bears two sons. The first is named Gershom ("sojourner"), because Moses is a stranger living in a foreign land. The second is named Eliezer ("God helps"), because God saved Moses from Pharaoh's sword.

God's Call and the 'Bridegroom of Blood' Incident: *A Summary of Ex 2–4*

Eventually the Pharaoh of Moses' youth dies, but the Israelites still groan in slavery. In Midian, Yahweh appears to Moses as a fire blazing from a bush, and commands him to rescue his people. Only when Yahweh permits Moses to take along his brother Aaron to do the public speaking does Moses set out, together with his wife and sons. On the journey, while they are encamped for the night, Yahweh accosts Moses and wants to kill him. But Zipporah picks up a sharp flint, cuts off her son's foreskin, and touches Moses' genitals with it. As she does this, she cries out, "You are my blood-bridegroom!" Appeased, Yahweh refrains from harming Moses.

The Exodus: *A Summary of Ex 5:1–18:5*

In Egypt, Yahweh works great wonders that terrify and demoralize the Egyptians. During this time, Moses sends his wife and children home to Jethro, his father-in-law. The tenth plague, the death of the firstborn, drives Pharaoh finally to release the Hebrews. God parts the sea so that the Hebrews may cross in safety, but closes the waters over the chariots and cavalry of Pharaoh. Then the prophet Miriam takes up her tambourine, and all the women follow her, dancing, as she leads them in song: "Sing to our God who is gloriously triumphant; horse and rider God hurls into the sea" (Ex 15:19–21). The Hebrew people then begin what extends into a forty-year journey in the wilderness. Meanwhile, word of all that Yahweh has done for Israel spreads even to Midian. Jethro brings Moses' wife and sons to visit him (Ex 18:2–5), but they apparently then return to Midian, for no further mention is made of them.

Miriam and Aaron Criticize Moses: *A Summary of Num 12:1–15 and 20:1*

Time passes. Moses takes a Cushite wife, and Miriam and Aaron criticize him for choosing a non-Hebrew. They complain, "Is Moses the only one by whom [Yahweh] has spoken? Has God not spoken by us as well?" Yahweh at once orders Moses, Aaron, and Miriam to appear at the Tent of Meeting. There Yahweh descends upon them in a pillar of cloud and denounces Aaron and Miriam for criticizing Moses. Still hot with anger, Yahweh departs in the cloud, leaving Miriam standing there with her skin diseased and white as snow. Appalled, Aaron pleads with Moses to do something. Moses cries out to Yahweh, "Not this! Heal her, I pray." Yahweh responds by commuting the duration of the disease to seven days, during which time Miriam must be ostracized. So Miriam is "shut outside" for seven days, and the people do not strike camp until she is readmitted (Num 12:15). Years later, Miriam dies and is buried in the wilderness of Zin, seventy miles south of Hebron (Num 20:1).

Reflection

For Moses, the books of Exodus, Leviticus, Numbers, and Deuteronomy unreel a saga. For the women in his life, Exodus and Numbers offer snapshots: • In a palace courtyard stand two Egyptian midwives, blithely concocting lies about their active role in saving the lives of Hebrew baby boys. • Among the reeds on a lush river bank crouches a competent little girl, guarding the cranky baby her mother has set afloat in a papyrus basket. • On the same bank stands a princess, adorned in gold and clothed in fine white linen, handing over the care of her newly claimed son to his own mother. • A bloody knife flashes in the firelight as another woman rescues her husband from a deadly night-terror. • Cymbals sparkle in the sun as Miriam the Prophet leads ten thousand Israelites in song and dance. • Miriam's skin erupts with disease, and shock registers on the faces of her people.

When the midwives Shiphrah and Puah defy Pharaoh's orders, they face a stiff reprimand. Obedient, however, to an inner law of nurturing life that they place above mere human commands, they cannot be intimidated. In fact, the clever tale they concoct to explain their noncompliance seems designed mainly to enable a ranting official to save face. Jochebed, the mother of Moses, never speaks. But her actions display her determination to do everything within her power before entrusting her son to others. With her husband's tacit approval, she conceals the baby, perhaps among the clay pots of a storeroom. When the baby becomes too active for concealment, she weaves a tiny ark from stems of the papyrus, a water plant said to repel even crocodiles. She waterproofs her ark, much as Noah sealed his, and sets her son adrift in it. But she posts as sentinel the watchful Miriam, a stalwart ally even at age seven.

Jochebed and Miriam must already know the bathing habits of Pharaoh's daughter, and something of her character, too, for young Miriam shows no surprise when the Egyptian woman takes pity on the occupant of the tiny ark. One can easily imagine the princess guessing the identity of the conveniently available wet-nurse and relishing the ironies: she proposes to pay Moses' mother to care for her own child until he is about seven, and then to feed, clothe, and educate the boy royally—all at the expense of the very man who has demanded the boy's death.

Except for the bizarre "bridegroom of blood" incident, Zipporah, Moses' first wife, remains a shadowy figure. What actually happens in this scene of darkness and violence? Is Moses really attacked, or is he overcome with a hallucinatory illness? Does Zipporah really circumcise her son on the spot? Regardless of how the incident is read, Zipporah emerges as a woman who, in order to save her man's life, will confront even a supernatural force with raw courage.

And finally there is the adult Miriam who leads her people in ecstatic song and dance, giving focus to their dream of freedom. Like her brothers she speaks for Yahweh—until the day she and Aaron condemn Moses' marriage. As the story is imagined by Renita J. Weems, an ordained elder of the African Methodist Episcopal Church, when Moses marries, Miriam resents the loss of her role as his confidante. But her disapproval springs also from her desire to shield him from criticism. After all, his new African wife could be viewed as a distant relative of the people's recent oppressors.[5]

In the story of Miriam's and Aaron's complaining, the fact that Miriam's name comes first and that only she is punished suggests either the degree of power Miriam held, or the desire of the later editor to denigrate a woman. To their credit, both brothers protest Yahweh's harshness, and surely Miriam recognizes the injustice of a punishment inflicted on her alone. As she wanders in loneliness outside the camp, however, her brothers' devotion and awareness of her own importance to her people must provide cold comfort. A century ago, suffragist Elizabeth Cady Stanton cited the patriarchal attitudes the story reveals: "As women are supposed to have no character or sacred office, it is always safe to punish them to the full extent of the law."[6] We hear no more of Miriam's leadership after this event, though Stanton tartly opines that if Miriam had been in charge, the Israelites would have reached Canaan in forty days instead of forty years. Tradition holds that when Miriam dies in a place where no water is available, the people nevertheless remain encamped for thirty days in order properly to solemnize her death.

❖ ❖

Even in mere snapshots, these women are memorable. Moses may have seen the burning bush, but banked fires smolder in their very souls. And if he is God's agent, so are they. Instead of securing their own safety by cowering in

5. *Just a Sister Away* (1988), 75–76.
6. *The Women's Bible*, Part I (1895), 102.

fear or obeying immoral commands, they risk everything to save life and, especially in Miriam's case, to inspire it with celebration of God's creative and redeeming actions.

Perhaps women who protest nuclear proliferation and other threats to women and children are the Shiphrahs and Puahs of today. Women who nurture inconvenient or discarded children may be among today's Jochebeds and daughters of Pharaoh. Today's Zipporahs include women who struggle simply to ensure their families' physical survival. And today's Miriams surely include all women who inspire others to spiritual fullness of life, even if their church denies them the exercise of leadership. As Denise Lardner Carmody writes of Roman Catholicism, "My church is not a place where excellence is rewarded. It rules out women and married men for leadership roles, sinfully diminishing its talent pool."[7] Women like these, like the women around Moses, can take their needs to the God who calls by name not only men, but each one of them:

Prayer

> In you alone, O God, we take shelter.
> Let no one say to us, "Fly back to your cage!"
> You lifted the burden of bondage
> from the shoulders of our ancestors;
> you fed them with finest wheat
> and honey from the rock.
> You called us and kindled our yearning for freedom;
> let your life-giving justice now descend like the dew,
> your fiery power rise in us to a brilliant dawn.
>
> God of the Exodus, stand not apart in our time of trouble.
> Ease the tyrannies of our lives;
> grant us your bright promise of freedom.
> Release all women from cages of doubt and fear.
> God of our mothers, lead us to the land of promise.
> And as we pass through bitter valleys on our way,
> help us to make of each a place of springs.[8]

Connections

1. A whole company of women works together to save the life of the infant Moses. Are you sometimes tempted to solve all problems on your own? Or do you draw strength and inspiration from working with others?

---

7. *Biblical Woman* (1989), 75.
8. Based on Isa 45:4–8 and 58:10, and on Ps 11:1 and 84:6.

2. Miriam's banishment from camp must have seemed the darkest moment of her life. When have you experienced overwhelming rejection or loneliness?

3. Like Miriam, many talented women find official religious leadership denied them. Just as Miriam never reached Canaan, they may never reach the promised land of gender equality. Even so, how might they extend their current use of their gifts for leadership?

4. Zipporah is passed back and forth between her father and her husband. Another woman, Moses' Cushite wife, is mentioned only as an occasion of debate. How is their subordinate status reflected in the lives of women today?

For Further Reading

Alter, Robert, *The World of Biblical Literature* (1992), 120.

Carmody, Denise Lardner, *Biblical Woman* (1989), 75.

Deen, Edith, *All of the Women of the Bible* (1955), 45–61, 289, 294–95, 310–11.

Exum, J. Cheryl, "Mothers in Israel," in *Feminist Interpretation of the Bible* (1985), ed. Letty M. Russell, 80–82.

Greeley, Andrew M., and Jacob Neusner, *The Bible and Us* (1990), 152–153.

Johnson, Ann, *Miryam of Nazareth* (1984), 56–69.

Kirk, Martha Ann, "A Story of Miriam," *God of Our Mothers* (1985), audiotape.

Mollenkott, Virginia Ramey, *The Divine Feminine* (1983), 32–35.

Nunnally-Cox, Janice, *Foremothers* (1981), 26–36.

Stanton, Elizabeth Cady, *The Woman's Bible*, Part I (1895), 102.

Trible, Phyllis J., "Bringing Miriam out of the Shadows," *Bible Review* 5 (February 1989), 14–25, 34.

Weems, Renita J., *Just a Sister Away* (1988), 71–83.

Winter, Miriam Therese, *WomanWisdom* (1991), 74–81, 124–32.

Yamasaki, April, *Remember Lot's Wife* (1991), 13–16.

10 Rahab the Prostitute: Survivor in Faith

Joshua 2:1–21 and 6:20–25

"... a token of good faith ..."

Background

Miriam, Moses, and Aaron lead the Israelites to the edge of Canaan, but it is Moses' successor, Joshua, who leads them into the land. He does so after Rahab, a Canaanite prostitute, saves the lives of the men he sends to spy out the territory. Rahab's actions earn her such esteem that she is mentioned even in the New Testament. Heb 11:31 enrolls her (along with only one other woman, Sarah) among the heroes of faith; Jas 2:25 celebrates her faith and her works; and Mt 1:5 lists her as an ancestor of Jesus.

Rahab lived at the beginning of the period during which the Israelites left the desert and sought a new home in Canaan, the land they believed Yahweh had promised them. Often called "The Conquest," this period lasted from about 1200 to 1000 BCE. As it is reported in the Books of Joshua and Judges, it does not make for pleasant reading. Patriarchal peoples of that time interpreted their deities' commands to take territory as requiring the elimination of the people already living there; and the Israelites, too, are depicted as believing that the peoples of Canaan were to be "annihilated and utterly destroyed without mercy" (Josh 11:20). On the basis of archaeological findings and indications within the books themselves, however, scholars now believe the Conquest represents a later writer's compression and theologizing of a long process—a process characterized as much by gradual infiltration as by bloody battle. Thus the story of the peaceable absorption of Rahab's family by invading Israelites is presented as an exception to the general rule of conquest. The initiative for the exception comes from Rahab herself, a woman of Canaan who bargains for security for her family in exchange for having already protected Joshua's agents.

Rahab's story appears in the Book of Joshua. It was assembled from earlier writings about five hundred years after Rahab's time, and revised to its present form two or three hundred years after that. During these centuries, tales of ancient cataclysms—like stories of conquest—were reworked several times. Overlapping the period of conquest, the era between 1500 and 1100 BCE was marked with natural disasters throughout the Mediterranean arena. Volcanic eruptions, earthquakes, and tidal waves account for stories like the sinking of Atlantis, and also for some of the wonders wrought by

Yahweh on Israel's behalf. For example, the story of Rahab includes a report that loud cries and trumpet blasts cause the collapse of the walls of Jericho. Archaeological evidence confirms such a collapse, followed by a fire that consumed the city—but these events occurred at least two hundred years before the Israelites arrived. The Bible's account of the fall of Jericho reads more like stylized liturgy than history, a fact which supports the theory that an old tale of the city's destruction was revised in the light of later writers' religious convictions.

Over the centuries, writers, assemblers, and interpreters of the book of Joshua also struggled with Rahab's alleged occupation of prostitution. In her time, peoples throughout the Middle East held temple prostitutes in high regard, and considered the occupation of harlot (paid prostitute) neither shameful nor illegal. For centuries, even Israel tolerated prostitution. By the time the Book of Joshua reached final form, however, all types of prostitution had come to be condemned within Israel, and men were warned neither to marry prostitutes nor to allow their daughters to become harlots. In fact, the word most frequently used by the prophets to explain the cause of Israel's ruin and exile at the hands of a series of foreign powers was that her people had "whored" after foreign gods; and the most arresting metaphor for Yahweh's love of Israel had become that of the passionate, foolish prophet Hosea, who repeatedly welcomed back his promiscuous wife.[1]

Given changes in attitude toward prostitution, it is little wonder that rabbis of late Old Testament times and the early centuries of the Common Era struggled with the story of Rahab. Some argued that because the text does not specify that Rahab has sex with Joshua's spies, she was really only an innkeeper—a profession suspect only of dishonest trade. In contrast, other rabbinic commentators chose to magnify her profligacy in order to enhance the wholeheartedness of her conversion to Israel. Some even made her a prophet in her own right, the ancestor of nine prophets (including the renowned Jeremiah and the female prophet Huldah), and the wife of Joshua himself—a man revered as a second Moses.

The Story of Rahab as Told in Joshua

Rahab Conceals Two Israelite Spies: *A Summary of Josh 2:1–21*

Joshua, the son of Nun, sends out two spies with orders to reconnoiter the land of Canaan, especially the city of Jericho. The men come to the house of a prostitute named Rahab to spend the night there. When the king of Jericho learns that they have arrived, he sends word to Rahab to bring them out, "for they have come to spy out the whole country." Rahab

---

1. Texts underlying this paragraph include Lev 19:29 and 21:7–9; Deut 23:17–18; Prov 2:16–22, 29:3, and 31:3; Hosea; Jer 3:6–4:4; and Ezek 16:1–63.

replies that the men did visit her, but she did not know who they were, and they left before the city gate was closed for the night. "I do not know where they were going," she adds, "but if you hurry after them you may overtake them." In fact, she has concealed the men on the roof of her house among the stalks of flax she is drying in rows. The king's messengers head toward the fords of the Jordan in pursuit of the spies, and the gate is closed behind them.

The men have not yet settled down when Rahab comes up to the roof to talk to them. She tells them her people are panic-stricken; they know that the God of the Israelites has given them the entire land. She reviews the mighty works of Yahweh and concludes, "Your coming has left no spirit in any of us; for . . . your God is God in heaven above and on earth below." She asks the men to swear by their God to protect her and to spare the lives of her entire family, just as she has kept faith with them.

Joshua's men assure her that when Yahweh gives them the country, they will deal faithfully with her, "so long as you do not betray our business." Rahab lets them down through a window by a rope, for her house is situated on an angle of the city wall. "Make for the hills," she says, "or the pursuers will come upon you. Hide there for three days until they return; then go on your way." The men tell her that when the invasion begins, she must gather her family inside the house and fasten a strand of scarlet cord in the window through which she lowered them. They cannot protect any family member who goes into the street, but if a hand is laid on anyone who stays indoors, the blood will be on their heads. "Remember too," they warn her, "that if you betray our business, then we shall be free of the oath you have made us take." "It shall be as you say," she replies. She sends them on their way and fastens the scarlet cord in her window.

Israel Takes Jericho and Spares the Family of Rahab: *A Summary of Josh 2:22–6:21 and 6:22–25*

The Israelite spies return safely to Joshua. The next day, the waters of the Jordan River part while the priests stand on the river bed holding the ark of the covenant, and the people cross into Canaan. For the next six days they unnerve the inhabitants of Jericho by marching silently and steadily around the city. On the seventh day, the priests blow a trumpet blast, the people release a mighty shout, and the walls of Jericho collapse. The fighters of Israel swarm into the city. Joshua directs the men he sent to reconnoiter the land to go to Rahab's house and bring her out with all who belong to her, as they swore to do. They bring out Rahab and her family and place them outside the Israelite camp. Then they set fire to the city and everything in it. Thus Joshua spares the lives of Rahab the prostitute, her household, and all who belong to her, because she hid the men he sent to scout the territory. They settle permanently among the people of Israel.

Reflection

The story of Rahab is set in a time marked by natural calamity and the atrocities of war. "Indeed," observes cultural historian Riane Eisler, "to the people living through these terrifying times, it must have seemed as though the very heavens, once thought to be the abode of a bountiful Goddess, had been captured by antihuman supernatural forces allied with their brutal representatives on earth."[2] In such a setting, the story of Rahab shows a striking lack of divine intervention. It depicts instead a woman who achieves her goals because she takes the steps demanded both by faith and by reason.

Rahab's profession remains in doubt, even though the story repeatedly identifies her as a prostitute. Since no husband is mentioned, she could have been a widow or an unmarried woman who supported her siblings and aging parents by running just such a business as an inn, a place toward which strangers would naturally gravitate. In fact, Rahab the innkeeper could have been labeled Rahab the harlot solely on the basis of opportunity to practice the trade. After all, male visitors would regularly have frequented her establishment. Proponents of such an interpretation tend to view the red cord as a literary symbol, its color signifying the "passing over" of her family, just as, during the Exodus, the angel passed over Hebrew houses marked with blood.

On the other hand, say some scholars, the handy scarlet cord may have functioned as a sign of the profession of prostitute, as in the "red light" districts of today. Even if Rahab was a prostitute, however, at least one strand within the traditions of Israel found in that fact nothing to condemn: "I shall not punish your daughters for becoming prostitutes or your sons' brides for their adultery," Yahweh says through the prophet Hosea, "because your men resort to whores and sacrifice with temple prostitutes" (4:14).

While the source of Rahab's income cannot be resolved, it is clear that she possessed keen intelligence and leadership ability. Perhaps, like Miriam, she was an older sister to whom her siblings naturally turned for advice or a helping hand. Clearly, too, she was industrious; she stored flax on the flat roof of her house in order later to weave linen from it. Her house seems to have enjoyed a well-protected location. It may have been situated between two walls, as in the fifteen-foot gap archaeologists found between the double walls of ancient Jericho. In addition, its position near the city gates would have made it possible for the politically astute Rahab to catch from customers and passersby the winds of fear that preceded the Israelites.

Sensitive to all she heard, Rahab must have weighed her alternatives long before chance—or Yahweh—lodged two Hebrew spies in her house. Her choices were loyalty to a possibly doomed king, or entrusting her future to the hands of the invaders. If she chose the latter, how could she guarantee

2. *The Chalice and the Blade* (1987), 57.

safety for herself and her family? The arrival of messengers from her king would seem to compound her dilemma. For merely housing the spies, her king might execute her; and no matter how strong an oath she might extract from the spies, her family could still die in the confusion of battle. Yet Rahab opts to defy her king even before she has struck any kind of bargain.

Rahab's choice—to risk all on the power of Yahweh and the dependability of Yahweh's agents—implies shrewd insight *and* a leap of faith. She emerges, too, as a woman of nerve. Her courage is reminiscent of that of the ordinary French, German, and Dutch citizens who risked their own lives to shelter Jewish refugees during World War II. Today, Rahab can serve as model to women living in all war-torn places, including inner cities. Such women, in order to create oases of life in the midst of violence, must balance one danger against another. They must decide whether to trust in the promises of police and social workers, or the protection of violence-prone gangs. They must discern whether to stay with an abusive but known male partner, or to risk life without a masculine protector. They must listen with silent savvy, yet ultimately act as their conscience dictates.

Rahab was rewarded for proceeding with the actions her leap of faith demanded; she and her family were absorbed into the confederation of Israel. Whether or not the Rahabs of today achieve secure reward, perhaps they can identify with that time of confusion *before* Rahab committed herself to Yahweh and to Israel. With Rahab, they may at present be able to focus only on a perennial human frustration—how to cope with the mundane in the very midst of disaster:

Prayer

> God or Goddess, what chaos!
> Between your thunderous quakes and the clash of weapons,
> I can barely think.
> When will the smoke wash out of my hair,
> the world cease rocking under my feet?
> Amid the bedlam, I watch and wait.
> I endure grasping hands;
> I try to accommodate raucous demands for service.
> At threats and bluster I take no offense.
> Though people look at me askance,
> I diligently tend my hearth; I weave my cloth:
> I support my own.
>
> But oh, Great One, I am so sick of chaos
> and so tired of routine.
> Must the earth forever tremble?
> Must I dance forever to the piping of others?

When will you wipe away my tears, ease the load I carry
and let me live in peace?
O Great One, grant me some lightness of heart—
some small, sweet taste of gladness!

Connections

1. Rahab risked everything in her leap of faith. Toward what risks, great
   or small, is your faith urging you?

2. Rahab can also be viewed as having worked out her own survival.
   What specific qualities make her a good model for women living under
   the threat of violence? *Thought on her feet + ahead*

   Didn't panic

3. Whether Rahab was "just" an innkeeper or "just" a prostitute, both
   were low-class occupations. How quick are you to judge others—or
   yourself—on the basis of profession or socioeconomic status?

For Further Reading

Deen, Edith, *All of the Women of the Bible* (1955), 65–69.

Eisler, Riane, *The Chalice and the Blade* (1987), 57–58.

Greeley, Andrew M., and Jacob Neusner, *The Bible and Us* (1990), 155–56,
161–62.

Nunnally-Cox, Janice, *Foremothers* (1981), 42–45.

Schaberg, Jane, *The Illegitimacy of Jesus* (1990), 20–22, 25–26.

Deborah and Jael: Fiery Women

Judges 4:3–23 and 5:1–31

"Champions there were none, until you . . . arose . . ."

Background

Of all the battles recorded in the Book of Judges, the one involving Deborah and Jael especially captivated Israel. The finely crafted story is filled with dramatic reversals: a weak-kneed Israelite military commander is roused by a woman; a people armed with light weapons routs an enemy that boasts iron chariots; and victory arises not through military prowess, but through Yahweh's employment of cosmic forces and a woman's wielding of common household implements.

The story of Deborah and Jael is set in a region southwest of the Sea of Galilee. The story opens at a time when the Israelites have long been oppressed by a Canaanite army under the command of Sisera. The judge (acknowledged political authority) in Israel at that time is a woman, Deborah. The Israelites are so cowed by the powerful iron chariots of Sisera that when Deborah gives their general, Barak, Yahweh's command to fight, Barak refuses to engage the enemy unless Deborah accompanies the troops. Under her guidance—and aided by a fierce storm of hail, sleet, and pounding rain—the Israelites rout the forces of Sisera on the Plain of Esdraelon.

Sisera himself escapes. He takes refuge in the tent of Heber, a non-Israelite—one of the nomadic Kenites, metal-workers related to the Midianites of northern Sinai. As a smith, the absent Heber might even have worked on the iron chariots of the Canaanites; Sisera, at any rate, expects and receives a friendly welcome in his tent. But once Sisera falls asleep, Jael, the wife of Heber, kills him. The defeat of the Canaanites, begun on a stormy field of battle, is completed inside a modest tent.

Although the Book of Judges praises Jael for her valor, she grossly violates customs of hospitality then practiced throughout the Middle East.[1] When hospitality had been offered and accepted, the guest acquired the right of protection at any cost. Yet Jael kills Sisera, adding insult to the defeat

---

1. In their book, *Social World of Ancient Israel 1250–587 BCE* (1993), 89–95, Victor H. Matthews and Don C. Benjamin contend that hospitality was not at issue. Basing their theory on male-female roles and on certain words in the text, they argue that Jael was repelling potential rape.

Sisera has already experienced, for death at the hands of a woman was considered the height of humiliation.[2]

These events immediately became the subject of the dramatic poem or song of Judg 5 (attributed to Deborah herself), and later the prose account of Judg 4. The song exalts both Jael and Deborah as national heroes. Cited as the oldest surviving Hebrew literary composition, it dates roughly to 1125 BCE, the time of the events it describes. Its vivid pace conveys the excitement of a battle in which cosmic forces aid the Israelites, and the conclusion of the poem juxtaposes two striking domestic scenes: Jael's assassination of Sisera, and the anxious peering of Sisera's mother through a window as she awaits the return of her son.

The prose account of Judg 4 presents Deborah as a woman unique in her world. In a society where military leadership, legal duties, and prophecy are the recognized preserves of male authority, she wields all three. As a military leader, she inspires to victory a coalition led by a male subordinate. As a judge—the only woman so identified in the Old Testament—she adjudicates legal cases. As a prophet—one of only four women so named—she speaks for Yahweh. By virtue of the poem attributed to her, she is remembered as a skilled poet and singer of tales.[3] She is further identified as *'eshet lappidot*—a phrase of uncertain meaning, usually translated as "Lapidoth's wife," even though there is no other evidence such a man existed, or that Deborah ever married. Many scholars now think *'eshet lappidot* means "spirited woman" or "fiery woman"—a translation well suited to the entire context of Deborah's story.

Nevertheless, in the past, patriarchal commentators often identified Barak, the timid general, as the judge of Israel at Deborah's time. Even today, Bible dictionaries cite "Deborah and Barak" as co-judges. The author of Judg 4 shows no such confusion. In fact, the storyteller takes great pains to stress the fact that Israel was led by a woman. Like Latin, Hebrew is an inflected language. Its noun endings indicate gender, and its verb endings imply the subject, he or she, depending on context. But the writer of Judg 4 repeatedly inserts awkward, grammatically unnecessary nouns and pronouns in order to stress femininity: "And Deborah, a prophet-*woman*, Lapidoth's *woman*, *she* was judging Israel at that time. And *she* would sit under the palm tree of Deborah. . . ."[4]

The Story of Deborah and Jael as Told in Judges

Deborah and Jael Defeat Sisera: *A Summary of Judg 4:3–23*

For twenty years Sisera, military commander for Jabin, king of Hazor, has oppressed Israel with his force of nine hundred iron-clad chariots. The

---

2. See, for example, Judg 9:54.

3. The other women named as prophets are Miriam, Huldah, and Noadiah. Poems or songs are associated with only two other Old Testament women, Miriam and Hannah.

4. As literally translated by Robert Alter, a professor of Hebrew and Comparative Literature, in his book *The World of Biblical Literature* (1992), 41. Emphasis added.

Israelites appeal to Yahweh, who at this time speaks through the prophet Deborah. She is a spirited woman who judges disputes under the Palm Tree of Deborah between Ramah and Bethel in the hill country of Ephraim—an area south of Jabin's seat of power. Deborah summons Barak, and gives him Yahweh's command: "Go and lead out ten thousand men from Naphtali and Zebulun and bring them with you to Mount Tabor. I shall draw out to you, at the wadi Kishon, Jabin's commander, Sisera, along with his chariots and troops, and deliver him into your power." Barak refuses the commission unless Deborah accompanies him, so she does so. But she tells him that because of his cowardice, Yahweh will cause Sisera to fall at the hand of a woman.

Fierce battle ensues at the wadi Kishon, where Yahweh throws Sisera and all his chariots and army into panic-stricken rout. Sisera himself, thirsty and battle-worn, escapes on foot. He approaches the tent of Heber, a Kenite, where he is received by Jael, Heber's wife: "Come in, my lord, come in here; do not be afraid." She gives him a place to rest, tucks a rug around him, and offers him a skin of milk.[5] He falls into an exhausted sleep. She picks up a tent peg and a mallet, creeps up to him, and drives the tent peg straight through his temple and down into the ground. When Barak passes by in search of Sisera, Jael calls out, "Come. I shall show you the man you are looking for." Barak enters the tent and beholds his enemy, "dead with the tent peg in his temple."

The Song of Deborah: *Selected Verses from Judg 5:1–31*

On that same day Deborah and Barak . . . sang this song:

> [When Yahweh] marched from the land of Edom,
> earth trembled; heaven quaked;
> the clouds streamed down in torrents.
> In the days of . . . Jael, caravans plied no longer;
> travellers . . . went round by devious paths.
> Champions there were none, none left in Israel,
> until you, Deborah, arose . . . as a mother in Israel.
> Then down marched the column and its chieftains,
> the people of [Yahweh] marching down like warriors.
> The stars fought from heaven . . . against Sisera.
> The torrent of Kishon swept him away. . . .
> Then hammered the hoofs of his horses,
> his chargers galloped, galloped away.

> Blest above women be Jael, wife of Heber the Kenite;
> blest above all women in the tents.
> He asked for water; she gave him milk,
> she offered him curds in a bowl fit for a chieftain.

---

5. A thick, yogurt-like drink.

She reached out her hand for the tent-peg,
her right hand for the . . . hammer.
With . . . a shattering blow she pierced his temple.
The mother of Sisera peered through the lattice,
through the window she peered and cried,
"Why is the clatter of his chariots so delayed?"
The wisest of her ladies answered her, . . .
"They must be finding spoil, taking their shares,
a damsel for each man, two damsels,
booty of dyed stuffs . . . to grace the victor's neck."

Reflection

The story is grisly, but it reports remarkable moments in the patriarchal Bible. Men may choose to deny women's gifts, but Yahweh does not. Still, identifying with Deborah and Jael poses a challenge for most American women. Most of us experience war at the safe remove of television, where missile deployment teams and bomber pilots devastate the lives of people far away. Most of us have never lived in a zone of terror, where travel is so disrupted that caravans cannot even replenish basic supplies. Most of us have never discovered an arrogant enemy knocking on our very door. Yet it takes little imagination to grasp how numb the Israelites must have grown, worn down by unceasing hostilities. Their fighting men had lost all nerve; the Kenites who lived among them must have felt trapped in a conflict not of their making.

Into this chaos step two remarkable heroes: Deborah, a woman of abundant talent, fired by devotion to Yahweh; and Jael, an ordinary homemaker, about whose motives we can only speculate. Deborah is a stunning character. She is gifted with commanding presence, oratorical power, a reputation as Yahweh's own spokesperson, and the sheer audacity to cry, "Enough!" The biblical word "arose" aptly characterizes her, observes commentator Edith Deen: "She did not sit at home and ponder the matter when the time came for action."[6] Whether or not Deborah married or had children of her own, the poem of Judg 5 rightly grants her the title of "mother in Israel," for she protects the terrorized Israelites and restores them to safety.

Nor does Jael sit and ponder when opportunity knocks; she, too, is a "fiery woman." Edith Deen criticizes the "hardness of character" Jael shows in her manner of killing Sisera; Elizabeth Cady Stanton condemns Jael outright: "The deception and cruelty practiced on Sisera by Jael under the guise of hospitality is revolting. . . . [It is] more like the work of a fiend than of a woman."[7] Yet we have no conception of the unrelenting hardship and devastation that may have motivated Jael. Nor do Deen and Stanton seem to notice that Jael merely uses

6. *All of the Women of the Bible* (1955), 72.
7. Deen, *All of the Women of the Bible*, 270; Stanton, *The Woman's Bible*, Part II, 20.

the tools at hand—it was the woman's job to pitch and strike the tent—in order to dispatch an enemy warrior. Would a man in her position have done any less?

❖ ❖

Beneath the gore, the story of Deborah and Jael demonstrates that courage and genius know no gender. Yet prior to the twentieth century, few other women attained either the power or the moral authority of a Deborah—perhaps Joan of Arc, who led the French to victory in the fifteenth century; or Catherine of Siena, mystic and papal diplomat of the fourteenth. In our era, great power has been exercised by Golda Meir of Israel, Margaret Thatcher of England, Indira Gandhi of India. Immense moral authority has been wielded by such women as Eva Perón of Argentina and Eleanor Roosevelt of the United States. Spirited women can also be found not only in politics, but in church chanceries and in all of the arts—painting, sculpture, dance, fiction, poetry, film, the nightly news.

But the women who rise to national or international prominence remain relatively few in number. Most women, like Jael, wield their power in the less public arenas of home, work, school, or church. Even though the biblical Jael remains, in Leonard Swidler's evocative phrases, a "deadly hostess" and an "ambivalent model"[8] of womanhood, women of today can adopt her quickness to grasp the initiative. Recognizing their own capacity for wisdom and inspiration, women can emulate both Jael and Deborah by rising up to oppose all forms of domination. They can battle discriminatory practices that impoverish women and children; nuclear proliferation that threatens the peoples of all nations; environmental degradation that endangers the entire planet.

Yet knowing full well how little individual power they still possess, women of today need also to withdraw for the sustenance of prayer. Like Deborah and Jael, they need to draw strength from contemplation of a deity who knows no limitations:

Prayer

> Glorious God, who but you has measured the seas in one hand
> and stretched out the skies like a curtain?
> Who has held all the soil of the earth in a basket,
> or weighed the hills on a jeweler's scales?
> Who has ever directed your spirit,
> or instructed you in the ways of wisdom?
> Nations before you scatter like dust motes;
> mighty powers appear as tiny seeds:
> scarcely are they planted, scarcely sown,
> before they wither and you whirl them off like chaff.

8. *Biblical Affirmations of Woman* (1979), 111.

What picture can we form of you,
you who sit enthroned on the roof of the world
yet lead your children safely by the hand?
There is none like you, no one is your equal.
When we lift our eyes to your heavens,
the stars you created and summoned by name,
how can we imagine our lot is hidden from you?

You never tire; your enthusiasm is boundless.
Our young may grow faint, the fittest of us may stumble,
but you give strength to the weary, vigor to the depleted.
You gather us from the corners of the earth;
you call us daughter and friend.
Work in us, that rivers may open on the arid heights
and refreshing springs slake our thirst for justice.
Work in us, that one day all may know you use the powerless
to craft a world of beauty and peace.[9]

Connections

1. The Book of Judges is silent on *how* Deborah rose to prominence. Do you believe she succeeded only because men had abdicated leadership, or for other reasons?

2. Deborah raised an army; Jael assassinated an enemy chieftain. In the Persian Gulf War of 1991, American servicewomen took part in combat. Do you think gender equality demands that women serve as soldiers?

3. Even though Deborah and Jael were heroes in their own milieu, they can be difficult to admire. Still, what qualities of theirs could you afford to imitate?

4. As a poet, Deborah inspired Israel. In what women's writings of today do you find strength and inspiration?

For Further Reading

Alter, Robert, *The World of Biblical Literature* (1992), 41–45.

Carmody, Denise Lardner, *Biblical Woman* (1989), 27–31.

Deen, Edith, *All of the Women of the Bible* (1955), 69–74, 269–70.

Exum, J. Cheryl, "Mothers in Israel" in *Feminist Interpretation of the Bible* (1985), ed. Letty M. Russell, 82–85.

Nunnally-Cox, Janice, *Foremothers* (1981), 45–51.

Stanton, Elizabeth Cady, *The Woman's Bible*, Part II (1898), 19–22.

Swidler, Leonard, *Biblical Affirmations of Woman* (1979), 85–87, 111–12.

9. Based on Isa 40 and 41.

12 The Daughter of Jephthah: Sacrificed Virgin

Judges 11

"She was his only child . . ."

Background

Judg 11 reports the tragic story of a military commander named Jephthah and his only child, a daughter. Before Jephthah leads a battle against the Ammonites on behalf of the people of Gilead, the spirit of Yahweh comes upon him, guaranteeing him success. Yet Jephthah, lacking faith, attempts to manipulate Yahweh by vowing that *if* he wins, he will sacrifice the first creature that comes out to greet him on his return home. His victory turns to grief when his young daughter dances out to welcome him. Like Jephthah himself, she seems not even to consider the idea of his abandoning the vow. She does, however, create her own memorial by requesting a deferral of the sacrifice so that she and her friends may mourn her lack of opportunity ever to bear children.

Although Judg 11 leaves no doubt that the daughter of Jephthah is put to death, some commentators have imagined a less terrible ending for the story. They suggest that Jephthah fulfills the intent of his vow by consecrating his daughter to Yahweh for life. Besides the text itself, however, the culture of ancient Israel contradicts such an interpretation. Deliberately chosen virginity was inconceivable to a society that prized family and descendants; the very concept of virginal consecration was unimaginable.

Human sacrifice was known, however, though not condoned. It was forbidden by the Law of Moses on the basis of the incident in which Abraham is prevented from sacrificing his son Isaac (Gen 22). Leviticus 20:5 states that "giving a child to the fire profanes the very name of Yahweh." Nevertheless, child sacrifice was practiced not only by the neighbors of Israel, but even by some Israelites as late as the sixth century BCE, as evidenced by scathing denunciations of the practice in the writings of the prophets Jeremiah, Ezekiel, and Micah.[1]

Past interpreters of the story of Jephthah's daughter often focused on Jephthah's grief, since Israelites regarded vows (like blessings and curses) as irrevocable. These readers missed the lack of faith implied by Jephthah's vow. Perhaps inspired by the New Testament author of Hebrews, who praises

---

1. The Law: Lev 18:21 and 20:2-5; Deut 12:31 and 18:10. The Prophets: Jer 7:31, 19:5; Ezek 16:21, 20:26, 20:31, 23:37; Mic 6:6-7.

Jephthah as a paragon of faith (Heb 11:32–34), they exalted the nobility of Jephthah's commitment to God, even as they decried the foolishness of his vow. More recently, critics have focused on the period of mourning observed by the daughter and her friends. This element of the story explains an otherwise obscure mourning rite regularly enacted during Old Testament times by the women of Gilead. Either a real Jephthah did sacrifice a daughter, around whom the ritual developed; or the story arose to explain a rite whose origins had been forgotten—perhaps an ancient cult that once honored a sacrificed goddess.

Certain elements of Jephthah's own story increase the poignancy of his daughter's story. He was an illegitimate child who was driven from his home by the taunts of his half-brothers, and who then spent his early adulthood as the leader of a gang of desperadoes. As scripture theologian Phyllis Trible observes,

> If Jephthah suffered for the sins of his parents, how much more shall this child bear because of the machinations of her father. Unfaithfulness reaches into the third generation to bring forth a despicable fruit. "Is there no balm in Gilead?" (Jer 8:22).[2]

As for the Ammonites Jephthah defeats in the story, they were never permanently subdued by Israel. Their distant kinship with Israel was both recognized and maligned in the story of their incestuous descent from Lot and one of his daughters. Their capital city, Rabbah, dominated the King's Highway—a caravan route that stretched from the Gulf of Aqaba in the south to Damascus in the north. Late in Old Testament times the city was redesigned, enlarged, and given the name by which it was known in New Testament times, Philadelphia. Today the city bears a name that reflects the uninterrupted survival of the ancient Ammonites. It is Amman, capital of Jordan. Ruins from biblical times survive within the city at Citadel Hill.

The Story of the Daughter of Jephthah as Told in Judges

A Summary of Judg 11:1–40

Jephthah of Gilead is an intrepid warrior, the son of Gilead by a prostitute. Gilead's legitimate sons drive Jephthah away by taunting him as a bastard. Jephthah flees to the land of Tob, where a number of worthless fellows rally to him. A time comes when the Ammonites launch an offensive against Israel. When the fighting begins, the elders of Gilead go to fetch Jephthah. "Come and be our commander so that we can fight the Ammonites," they say. When Jephthah points out that they once drove him off in hatred, they enlarge their offer, inviting him to become head over all of Gilead.

Jephthah accepts the commission and attempts to negotiate a settlement with the Ammonites, but the effort fails. On the eve of battle Jephthah vows to Yahweh, "If you will deliver the Ammonites into my hands, then the first creature that comes out of the door of my house to meet me when I return from

2. *Texts of Terror* (1984), 100.

them safely shall be [yours]; I shall offer that as a whole-offering." Jephthah crosses into Ammonite territory to attack, and Yahweh delivers the Ammonites into his hands. Jephthah routs them with great slaughter, taking twenty towns.

When Jephthah arrives home in Gilead, his daughter dances out to meet him, shaking her tambourine. She is his only child; he has no other son or daughter. At sight of her, he tears his clothes and cries out, "Oh, my daughter, you have broken my heart! Such calamity you have brought on me! I have made a vow . . . and I cannot go back on it." She replies that if he has made a vow, he must fulfill it, since Yahweh has avenged him on his enemies. "But, father, grant me this one favor: Spare me for two months, that I may roam the hills with my companions and mourn that I must die a virgin."

"Go," he says, letting her depart. Accompanied by her friends, for two months she mourns her unmarried state in the hills. She then returns to her father, and he fulfills his vow. She dies a virgin. It becomes a tradition for the women to go into the mountains for four days every year to commemorate the daughter of Jephthah the Gileadite.

Reflection

The key sound of this story is not the clash of spears, but the mournful wail of women's voices. The story is a tragedy both for child and for parents. In a patriarchal world, it is not only the daughter who comes to a dead end, but also the father and the never-mentioned mother, for the carrying out of Jephthah's vow forever deprives them of descendants—the greatest blessing they can imagine.

The tragedy arises from Jephthah's central flaws: his faulty grasp of the will of Yahweh, and his iron inflexibility in carrying out a vow. But if Jephthah's rigidity strikes today's readers as difficult to believe, his daughter's calm acceptance of a sacrificial death seems nothing short of astonishing. Since a woman of Israel could suffer no greater disgrace than to die childless, it is nearly impossible to imagine her complying as readily as the story suggests.

The very nature of the vow contributes a further air of surrealism to the situation. Since quarters for small cattle were commonly attached to people's houses at that time, some readers argue that Jephthah expected a cow to come out of his house. Surely it is far more likely that the sounds of a victor's return would draw forth a human being—not an animal. Yet unlike Abraham, who worked to conceal from Isaac the fate intended for him (Gen 22:8), Jephthah has the gall to hurl accusations at his *daughter*; to blame *her* for forcing him to kill her. And, according to this story, she accepts her fate.

Commentators of the past have eulogized the daughter's great virtue. Edith Deen praises the daughter of Jephthah as "a courageous young woman who was both meek in spirit and patient in suffering." In fact, Deen subtitles her chapter "Example of Noble Submission."[3] The recorder of the story may indeed have perceived the daughter's obedience as a virtue. But in the fullest

3. *All of the Women of the Bible* (1955), 74, 78.

scope of Judaeo-Christian tradition, both Jephthah's adherence to his word and his daughter's submission can be taken only as virtue distorted to the point of nightmare. God never appears to Jephthah, never requests such a sacrifice. The story is a *human* tragedy, rooted in twisted thinking and misplaced loyalties. It merits the remark written by Elizabeth Cady Stanton a century ago: "I would that this page of history were gilded with a dignified whole-souled rebellion."[4]

One slight recognition of wrongness, one slight suggestion of rebellion, is implied even by the patriarchal writer or editor, however: he retains the story of the young women's pilgrimage into the hills to grieve a life unfulfilled. These young women experienced a sorrow unknowable to the men of their world, yet every friend of Jephthah's daughter knew that her fate could descend without warning upon any one of them. And so they mourned the tragic foolishness of a world organized in terms of power and dominance—a folly that continues into our own time.

❖ ❖

Who is the daughter of Jephthah today? She is anyone whose fate appears to be sealed, whether by financial catastrophe, terminal illness, or a legally imposed death sentence. In a broader sense, she is anyone who mourns. The death or departure of a friend or family member still changes irrevocably the texture of a life. An unexpected pregnancy or an inability to conceive can end a dream of the shape of a family. The abandonment even of an addiction or a sick relationship creates an inner emptiness.

More specifically, the daughter of Jephthah lives on in any child whose potential is sacrificed by adults preoccupied with personal ambitions. She is any girl whose talents are sacrificed in a religious or educational system that favors males. She is any young woman so impoverished that her search for meaning ends in death from anorexia nervosa, drugs, or suicide. She is any child slaughtered in a random shooting. She is any child growing up in a place torn by war. And she is, especially, the woman of any age who flees a home that has become a place not of security, but of random, unpredictable violence.

Just as God neither requests nor desires the death of the daughter of Jephthah, so God wishes neither injury nor death upon anyone else. Identifying with Jephthah's daughter, we need to gather our friends and join with her in grieving all waste of life:

Prayer

I am one who has known affliction.
My flesh will soon be wasted, my bones broken.
Cruel words lock me in place and cast me into darkness
with those already dead.
Fetters weight my arms; blocks of stone bar my road.

4. *The Woman's Bible*, Part II (1898), 25.

Shunted aside, I am fed on ashes;
I am given bitter herbs to drink.
Peace has fled my life; I cannot recall good fortune.
My eyes stream with tears; my dancing turns to mourning.
The garland slips from my head, the tambourine from my fingers.
My heart aches for every daughter of Zion.

I cannot even find my God.

Yet surely God's love is not exhausted,
nor all God's compassion spent.
To deprive someone of life in God's own name—
such a thing Yahweh has never approved.
And so I lift my hands and my heart
to the God I neither see nor feel, yet who is all I have—
Yahweh, who is good to all who seek comfort;
Yahweh, in whose hands I place my life.[5]

Connections

1. What sources of grief exist in your life? How might you gather your friends for mourning?

2. Like abused children of today who defend their parents to outsiders, the daughter of Jephthah accepts her father's actions as correct. How can children be educated *not* to submit to abuse?

3. At what point should a woman let go of rage toward an abuser? How can she move on from the guilt and shame she has internalized to a renewed sense of wholeness and worth?

4. In a sense, each of us contains both Jephthah and his daughter. In our efforts to become respected, independent adults, we sometimes kill the playful child within us. How do you treat the child within you?

For Further Reading

Alter, Robert, *The World of Biblical Literature* (1992), 56–65.

Deen, Edith, *All of the Women of the Bible* (1955), 74–78.

Nunnally-Cox, Janice, *Foremothers* (1981), 51–54.

Stanton, Elizabeth Cady, *The Woman's Bible*, Part II (1898), 24–25.

Trible, Phyllis J. *Texts of Terror* (1984), 93–116.

Weems, Renita J., *Just a Sister Away* (1988), 53–69.

Winter, Miriam Therese, *WomanWisdom* (1991), 140–41, 146–47.

Yamasaki, April, *Remember Lot's Wife* (1991), 19–20.

5. Based on Lam 3 and 5:15–17.

13 The Wife of Manoah, and Hannah: Mothers Chosen by God

Judges 13:2–25, 1 Samuel 1:2–28 and 2:1–26

". . . she conceived, and . . . bore a son . . ."

The Wife of Manoah: The Mother of Samson
Hannah, Wife of Elkanah: The Mother of Samuel

Background

The unnamed wife of Manoah and Hannah, the wife of Elkanah, lived during the era of the Judges (c. 1200–1000 BCE). Both were women who, with God's aid, conceived and bore remarkable sons. The stories of both women echo those of the great matriarchs of Israel. The story of the wife of Manoah, with its angel who promises that a son will be conceived, parallels that of Sarah. The story of Hannah, with its rivalry between barren and fruitful wives, parallels that of Rachel and Leah. The wife of Manoah becomes the mother of Samson, who later harasses the Philistines. Hannah becomes the mother of Samuel, the prophet who anoints the first two kings of Israel.

The stories of these women occur during intervals of peace in an era that was often characterized by war. These interludes offer glimpses of the ancient beliefs and worship practices of Israel. The story of the wife of Manoah involves the ancient belief that to see God or a visible manifestation of God—an angel—is to die. This belief is cited in other Old Testament passages as well, including the story of Hagar (Gen 16:13) and the story of Jacob's wrestling with a supernatural being (Gen 32:30). The story of the wife of Manoah also features the ancient practice of offering sacrifice to Yahweh on large rocks that serve as open-air altars.

The story of Hannah and her husband Elkanah is set somewhat later. In their time, Shiloh—a village about twenty miles north of the later capital, Jerusalem—serves as the religious and administrative center of the loosely confederated tribes of Israel. A shrine at Shiloh houses the ark of the covenant, a portable chest containing the tablets of the Law thought to go back to the time of Moses. Hereditary priests maintain the shrine, and each year Hannah and Elkanah attend a harvest festival celebrated there—probably the Feast of Tabernacles, a week-long celebration during which the people live in freshly erected leafy booths.

The stories of both women suggest that their sons are reared as Nazirites—people dedicated to God and, as signs of that dedication, barred from drinking alcohol, cutting or shaving their hair, or touching the dead (Num 6:1–21). Nazirite vows were usually made for a limited time, but the angel who appears to the wife of Manoah directs her to consecrate her son Samson for life. Since that consecration begins in the womb, the wife of Manoah is herself forbidden the use of alcohol. Hannah also consecrates her son Samuel to Yahweh for life, and her story mentions alcohol, but it is not clear whether Samuel becomes Nazirite, priest, or both.

Overall, the wife of Manoah is depicted as a ready listener and receiver of God's word. Her husband keeps attempting to seize the limelight, but God refuses to allow her to be overshadowed. Hannah is depicted as a woman of prayer. Though it was probably placed on her lips by a later writer, the psalm Hannah sings on dedicating her son to God suits her situation perfectly. Paralleling the content of Job 12:13–25, it celebrates Yahweh as one who grants favor to the lowly. Hannah's song of praise serves as a basis for the Magnificat of Mary, Mother of Jesus, in the New Testament (Lk 1:46–55).

The Story of the Wife of Manoah as Told in Judges

A Summary of Judg 13:2–25

Manoah, a man of the tribe of Dan, has a wife who has no child. The angel of God appears to her and tells her that she will conceive and give birth to a son. "Now be careful to drink no wine or strong drink, and to eat no forbidden food," the angel tells her; "no razor must touch his head, for the boy is to be a Nazirite, consecrated to God from birth. He will strike the first blow for Israel's freedom from the power of the Philistines." The woman immediately tells her husband that she has been visited by a "man of God" whose "appearance was that of an angel of God, most terrible to see." She reports to Manoah the promise of a son and the Nazirite instructions, but omits what was said about her son's future mission.

Excited, Manoah prays that the man of God may appear again, to him and to his wife. Yahweh does send the angel again—to the woman, who is sitting in a field. She runs to get Manoah, who returns with her at once. Manoah approaches the visitor and asks whether he is the same man who previously spoke with his wife. Assured that he is, Manoah goes on: "Now when your words come true, what kind of boy will he be and what will he do?" The angel tersely summarizes the Nazirite instructions, but omits all reference to the child's mission against the Philistines. Manoah next urges the man to stay for a sacrificial meal. The angel declines the meal, but urges Manoah to go ahead and make an offering to Yahweh if he wishes. Manoah persists with his questions, asking, "What is your name? For we shall want to honor you when your words come true." The angel replies, "How can you ask my name? It is a name of wonder."

Finally Manoah desists. On a rock, he sets up a sacrifice to Yahweh of a young goat and the appropriate grain offering. As he and his wife watch, the fire suddenly flares toward heaven, and the angel ascends in the flames. Both

Manoah and his wife fall face downward to the ground. Finally realizing that he has seen an angel, Manoah says to his wife, "We are doomed to die, for we have seen God." She replies that if Yahweh had wanted to kill them, they would never have been selected to "see and hear all this." She conceives and bears a son, and names him Samson.

The Story of Hannah as Told in the First Book of Samuel

A Summary of 1 Sam 1:2–28 and 2:1–11, 18–21

Elkanah, a man from the hill country of Ephraim, has two wives: Peninnah, who has children, and Hannah, who is childless. Yet Hannah is the one Elkanah loves. Every year, Elkanah takes his family to Shiloh to offer sacrifice to Yahweh. He always gives several shares of the meat to Peninnah, "with all her sons and daughters," but to Hannah he gives a single share. Every year Peninnah torments Hannah about her childlessness until Hannah bursts into tears and cannot eat. Elkanah asks, "Hannah, why are you so miserable? Am I not more to you than ten sons?"

Finally, one year, Hannah rushes from the meal to the Tent of Yahweh. Weeping bitterly, she vows that if she is granted a son, she will give him to God for life, and no razor will ever touch his head. Her lips move, but her prayer is silent. Watching her as she goes on in this manner for some time, the priest Eli concludes that she is inebriated. "Enough of this drunken behavior!" he bursts out. "Leave off until the effect of the wine has gone." When Hannah courteously explains that she is praying, not drunk, Eli sends her off in peace. "And may the God of Israel grant what you have asked."

The family returns home, and Elkanah has intercourse with Hannah. Yahweh remembers her, and she conceives. In due time she bears a son whom she names Samuel ("asked of God"). Elkanah and his household continue to make the annual trip to Shiloh, but Hannah does not accompany them again until she has weaned Samuel.[1] Then she takes the boy to Eli and tells him that she is the woman who stood beside him praying to Yahweh. "It was this boy that I prayed for and [Yahweh] has granted what I asked. Now I make him over to [God]." Then Hannah sings praise to Yahweh:

"My heart exults in Yahweh; in God I lift high my head. The strong stand mute in dismay, while those who faltered put on new strength. Those who had plenty sell themselves for a crust, and the hungry regain their strength. The barren woman bears seven children, while the mother of many languishes. Poverty and riches both come from Yahweh, who raises the lowly from the dust to give them a place among the great."[2]

---

1. Weaning usually occurred at about age three.
2. A summary-paraphrase. See the full poem in 1 Sam 2:1–10.

The boy Samuel remains behind to serve Yahweh under the guidance of Eli, and grows up in Yahweh's presence. Elkanah and Hannah return home to Ramah. Every year Hannah makes her son a little cloak and takes it to him when she and Elkanah go up to Shiloh for the annual sacrifice. God shows regard for Hannah, and she conceives and gives birth to three more sons and two daughters.

Reflection

Elizabeth Cady Stanton once commented, "The one sorrow which overtopped all others with the Bible women was in regard to children. If they had none, they made everybody miserable. If they had children, they fanned the jealousies of one for the other."[3] Within Israel, the bearing of sons was more than a matter of social acceptance; it carried the further connotation of the favor—or disfavor—of Yahweh.

In the first story, it seems that Yahweh chooses to favor the wife of Manoah when she is quite young, since nothing indicates that she considers her barrenness critical. She has not reached menopause, like Sarah; she does not grieve long-term barrenness, like Rachel; and she does not offer her husband a serving woman, like Sarah, Rachel, or Leah. Her youth is also suggested by her need to keep reporting to her husband. At one point she even leaves an angel standing in a field in order to run and fetch him. Even so, it is the *woman* God favors. In fact, God's angel seems barely able to tolerate the meddlesome Manoah. And from the first, it is the woman alone who is entrusted with knowledge of God's plan for the son to come. In contrast with her self-important husband, she is the one who emerges as a true responder to God's creative word.

In the second story, Hannah seems to be past her youth, but still well within childbearing age. Scorned by Peninnah, a rival in her own household, she is one of a long line of barren women God gifts with unusual sons. Unlike Sarah or Rebekah, however, Hannah shows signs of conditioning in submissiveness. She vents no displays of anger toward Peninnah, and when the priest Eli makes offensive assumptions about her behavior, it is she who takes pains to show him courtesy. Eli's own sons have gained notoriety as scoundrels who care little for Yahweh (1 Sam 2:12), yet when Hannah brings her child to Eli, she does not so much as hint that she questions his ability to rear him properly. Only in prayer does Hannah's true strength emerge. She is a woman of faith and hope who boldly pours out her need and desperation to a God she knows personally. She does not think of prayer as a genteel exchange between a proper matron and a mighty king. Like Sarah who laughs and Deborah who exults in bloody victory, Hannah gives God what

---

3. *The Woman's Bible*, Part II (1898), 46.

she feels at the moment. In this very dropping of her shields, she releases whatever has prevented conception, making it possible for God to help her. Not one to turn to God only in need, however, she prays again in the happy aftermath, singing praise to the One she recognizes as a reverser of ordinary human judgments.

❖ ❖

It could not have been easy to be a mother in Israel during the era of the Judges. Then, as now, mothers gave birth with the dragons of war standing by to devour their children. Whatever momentary truce might prevail, the prospect of bloody battle crept always upon the horizon. Though sanctified by the concept that war was dictated and led by God, these campaigns were candid matters of brutal combat followed by looting and burning of the defeated village, execution of anyone considered a threat (usually all of the men), and enslavement of the women and children. Nothing was disguised as a "surgical strike"; no one calculated "acceptable losses." In its totality, this form of war differed from today's threat of nuclear annihilation only in its more limited scope. Then, as now, thinking women must have needed immense faith and hope to bring children into the world. Even as they longed for children, they must have worried, Will my son survive to adulthood? Will my daughter know peace and security? Then, as now, racked with concern for all women's children, they must fiercely have longed for peace, and brought their concerns to Yahweh:

Prayer

Mothers: How can we sing, to you, Mother of Israel?
Never having known the weight of a child,
how can we enlarge the spaces of our dwellings,
extend our tent curtains to the full,
believing that our children will possess this land?
Even if you give us sons, may their roads not lead to death?
May our daughters' joy not one day corrode to sorrow?

Yahweh: Will the pot contend with the potter,
the clay with the hand that shapes it?
Will the child say to her maker, "You have no skill?"
In the groaning of labor, I gave birth to your earth
and fashioned humankind upon it;
I established the heavens and all their host.
Come to me; urge your case, but remember—
I am God; there is no other.

Mothers: Creator-Mother, we praise you,
for all your works are wonderful.

We remember your works from of old;
we know that you will uphold us always
and carry us and ours to safety.
Deepen our faith in your enduring love.[4]

Connections

1. What areas of accomplishment are recognized for women of today? In what lingering ways do childless women still find themselves reproached as inadequate?

2. Use of alcohol is mentioned in the stories of both mothers in this chapter. How is the value of abstinence from alcohol during pregnancy corroborated by today's awareness of problems deriving from fetal alcohol syndrome?

3. Are there any causes of today behind which you believe mothers should especially rally? What leads you to select those specific issues?

4. Many other aspects of these stories could be discussed—among them, patronizing husbands, petty sniping among women, releasing a beloved child to someone else's care, and the power of prayer. Which elements strike you? What is their connection with your life?

For Further Reading

Carmody, Denise Lardner, *Biblical Woman* (1989), 38–43.

Deen, Edith, *All of the Women of the Bible* (1955), 87–92, 325–26.

Exum, J. Cheryl, "Mothers in Israel" in *Feminist Interpretation of the Bible* (1985), ed. Letty M. Russell, 82–85.

Nunnally-Cox, Janice, *Foremothers* (1981), 54–58, 60–64.

Stanton, Elizabeth Cady, *The Woman's Bible*, Part II, (1898), 28–30, 44–46.

Winter, Miriam Therese, *WomanWisdom* (1991), 163–69.

---

4. Based on Isa 45:9–12, 21–22, and 46:3–5, 10–11.

14 Delilah and the Wife of Samson: Pawns in the Hands of Men

Judges 14, 15, 16

"... Cajole him and find out ..."

Background

two choices

People tend to remember Samson as a valiant hero who killed scores of brutal Philistines in hand-to-hand combat, and Delilah as the evil, scissors-wielding love of his life, a prostitute who betrayed him. In actuality, however, the stories told in Judges reveal Samson as a murderous bandit involved in the escalation of a petty feud, and Delilah as a woman who faced a life-or-death choice. Her occupation is never mentioned; nor is she the only woman who became entangled with Samson.

Samson's feud with the Philistines begins with a gambling debt incurred at his wedding. To pay it, Samson kills thirty Philistine men, steals their clothing, pays his debt and stalks off, apparently abandoning his Philistine wife. Next, on learning that his wife has been given in marriage to another man, he burns down acres of Philistine crops, vineyards, and olive groves. When the Philistines attempt to appease him by killing both his wife and her father, he retaliates by slaying thousands of Philistine men. Many years later, when the leading men of Philistia approach their countrywoman Delilah with a plan for capturing the still formidable strong man, he finally meets defeat, because she sides with her own people in order to ensure her own survival.

Who were these Philistines Samson harasses? Their origin is obscure. But some time between 1200 and 1000 BCE, these "Sea Peoples" advanced across the Mediterranean from the Greek mainland and Aegean islands, and claimed the strip of coastal land that runs from Gaza to Tel Aviv in modern Israel. This strip lay upon a valuable commercial crossroad between Egypt and Asia. Some of the land could be cultivated, but swamps and sand dunes covered other sections. Consequently the Philistines sought to expand inland, into Israelite territory.

Stories of Samson and the Philistines thus occur at a frontier. Samson's people, the tribe of Dan, live north of the Philistines. Israelites of the tribe of Judah live south of Dan, east of Philistia. Philistines, Danites, and Judahites move freely back and forth among each other's villages, and sometimes even intermarry. As in stories of the American Old West, however, hostilities may erupt at any moment, especially if a man emerges who is strong enough to terrorize whole towns. Samson—a veritable giant—is just such a figure.

Although he is later called a judge of Israel, he never commands an army, speaks for Yahweh, or dispenses judgment. Instead he pursues against the Philistines a long-term vendetta occasioned by his erotic obsession with Philistine women.

Yet just as a movie like *Bonnie and Clyde* glamorizes criminals, Samson's exploits so thrilled his contemporaries that legend exaggerated his deeds to epic proportions. By the time the Book of Judges was assembled, the brutality of the stories was recognized, but the compilers managed to give the tales a religious gloss by inserting a story of Samson's miraculous origins[1] and by saying of his fits of rage that he was "seized by the Spirit." Although this phrase identified God as the source of Samson's strength, the editors took care never to imply that Yahweh desired or approved Samson's actual deeds.

From early times, Samson's strength was compared with that of the Greek hero Herakles (Hercules). In fact, not cutting one's hair, the one condition of Nazirite consecration to Yahweh that Samson honored, is an example of a widespread ancient belief that long, thick hair on a male god or hero indicated vitality and power. (Besides Samson, examples include Shiva in India and the sun god Apollo in Greece.) Another widespread ancient myth featured a moon goddess who seduced a sun hero and destroyed his vital force by cutting off his hair. The story of Samson and Delilah picks up elements of these pervasive ideas. The name "Samson" comes from the Hebrew word *shemesh*, "sun," and "Delilah" appears to derive either from the Hebrew *laylah*, "night," or the Arabic *dalla*, "to behave amorously or seductively."

In later times, Christian commentators came to present Samson as a "type" of Christ, a figure foreshadowing him. Ultimately, Samson dies for his people, and Delilah, his betrayer, parallels Judas, the betrayer of Jesus. Nonetheless, seeking inspiration rather than gore from the Bible, many readers of today agree with an evaluation offered by Episcopal priest J. Ellen Nunnally. She considers the Samson saga one "which could happily vanish" from the biblical record.[2]

The Story of the Wife of Samson as Told in Judges

A Summary of Judg 14:1–15:16

A Philistine woman of Timnah catches Samson's eye. His parents protest his seeking a wife from among the "uncircumcised Philistines," but Samson gets his way. One day, as he walks to Timnah to visit his wife,[3] a lion bounds toward him. Seized by the Spirit, Samson tears it apart with his bare hands. Later, en route to his wedding feast, he notices that the carcass is filled with bees and honey.

1. See chapter 13, the story of the wife of Manoah (Judg 13).
2. *Foremothers* (1981), 57.
3. A man and woman were considered espoused from the time of betrothal.

As the week-long celebration begins, the Philistines give Samson the customary escort of thirty young men. Samson enters into the spirit of the festivities by proposing a riddle to them: "Out of the eater came something to eat; out of the strong came something sweet." He says that if they can solve his riddle by the end of the feast, he will give each of them a length of linen and a change of clothing. If they cannot solve it, each of them must give him a length of linen and a change of clothing.

Unable to guess the answer, the Philistine men threaten to kill Samson's wife and burn down her father's house unless she coaxes the explanation from Samson. She sobs on Samson's shoulder day after day, begging him to prove his love by telling her the answer. On the final day of the feast Samson yields, and tells her about the lion and the honey. She passes the word, and the young men confront Samson with the solution. He retorts, "If you had not plowed with my heifer, you would not have solved my riddle." Seized by the Spirit, he goes to the Philistine town of Ashkelon where he strikes down thirty men and strips them. He returns to Timnah, pays his debt with their clothing, and stalks home "in a furious temper." The father of the bride, considering his daughter abandoned, gives her in marriage to Samson's groomsman.

By the time of the wheat harvest, Samson's temper has cooled. He goes to visit his wife, only to find her married to another man. Enraged, he vows to do the Philistines "some real harm." He captures three hundred foxes, ties them tail to tail in pairs, fastens and lights a torch between each set of tails, and sets the foxes loose in the Philistine fields. Everything burns—standing grain, grain gathered into sheaves, vineyards, even ancient olive groves. Realizing it was the giving of Samson's wife to another man that sparked the havoc, the Philistines burn both the woman and her father to death in an attempt to appease Samson. He views this act as a further outrage, and retaliates by smiting them "hip and thigh," slaughtering many. Finally he retreats to a cave in the hill country of Judah, but now the Philistines seek revenge. They threaten Judah by setting up an armed camp, thereby coercing three thousand Judahites into promising to hand Samson over. Samson allows the men of Judah to bind him and deliver him to the Philistines, but when they begin to shout in triumph, he is once more seized by the Spirit. He bursts his ropes, grabs the jawbone of an ass, and uses it to slaughter a thousand men.

The Story of Delilah as Told in Judges

A Summary of Judg 16:1–30

After twenty years of peace, Samson one day visits a prostitute in the Philistine town of Gaza. The men of Gaza lie in wait near the city gates, planning to kill Samson at dawn when the gates are unlocked, but Samson foils them. At midnight he grasps the gates and tears them loose—posts, bar, and all—and hoists the massive pieces onto his shoulders. He deposits them thirty miles away on the top of a hill in Judah.

Then Samson falls in love with a Philistine woman named Delilah. The leading men among the Philistines urge her to find out for them what gives Samson his enduring strength, and how he can be rendered helpless. "We shall each give you eleven hundred pieces of silver," they tell her. On three different occasions, Samson appears to give Delilah the answer, and with men of Philistia lying in wait, she tests the sleeping Samson. But each time, when she cries out to Samson that the Philistines are upon him, he easily shakes himself free of his bonds.

At last Delilah complains. "How can you say you love me when you do not confide in me? This is the third time you have made a fool of me and have not told me what gives you your great strength." Yielding to her persuasion, Samson tells her that no razor has touched his head since birth. "If my head were shaved, then my strength would leave me." Delilah again notifies the Philistine men. Then she lulls Samson to sleep with his head on her lap, and summons a barber. When Samson's hair is shorn she again cries out, "Samson, the Philistines are upon you!" This time his strength has left him. The Philistines capture him, gouge out his eyes, and imprison him at Gaza. There they use him as a beast of burden to operate a grain-grinding mill.

Some time later, the Philistines decide to exhibit Samson at a festival in honor of their god, Dagon. Not realizing that Samson's strength has returned with the growth of his hair, his guide agrees to position him near the pillars that support the temple. At the height of the festivities, when the temple is filled and another three thousand men and women look down into the central courtyard from the roof, Samson pushes the pillars with all his might. The temple collapses, killing Samson and all the Philistines.

Reflection

The Philistine woman of Timnah has no idea what she is getting into when she agrees to marry an outsider. Samson has courted her, so she knows that the brawny Israelite possesses a certain charm. But with his snickering way of referring to women as cattle and his incessant boasting about his hunting feats, he sounds more like an adolescent than a grown man. Does he even love her, she wonders, or merely lust for her? Is his violence limited to tearing wild animals limb from limb, or will he someday slap her around as well? Still, he is only one man, as compared with thirty Philistine men who threaten immediate violence. Besides, the fuss about the riddle strikes her as nothing more than a harmless game. The price of her error is life itself. Flames searing her flesh, the woman of Timnah dies in agony, a pawn to men's games.

By Delilah's time, surely every woman of Philistia knows about Samson's brutal rages; and their own men's savage execution of Samson's wife has undoubtedly bred equal terror in their hearts. Yet the men of Philistia continue to cultivate their hatred of Samson and to seek revenge. Samson's obsession with Delilah offers them the opening they seek. Delilah seems to be a well-born woman or, if a prostitute, no ordinary one, but rather a high-class courtesan, for she deals familiarly with the leading men of Philistia. Just as they still harbor their long-term resentment of Samson, however, perhaps she still nurtures grief over the fiery fate of Samson's wife. If she is a prostitute, perhaps she has worked her own subtle vengeance for the other woman's death by milking her clients of the heftiest fees she can command. In any case, she has become known as someone who can be bought—for a generous price. That reputation saves her. Would men willing to spend so much on Samson balk at taking the life of anyone who thwarted them? Although the threat is veiled, Delilah knows it is there, and her sin, if sin exists, is to place a higher value on self-preservation than on loyalty to an outsider. As commentator Mary Cartledge-Hayes wryly observes, "Delilah typifies the fact that women may be powerless, but they don't have to die as a result. Sometimes they get lucky: They escape with only the hatred of generations to come."[4]

❖ ❖

The woman of Timnah dies for having underestimated the macho interpretation of a party pastime. Delilah earns the scorn of centuries of readers for having opted to protect herself. These women typify eons of subordination of women, including casual acceptance of men's "right" to abuse them. In the United States, violence against women not only continues, but has, according to the American Medical Association and the Surgeon General, reached epidemic proportions:

> Horrors on the homefront are the leading source of injury for women between the ages of 15 and 44. Each year 4 million women are severely assaulted by their current or former partner. Many of the victims fail to make it to the hospital in time: more than half of female murder victims are slain by their husband or boyfriend.[5]

Though emotionally and physically battered women often accept the blame for men's violence, they are not at fault. Abuse of women is men's sickness, and women can no more cure it than children can prevent child abuse. But women of today command far greater legal, economic, and political power than did Delilah or the wife of Samson. They can and do influence their environment far more profoundly than could any woman of Philistia. Whether a woman prosecutes an abusive man in a court of law, heartens a friend or neighbor to take advantage of available help, or donates time or money to a shelter for battered women and children, she is helping to prevent

4. *To Love Delilah* (1990), 44.
5. Jill Smolowe, "What the Doctor Should Do," *Time*, 29 June 1992, 57.

other women from suffering defamation of character like Delilah, or savage death like the wife of Samson.

❖ ❖

The nature of the deities worshipped by the women of Philistia is unknown to us, but in their time people conceived of deities who comforted as well as deities who destroyed. If Delilah escaped the carnage when Samson demolished the Temple of Dagon, perhaps she prayed:

Prayer

Mothering God, be with me and all women.
Bruised and violated,
we ask to be cradled in your loving hands.
Heal our wounds and deliver us from further violence.
You who calm the wild beast and gentle the roiling seas,
protect us from word-games that end in murder,
feuds that escalate to full-scale war.

Deliver us, too, from our own readiness to believe
what abusive men say about us.
And deliver us from the immobilizing chains
of our own anger.
Help us focus our efforts that, together,
we may walk in ways that lead to peace.

Connections

1. What choices were available to the woman of Timnah? What would you have done in her situation?
2. What courses of action were open to Delilah? Considering the choice she made, do you view her more as betrayer or as survivor? Why?
3. In these stories, anger and violence escalate. Similar escalation of quarrels occurs within families. What can one member of a family do to break the cycle of violence?

For Further Reading

Cartledge-Hayes, Mary, *To Love Delilah* (1990), 36–45.
Deen, Edith, *All of the Women of the Bible* (1955), 78–81, 326–28, 358.
Nunnally-Cox, Janice (J. Ellen Nunnally), *Foremothers* (1981), 54–58.
Winter, Miriam Therese, *WomanWisdom* (1991), 156–62.

15 Ruth and Naomi: Devoted Friends

The Book of Ruth

". . . better to you than seven sons . . ."

Background

Though set in "the days of the judges," the Book of Ruth offers a welcome respite from stories of blood and conquest. It introduces no villains, preaches no hatred of foreigners, depicts no battles. Instead it presents a peaceful countryside where cooperation is the norm. In the book, a family journeys from Judah to Moab during a time of famine. The father dies, the sons marry Moabite women, and then the sons die. Three women are widowed—Naomi and her daughters-in-law Orpah and Ruth. At Naomi's urging Orpah remains in Moab, but Ruth insists upon returning to Judah with Naomi. At first Ruth supports the two of them, but after a time Naomi guides Ruth in invoking the levirate customs of Israel. These customs require a close male relative of a dead man to marry his widow and sire sons in the dead man's name. Ruth marries a kinsman named Boaz, and from their union arises the line that produces King David.

The story is carefully orchestrated, building suspense much like a modern short story. It presents three characters who are especially admirable: the women Naomi and Ruth, and the man Boaz. Ruth occupies the spotlight. In terms of the plot, Orpah serves as foil or contrast to Ruth, and an unnamed kinsman serves as foil to Boaz. Three "choruses" also participate in the action: the women of Bethlehem, workers in the fields of Boaz, and elders at the city gate.

The story is unusually woman-centered both in language and in plot. Naomi uses an old name for God, Shaddai, usually translated "God Almighty" but originally "God of the Fruitful Mountains" (that is, "God of Breasts"). She also urges each of her daughters-in-law to return to her "mother's house"—a substitute for "father's house" found only here and in Song 3:4. In the plot of the story, no angel ever appears, God never intervenes, no man rushes to the rescue. Although Naomi and Ruth live in a culture where childless widows are nonentities, this old woman and her young daughter-in-law bear their own burdens and build their own future. In the end, the reason Ruth agrees to seek marriage is, perhaps, that people of her time did not believe in an afterlife in the Christian sense. The only way they could achieve immortality was to live on in their children. Even then, it is Ruth who proposes to Boaz.

In literary terms, the story is historical fiction, with an ending that connects it with a tradition that David's ancestors included a Moabite woman. The story circulated orally for some time, and may first have been written down shortly after David's time. It reached final form only after the Babylonian Exile—six hundred years after the events it celebrates. For Israelite readers, Ruth's nationality was of prime importance. She came from Moab, a table land east of Judah on the other side of the Dead Sea (today's southwestern Jordan). Although the language and culture of Moab and Israel were almost identical, Israelites despised Moabites for their numerous deities and fertility rituals. Genesis makes the Moabites the product of an incestuous union between Lot and one of his daughters; Deuteronomy decrees that no Moabite may be admitted to the assembly of Yahweh; Isaiah and Jeremiah record oracles against Moab; and after the Exile, Ezra and Nehemiah urge Israelite men to rid themselves of Moabite and other foreign wives.[1]

Overall, then, the title character comes from a despised race, the lowest economic class, and the gender that is subordinate in a world dominated by men. Yet Ruth emerges as a shining example of womanhood and as a model of faith comparable only to Abraham, founding father of Israel, who also abandoned all at God's call.

The Story of Ruth and Naomi as Told in the Book of Ruth

Ruth Moves to Bethlehem with Naomi: *A Summary of Ruth 1*

In the days of the judges, famine drives a family from Bethlehem in Judah to the country of Moab. They are Elimelech, his wife Naomi, and their sons Mahlon and Chilion. Elimelech dies in Moab. Some time later, Mahlon and Chilion marry Moabite women named Ruth and Orpah. When the family has lived in Moab about ten years, both Mahlon and Chilion die. The grieving Naomi eventually hears that food is again plentiful in Judah, and sets out for home. When her daughters-in-law accompany her onto the road, Naomi prays that God may deal kindly with them in the same way that they have kept faith with the dead and with her. Then she urges them to return to their mothers' houses and seek new husbands. At first they refuse. Naomi weeps and reasons with them until, at last, Orpah kisses Naomi and turns back. Ruth, however, persists: "Where you go, I shall go, and where you stay, I shall stay. Your people will be my people, and your God my God. Where you die, I shall die, and there shall be buried. I solemnly declare . . . that nothing but death will part me from you." Naomi protests no further, and she and Ruth travel together, reaching Bethlehem at the beginning of the barley harvest. Barely recognizing Naomi, the townswomen cry in excitement, "Can this be Naomi?" She responds, "Do not call me Naomi; call me Mara, for . . . I went away full, and [Shaddai] has brought me back empty."[2]

Ruth Comes to the Attention of Boaz: *A Summary of Ruth 2*

Ruth gains Naomi's assurance that she is permitted to glean behind the reapers who cut the grain and bind it into sheaves. The field she chooses belongs to a

---

1. Gen 19:30–38; Deut 23:3–4; Isa 15 and 16; Jer 48; Ezra 9 and 10; Neh 13:1–3.

2. Naomi means "delight" or "pleasantness"; Mara means "bitter." Ruth may be a contraction of *retût*, "lady friend" or "beautiful friend."

man of substance named Boaz. At mid-day Boaz asks his foreman, "Whose girl is that?" The man tells him Ruth's story, and adds that she has been on her feet all day, with hardly a moment's rest. Favorably impressed by Ruth's devotion to Naomi and by her industry, Boaz tells her to glean only in his fields, together with his servant women. He orders his men not to bother Ruth and tells her to drink from his crew's water jars any time she is thirsty. In the evening Boaz invites her to eat with him and his workers. After the meal he instructs his crew to let her glean right among the sheaves, and even to drop ears of grain for her.[3] Ruth threshes the barley she has gathered and takes it home. Amazed at the amount, Naomi asks Ruth where she has been gleaning. When Ruth names Boaz and describes his kindness, Naomi blesses him for keeping faith with the dead as well as the living, for he is a "very near" relative of her dead husband. Ruth continues to glean in Boaz's fields until the end of the barley and wheat harvests.

Naomi and Ruth Invoke Levirate Customs: *A Summary of Ruth 3*

One day Naomi tells Ruth that she wants to see her happily settled. She says that Boaz will be winnowing barley at the threshing floor that night, and directs Ruth to anoint herself with perfumed oil, dress attractively, and go to the threshing floor but conceal herself from Boaz. "When he lies down, make sure you know the place where he is. Then go in, turn back the covering at his feet and lie down. He will tell you what to do." Ruth replies, "I will do everything you say."[4]

That evening, drowsy with food and drink, Boaz curls up in his cloak and falls sound asleep on a heap of grain. About midnight he awakens to find a woman at his feet! "Who are you?" he asks. "Sir, it is I, Ruth," she replies. "Spread the skirt of your cloak over me, for you are my next of kin."[5] Boaz calls upon God to bless her, for the whole town knows what a fine woman she is. "You are proving yourself more devoted to the family than ever by not running after any young man, whether rich or poor." He goes on to explain that although he is a near kinsman, another man is even more closely related. If the other man will act as next of kin, well and good. If not, Boaz will act as kinsman-redeemer. At Boaz's invitation, Ruth spends the rest of the night at his feet. Before it is light enough for anyone to recognize her, he fills her cloak with six measures of barley and sends her home. Ruth tells Naomi everything that was said and done, and Naomi assures her that Boaz will settle the matter that very day.

3. Lev 19:9–10, 23:22 and Deut 24:19–22 direct owners of fields not to reap too thoroughly or go back to pick up anything that was missed, but to leave the remainder for the widowed, the poor, and the alien, because the people of Israel were once aliens themselves in Egypt. Boaz goes well beyond these directives.

4. Turning back the covers over Boaz' lower body is provocative and ambiguous, since "feet" is sometimes a euphemism for "genitals" (e.g., Ex 4:25). At the very least, Ruth risks a charge of promiscuity if she is discovered. Tradition asserts that Ruth's encounter with Boaz did not involve intercourse.

5. In effect, "Honor custom and marry me." Ruth is asking Boaz to act as a redeemer by spreading protection over her as Yahweh spread his wing over the Israelites in the desert.

Boaz Marries Ruth: *A Summary of Ruth 4*

Boaz, meanwhile, goes to sit at the town gate. When the other relative appears, he invites the man and ten town elders to join him. Boaz reminds his audience of a strip of field belonging to Elimelech. "Naomi is selling it," he says, "now that she has returned from Moab." He asks his kinsman whether or not he plans to do his duty and buy it. When the man says that he will, Boaz points out that he must at the same time marry the widow Ruth and raise up sons with her to keep the land in Mahlon's line. The man responds that then he cannot act, lest Mahlon's property rights become entangled with his own to the detriment of his heirs: Boaz must redeem the land and the woman. The two men perform a symbolic exchange of sandals.[6] Boaz then calls upon all who are present to witness his purchase of the land and his taking of "Mahlon's widow, Ruth, the Moabite, to be my wife, in order to keep alive the dead man's name on his holding." The witnesses invoke God's blessings upon Ruth, citing the memory of Rachel and Leah, the mothers of the twelve clans of Israel; and the widow Tamar, who bore twin sons to Judah. So Boaz and Ruth marry, and God blesses Ruth with a son. The women tell Naomi that the child will renew her life and serve as a "support and stay" in her old age, "for your devoted daughter-in-law, who has proved better to you than seven sons, has borne him." Acting as a guardian, Naomi lays the boy in her own lap and accepts for him the name Obed, proposed by the women of Bethlehem. Obed becomes the father of Jesse, who becomes the father of David the King.

Reflection

The story of Ruth is rich with drama: women debating in a public road, a chance meeting in a grain field, a daring rendezvous on a threshing floor, a legal case argued at the city gates. Through it all, the story focuses on women supporting women—carrying on after the deaths of spouses, taking the initiative in difficult times, calling upon others to fulfill their duty. A story that begins in emptiness ends in abundance.

Above all, the story speaks of Ruth's devotion to Naomi. Not only does Ruth break with family, country, and faith, but in a world where women depend on men for their very lives, she abandons any search for a young man in order to bond with an old woman. Ruth's pledge is to nothing Naomi can offer, nor to the memory of their husbands. It is simply to Naomi the woman. Even the God to whom Ruth pledges fidelity is known to her only through Naomi, yet the deepest element of her friendship with Naomi seems to lie in their union of heart about spiritual matters.

---

6. Marking a property deal by exchanging sandals (Ruth 4:7–8; Am 2:6) may have arisen from the practice of claiming title to land by walking its boundaries or casting a shoe upon it (Ps 60:8). In another connection between sandals and levirate customs, a man who refused to do his duty suffered enduring humiliation if the aggrieved widow removed his sandal in front of witnesses (Deut 25:9–10).

The friendship is so profound that Ruth is able to allow Naomi time to work out the depression she is suffering when they arrive in Bethlehem. As the one contributing the work, never does Ruth use her economic edge to dominate Naomi. Instead she welcomes Naomi's knowledge of the customs of Israel and her wisdom in determining when and how to invoke them. Even when Ruth marries Boaz, the friendship between the two women endures. Neither abandons the sustenance it offers solely because Ruth has established a similar partnership with a man.

In contrast with Bible stories where women compete for status, power, or men, the story of Ruth and Naomi testifies to the strength of women's bonding. As ordained Methodist elder Renita J. Weems writes,

> Their relationship typifies the special friendship that can often develop between women, despite differences in age, nationality, and religion. Ruth and Naomi's legacy is that of a seasoned friendship between two women, a friendship which survived the test of time despite the odds against women as individuals, as friends, as women living without men.[7]

Given the story of Ruth and Naomi, one wonders what additional instances of women's bonding occurred in Old Testament times—what other examples of networking and mentoring (to use today's terms) occurred that no man cared to record for posterity.

Today, women continue to nurture sustaining friendships with other women—mothers, grandmothers, sisters, cousins, aunts, neighbors, coworkers, members of the same faith community or support group. Women gather for fun and for comradeship. They turn to each other in times of joy and pain; they celebrate life and mourn death. Together they work for a world where it is sharing, not winning, that matters. And in the deepest of these women's circles, it is a God who transcends pettiness and human divisions who provides the staying power. Like Ruth and Naomi who honored Shaddai, today's women pray in praise of a faithful, fruitful God:

Prayer

> We praise you, God of those in need,
> for your love endures forever.
> Gathered from east and west, north and south,
> we cry to you in our emptiness,
> and you fill us with what is good.
> We cry to you in our fullness,
> and you deepen our joy.
> You turn bitter desert to pleasant springs;
> you lift us from seas of distress
> and lead us to safe harbor;

7. *Just a Sister Away* (1988), 24–25.

you light our way along roads of darkness
to places where we can thrive.

Faithful God, make us present to each other
in times of pleasure and times of bitter choice.
As Ruth and Naomi supported each other,
so may we, together,
work our fields and renew our households.
May we be bold like Ruth, wise like Naomi.
May we gift those around us
with the wonder of your enduring love.[8]

Connections

1. The story presents three major women, Naomi, Orpah, and Ruth. With which woman do you most strongly identify? Why?

2. Naomi sees Shaddai reflected in the behavior of her daughters-in-law, and they know Naomi's God through Naomi. If you were set down in a distant place, what would people deduce about your God from your behavior?

3. The passage "Where you go, I will go" is often read at weddings, as if spoken between woman and man. What do you find interesting or ironic about the actual origin of the words?

4. When have you experienced friendship as deep as that between Naomi and Ruth? When have other women comforted you or celebrated with you? When have you in turn enveloped them in compassion or joy?

For Further Reading

Alter, Robert, *The World of Biblical Literature* (1992), 51–52.

Carmody, Denise Lardner, *Biblical Woman* (1989), 32–37.

Deen, Edith, *All of the Women of the Bible* (1955), 81–87, 284–85.

Johnson, Ann, *Miryam of Nazareth* (1984), 49–55.

Kirk, Martha Ann, "A Story of Ruth," *God of Our Mothers* (1985), audiotape.

Mollenkott, Virginia Ramey, *The Divine Feminine* (1983), 54–59.

Schaberg, Jane, *The Illegitimacy of Jesus* (1990), 26–29.

Trible, Phyllis, *God and the Rhetoric of Sexuality* (1978), 166–99.

Weems, Renita J., *Just a Sister Away* (1988), 22–36.

Winter, Miriam Therese, *WomanWisdom* (1991), 286–89.

Yamasaki, April, *Remember Lot's Wife* (1991), 25–26.

8. Based on Ps 107 and the Book of Ruth.

16 Wives of David: Adjuncts of the Throne

1 Samuel 14, 18, 19, 25, 27–30; 2 Samuel 1–6, 11, 12;

1 Kings 1–2

". . . he took more concubines and wives in Jerusalem . . ."

Three Wives of David in order of appearance:
>*Michal:* Daughter of King Saul
>*Abigail:* Widow of Nabal of Carmel
>*Bathsheba:* Wife of Uriah the Hittite

Background

Several wives of King David are named in the books of Samuel and Kings, but their brief appearances are overshadowed by the tempestuous story of David himself. Although David was Yahweh's choice to succeed King Saul, Saul's insane jealousy forced David into a life of banditry, and his rise to kingship was stormy. Many of David's wives experienced war first hand. Further, even after David secured the throne and made Jerusalem his capital, his own ungovernable passions ignited problems within his family. He contributed to a spirit of rebellion that eventually found expression in attempted coups d'état by two of his sons, Absalom and Adonijah.

Whatever their innate talents or strength of character, David's queens possessed no power. They were little more than perks of monarchy, appendages of the throne. In the Middle East of 1000 BCE, large harems increased a ruler's prestige, and a king's women were set apart for his private pleasure. Indeed, seizing one of the king's women constituted a treasonous stab at the throne itself, and ascending a throne was usually marked by assuming the previous king's harem.

Even at the level of physical comfort, David's wives were little better off than the wives of prosperous tradesmen. He possessed neither the time nor the resources to beautify his capital, and the women of his harem were confined within a walled citadel made of earth and stone, living on a second floor, above storerooms and arsenals.

References in Samuel suggest that David's harem included at least twenty women. In addition to any women he may have "inherited" from Saul, eight wives are individually named; he takes additional wives and concubines when he seizes Jerusalem; and he leaves ten concubines behind when he flees the city during Absalom's rebellion (1 Sam 18:27; 2 Sam 3:2–5, 5:13–16,

11:27, 15:16). Of his wives, only three briefly take center stage: Michal, who rescues David from the wrath of Saul; Abigail, whose wise counsel prevents him from initiating a blood feud he will later regret; and Bathsheba, who becomes the mother of his successor, Solomon.

The Story of Michal as Begun in 1 Samuel

Michal Saves David: *A Summary of 1 Sam 14:49, 18:1–29, and 19:11–18*

The young warrior David succeeds so well that the people celebrate his victories more highly than those of King Saul. Saul reluctantly offers David his older daughter Merab as wife. But he expects David to die in battle with the Philistines, so he gives her to another man. Then David survives the campaign. Seeing that his younger daughter Michal has fallen in love with David, Saul decides that she can serve his purposes as well as her sister. As the bride price for Michal, Saul asks of David the foreskins of a hundred Philistines. But again David survives; in fact, he and his men slay twice that many Philistines, and David counts out two hundred foreskins to his prospective father-in-law. Saul allows the marriage to proceed, but his jealousy continues to fester. When he actually plans to assassinate his son-in-law, however, Michal comes to David's rescue. She catches wind of the plot and lowers him from their house through a window. She then places a household idol in his bed with a goat's hair rug at its head. Saul's agents mistake the dummy for David, sick in bed. The ruse is discovered when Saul demands that they bring him in, bed and all. Challenged by her father, Michal claims that David threatened her life if she did not help him.

The Story of Abigail and Michal as Told in 1 and 2 Samuel

Abigail Acts Wisely: *A Summary of 1 Sam 25:1–44 and 30:1–21*

Living in the countryside, David assembles an army of malcontents. He repeatedly evades capture by Saul. For a time his guerrillas occupy the stony wilds of Judah near Maon, where they protect the property of the wealthy Nabal—a mean and surly man who is married to the beautiful and intelligent Abigail. One day when Nabal is shearing sheep on his other property in Carmel, David sends a request to him for supplies. Nabal rails at David as a good-for-nothing rebel who deserves no aid. Incensed, David vows to annihilate Nabal's entire household. Meanwhile, however, one of Nabal's servants has rushed to Maon to report the clash to Abigail. She quickly packs several donkeys with bread, wine, mutton, grain, raisins, and figs, and sends the supplies to David's camp. She herself follows. On the way, she encounters David and four hundred armed men descending a ravine. She prostrates herself at David's feet and pleads (with great tact) for her household. Predicting that David's God will raise him to greatness, she argues that he will then regret having spilled innocent blood. David blesses Abigail for her good sense, accepts her gifts, and sends her home in peace.

At home, Abigail finds Nabal hosting a drunken banquet. She waits until morning, when he is sober, to tell her story. Nabal suffers a seizure, and ten days later he dies. When David hears the news, he sends a marriage proposal to Abigail, and she rides to his camp and marries him. By this time David has also married Ahinoam of Jezreel, but Saul has given David's first wife, Michal, to a man named Palti. Saul finally abandons his pursuit of David when David allies himself with Achish, the Philistine King of Gath. David earns Achish's trust by raiding desert nomads and passing off the booty as coming from Judah. But the other Philistines do not trust David, and when he accompanies Achish on a campaign into Judah, they demand that he be sent back home. David and his men reach their town to find it raided and burned by Amalekites from the desert, their wives and children captured. They pursue the Amalekites, soundly defeat them, and rescue all of the captives, including David's wives Ahinoam and Abigail.

Michal Despises David: *A Summary of 1 Sam 30 and 2 Sam 1–6*

While David is rescuing his wives in the south, the Philistines defeat Saul in the north. Saul dies on Mount Gilboa. Together with his wives and followers, David moves to Hebron where he is anointed king of Judah. During the time that he rules Judah from Hebron, each of the six wives then living with him— Ahinoam, Abigail, Maacah, Haggith, Abital, and Eglah—bears him a son. The sons' names are Amnon, Chileab, Absalom, Adonijah, Shephatiah, and Ithream. Meanwhile war drags on between David and Saul's son Ishbosheth (Ishbaal), who rules in the north. As the house of Saul weakens, David enhances his own position by negotiating the return of his first wife, Michal. On the day she is delivered, her husband Palti follows for miles, weeping. When Ishbosheth dies, David becomes king of Israel (the north) as well as Judah (the south). He rules the reunited kingdom from Hebron for seven years. Then he wrests Jerusalem from the Jebusites and makes it his capital. From Jerusalem, where he takes more concubines and wives and sires many more sons and daughters, he rules another thirty-three years.

David makes Jerusalem the religious as well as the administrative center of his kingdom by installing the ark of the covenant there. On its arrival from the backwater where it has been stored, he dances ecstatically before it, clad only in an ephod.[1] Michal looks down from a window, and despises him. When he returns to the palace, she upbraids him. "What a glorious day for the king of Israel," she says, "when he made an exhibition of himself in the sight of his servants' slave girls, as any vulgar clown might do!" David

---

1. An ephod was a sort of ceremonial apron, a light garment that covered the front of a high priest's body. David's ephod seems to have been merely a small skirt or loincloth.

responds that he shall always dance for joy before Yahweh, whatever disgrace it earns him in her eyes. To her dying day, Michal is childless.

The Story of Bathsheba as Told in 2 Samuel and 1 Kings

David Takes Bathsheba from Uriah: *A Summary of 2 Sam 11 and 12:15–25*

One spring David sends his commander Joab across the Jordan to besiege the Ammonites at Rabbah (the modern Amman, capital of Jordan). David remains in Jerusalem. Strolling around the roof of the palace one evening, he sees a beautiful woman bathing on another rooftop.[2] She is Bathsheba, wife of Uriah the Hittite. He sends for her and has intercourse with her, even though she is still purifying herself after her period, and then she goes home. She conceives, and sends word to David that she is pregnant.[3]

David summons Uriah and discusses with him the progress of the war. Then he sends him home, expecting him to sleep with Bathsheba. But Uriah observes a soldier's ritual abstinence from intercourse and sleeps with his men near the palace gate. Even when David gets him drunk the next evening, he stays away from his wife. Finally David sends him back to Ammon, carrying a letter that tells Joab to put him in the front lines, then fall back so that he will be killed. Joab does as David directs, and Uriah dies. Bathsheba mourns her husband, and when her period of mourning has ended, David brings her into the palace as his wife. She bears a son, but the child dies because of David's sins. As the prophet Nathan informs David, Yahweh is angry over David's arranging Uriah's death and taking his wife.[4] David consoles Bathsheba and lies with her again, and she bears a son whom God loves. She names him Solomon.

Bathsheba Plays Politics: *A Summary of 1 Kings 1–2*

When he is old, David cannot keep warm no matter how well his servants wrap him. They search throughout Israel and select Abishag, a young woman of Shunem, to lie in his arms and make him hot. Meanwhile, David's son Adonijah gathers support and lays claim to the throne. The prophet Nathan goes to Bathsheba, Solomon's mother, and advises her to say to David at once, "Did not your majesty swear to me that my son Solomon should succeed you as king, and that it was he who should sit on your throne? Why then

2. Presumably only the palace was high enough for gazing down upon other roofs.

3. Besides identifying David, not Uriah, as the father of Bathsheba's child, this passage establishes that Bathsheba was performing not an ordinary bath when David noticed her, but the ritual immersion required seven days after the end of a woman's menstrual period. Still practiced by Orthodox Jewish women, this bath signifies spiritual renewal and permits a woman and her husband to resume marital relations.

4. David's misfortunes multiply hereafter. They include pestilence, famine, the rape of one of his daughters, rebellions, and the death of his sons Amnon and Absalom.

has Adonijah become king?" Bathsheba goes to David and asks these questions. David immediately proclaims Solomon his successor and has him anointed as his regent. Adonijah flees to the sanctuary and Solomon spares his life, but vows to kill him if he ever makes trouble again. David dies soon after this. Still resentful at having been passed over for his younger half-brother, Adonijah goes to Bathsheba and asks her to petition Solomon to give him Abishag as his wife. Solomon hears his mother out, but he takes Adonijah's request as tantamount to another attack on the throne, and executes him.

Reflection

Three women stand out in David's story, each differing from the others. Michal is a princess, Abigail an estate manager, Bathsheba a soldier's wife. Michal at first loves David, though he seems to regard her solely as a political pawn. Abigail prostrates herself at David's feet, but confronts him as an equal. Bathsheba yields to David's lust and power.

The young Michal idolizes David enough to foil the plans of Saul, her own father. Judging by the presence of a household idol in her home, her family is not single-mindedly committed to David's Yahweh, but her youthful devotion to David is total. Years later, she has come to despise David. We are not told what causes her bitterness, but the sheer fact of being passed from one man to another must have contributed. Even though she is a princess, she is traded like a trophy. As Elizabeth Cady Stanton observes, Michal must have lived "in a quandary the chief part of the time."[5] David never rewards the courage and ingenuity she shows in saving his life; indeed, he forgets her for years.

Against the odds, Michal may have grown to love Palti: he, at least, mourns extravagantly when David yanks her from their marriage. Nor does David treat Michal as a princess on this second go-round, either: he lets her sink into anonymity among the other women of his harem. And as if having her entire life dictated by the whims of kings were not bad enough, she dies in disgrace, never having borne a child.

Abigail, in contrast, emerges as a confident, competent woman who acts as she pleases. She seems to manage Nabal's property, for no one shows surprise when she packs up a food train for David's guerrillas. Too sensible to allow her household to be destroyed because of her husband's shortsightedness, she flouts social codes and rides off alone to meet David. When her churlish husband suffers a stroke or heart attack—occasioned by shock at his close call with death, or at his wife's dispersal of his stores?—she loses no time in shattering custom again. Abandoning her estate (or bringing the portable wealth with her), she saddles up to go and marry David.

5. *The Woman's Bible,* Part II (1898), 49.

Abigail later experiences captivity at the hands of the Amalekites, rescue at the hands of David. From the first, apparently without rancor, she shares David with other wives. Gifted with diplomacy and unshakable self-confidence, she probably continued to thrive no matter how many wives David took. She apparently hands on her good sense to her son Chileab, for even though he is senior to his half-brothers Absalom and Adonijah, he is never said to have joined either of their plots against David.

The Bathsheba of the Bible, unlike the seductive exhibitionist of popular imagination, is a religiously observant woman and a political naïf who is manipulated by powerful men. When David first sends for her, she is not simply bathing, but observing a religious ritual in a secluded corner of her own rooftop. Having had little choice but to obey a royal summons, she rightly places the problem of the pregnancy that results squarely in David's hands. What storms of emotion engulf her as he proceeds to "solve the problem" by arranging the murder of her husband? Does she even know about David's hand in Uriah's death, or does she believe Uriah to be a genuine casualty of war?

The first child of David and Bathsheba dies, but David continues to love her, and he grants her favors into his old age. If it is the prophet Nathan who initiates Solomon's succession (we have no way of knowing whether or not David really promised the throne to Solomon), it is nevertheless Bathsheba to whom David listens. Bathsheba fares less well with the king when that king is her own son. When she conveys to Solomon his brother's request to possess Abishag, Solomon treats her as lacking all political insight. Instead of humoring her, he executes the man. No temptress or seducer is this Bathsheba, but a quiet woman who never quite emerges as a fully formed personality. No wonder tradition celebrates her role rather than her person: Judaism recalls her as mother of the house of David through Solomon; Matthew cites her as an ancestor of Jesus (Mt 1:6).

❖ ❖

In the circumstances of their lives, these women seem distant from women of our century. Yet in emotional reactions, their responses can still be seen among people of today. In difficult times, Michal resorts to bitterness; Abigail bends her talents to negotiation; and Bathsheba, though appearing to sway with every breeze, quietly prospers.

Each woman undoubtedly ponders the role of David and David's God in her life. Even Michal's story implicitly attests belief in the power of Yahweh, for her barrenness marks the rise of the house of David, who is beloved of Yahweh, at the expense of the house of Saul. Abigail seems genuinely to believe in Yahweh's future plans for the house of David. Bathsheba guarantees continuation of the dynasty through Solomon, the son God is said to love. Perhaps each, in her own way, ultimately finds greater peace and comfort in David's God than in David's person:

Prayer

I love you, Yahweh, my strength.
You are my only protector,
my fortress in whom I take refuge.
I call upon you, for you are worthy of praise.
When bitter torrents engulf me, you come down:
you mount the cherubim and soar on the wings of the wind.
You reach from on high to draw me from the depths of misery.
You rescue me and delight in me;
you bring me into a place of peace.

God of Israel, you are my light in darkness,
for who is true king but you?
Who is my Rock except you?
You sustain my life and establish me on the heights.
I praise you among the nations,
for you show unfailing kindness to your chosen.[6]

Connections

1. Michal lies to her father in order to protect David, Abigail thwarts her husband's wishes in order to prevent bloodshed, and Bathsheba violates her own marriage vows at the king's demand. What would you have done in their situations?

2. All three of these women experience marriage to another man besides David. On the basis of clues given in the stories, which marriage—Michal and Palti, Abigail and Nabal, Bathsheba and Uriah—would you guess to have been the happiest, before David disrupted it?

3. Can any one of these women serve as a role model for you? In what ways?

For Further Reading

Deen, Edith, *All of the Women of the Bible* (1955), 96–106, 112–17.

Moloney, Francis J., *Woman First Among the Faithful* (1984), 32–33, 44–47.

Nunnally-Cox, Janice, *Foremothers* (1981), 66–77.

Schaberg, Jane, *The Illegitimacy of Jesus* (1990), 20, 29–33.

Stanton, Elizabeth Cady, *The Woman's Bible*, Part II (1898), 49.

Winter, Miriam Therese, *WomanWisdom* (1991), 177–89, 340–54, 360–66.

6. Based on Ps 18 and its doublet in 2 Sam 22:1–23:7, attributed to David.

17 Tamar, Daughter of David and Maacah: Princess Discarded

2 Samuel 13:1–39

"Tamar threw ashes over her head . . ."

Background

The story of Tamar, daughter of David and Maacah, appears in the David cycle shortly after David orders Uriah killed in battle so that David can take Bathsheba as his own. The opening scene of Tamar's story focuses on Amnon, David's son by Ahinoam. Lusting for Tamar, his half-sister, Amnon lures her to his quarters and urges her into his bed. In protest, Tamar pleads that Amnon marry her instead.[1] Unlike David, however, who at least married Bathsheba and loved her after he dishonored her, Amnon rapes Tamar and then orders her out of his life.

When King David hears about his son's crime, he takes no action. David's moral paralysis leads Tamar's full brother, Absalom, to nurture a simmering hatred of Amnon. Finally Absalom invites all of his brothers to a dinner party, during which he has Amnon assassinated. Absalom flees Israel as a fugitive, and is killed a few years later during a rebellion he foments against David, his father. Of Tamar, nothing more is said.

The story of Amnon's rape of Tamar lies within a set of stories that dramatize the unruly passions corroding David's family. In the story, repeated use of the words "brother" and "sister" underscores the theme of family sickness: the very ties that should guarantee solidarity and safety are perverted to crime. After Tamar is assaulted by her own brother, she is ignored by her father. David loses himself in mourning the death of Amnon, his oldest son, while at the same time yearning for reconciliation with Absalom, the murderer. By showing no concern for Tamar, David in effect denies her importance—even her existence—and extends the wrong already done her. As in the Dinah story of Gen 33, Tamar's mother never appears, God does not speak, and Tamar herself is pushed to the periphery by the raging emotions of her brothers and the indecisiveness of her father. A

---

1. In Lev 20:17, intercourse between a man and his half-sister is punishable by eviction of the couple from the community of Israel. Either this law is not yet fully enforced, or Tamar assumes that her father, as king, can override it.

princess whose life was once enveloped in protective care finds herself dismissed and abandoned.

In addition to its similarities with the story of Dinah, the story of the rape of Tamar parallels Gen 39, where the wife of Potiphar attempts to seduce the young Joseph. Both the Tamar story and the Joseph story involve a virginal, attractive victim. Both stories note the victim's clothing. In both stories the aggressor speaks tersely ("Lie with me"; "Get out"), while the victim piles words upon words in an attempt to reason with the attacker. In outcome, however, the stories diverge, and the divergence points up the likelihood of greater tragedy when the one who is assaulted is a woman. Joseph is physically strong enough to flee his master's wife, and even though he is unjustly imprisoned, his fortunes later rise. For Tamar, anatomy is destiny. Physically overpowered, she loses everything.

The Story of Tamar as Told in 2 Samuel

A Summary of 2 Sam 13:1–39

The children of David have grown to young adulthood. They include his first-born, Amnon, son of Ahinoam; and the children of Maacah—David's third-born son, the handsome Absalom, and a daughter, the beautiful Tamar. Amnon develops a passion for his half-sister, Tamar, but he cannot figure out how to carry out his designs upon her.[2] Amnon is tormented by his passion until he consults his cousin Jonadab. Jonadab advises him to take to his bed, pretending to be sick. Then when his father, King David, comes to visit, he should request that David permit Tamar to come to his rooms to make him some appetizing food.

Amnon follows this advice, and it works. Tamar is sent to her half-brother's quarters. She kneads some dough, twists it into bread cakes, fries the cakes, and takes them out of the pan. But Amnon refuses to eat them. He orders everyone out of the room and asks Tamar to serve the cakes in his sleeping recess. When she does so, Amnon seizes her and says, "Sister, come to bed with me." Already pinioned by his arms, she pleads, "No, my brother, do not dishonor me. Such things are not done in Israel; do not behave so infamously. Where could I go and hide from my disgrace? You would sink as low as the most infamous in Israel. Why not speak to the king for me? He will not refuse you leave to marry me."

But Amnon refuses to listen. He overpowers Tamar and rapes her. Afterward, he is filled with a revulsion that is stronger than his previous desire. "Get out!" he says. When she points out that sending her away now is worse than the wrong he has already inflicted, he summons his attendant

2. As an unmarried princess, she is strictly supervised.

and says, "Rid me of this woman; put her out and bolt the door after her." At the time, Tamar is wearing a long ornamented tunic with sleeves, the usual dress of an unmarried princess. When the door is barred behind her, she tears her robe, throws ashes over her head as a sign of her grief and humiliation, and sobs aloud as she goes to the house of her brother Absalom.

Absalom is enraged at what has happened, but he advises the inconsolable Tamar, "Do not take it to heart." When King David hears the story, he is irritated, but he does nothing because he favors Amnon, his first-born. Absalom simmers in silence, nurturing a profound hatred for Amnon because of the dishonor he has done to Tamar. Some two years later, at the time of the sheep-shearing festival, Absalom invites his father, his father's retinue, and all of his half-brothers—especially Amnon—to attend a royal dinner he is hosting about twenty miles north of Jerusalem. David declines, but permits all of his sons to attend. At the dinner, Absalom directs his servants to wait until Amnon is merry with wine, and then kill him. They act as bidden, and the rest of the panic-stricken princes rush to their mules to escape.

While the young princes are on the road, David is told that Absalom has killed all of them. But even as David begins to tear his garments and throw himself to the floor in grief, Jonadab assures him that only Amnon is dead, for "Absalom has gone about with a scowl on his face ever since Amnon ravished his sister Tamar." The princes soon arrive, bearing out the accuracy of Jonadab's information. Absalom himself takes refuge east of the Sea of Galilee with his maternal grandfather, the king of Geshur. David mourns Amnon for three years, but he also yearns for reconciliation with Absalom.

Reflection

Once again, as in the story of Dinah, a victim of rape is lost to the political overtones of her story: Tamar's dishonor provides her brother with an incentive for vengeance that leads ultimately to civil war. Nothing is done for Tamar, however, beyond provision of shelter. Not even her powerful father, king of Israel, makes the slightest effort to ease her circumstances or find a suitable husband for so beautiful, articulate, and skilled a girl. Instead she is left shamed for life, a young woman last seen bewailing her fate, her fine robe hanging in tatters and her head covered with ashes.

In Tamar's time as in the centuries since then, rapes were divided into those that mattered and those that did not. In her world, the only rape really worth punishing was that of an unmarried girl, and even that was considered a property crime—the ruination of a marketable asset, for which the girl's father merited recompense (Deut 22:28–29). In cases of incest, the community was commanded to ostracize both partners (Lev 20:17). Yet no law is invoked for Tamar, either to help her or to punish her. Much like her ancestor and namesake Tamar, the widowed daughter-in-law whom Judah sent home to her parents, David's daughter Tamar is expected graciously to fade into the walls of a relative's house.[3]

❖ ❖

Obviously the rape of Tamar and its devastating aftereffects remain relevant today. But the relevance is even greater than commonly believed. Researchers Patricia Aburdene and John Naisbitt report that a chilling statistic circulated by the U.S. Justice Department, the rape of a woman every six minutes, "is completely out of date. According to . . . latest figures, at least one woman is raped *every minute*."[4] Nor is it a foregone conclusion that a jury of today would at least offer Tamar some emotional vindication. She did, after all, go to Amnon's apartment. In 1991 a poll conducted for *Time* and the Cable News Network revealed that forty-nine percent of those between the ages of eighteen and forty-nine still considered such a woman partly to blame for her own victimization.[5]

Given these statistics, it is little wonder that women circumscribe their lives with precautions designed to ensure their safety. Things might be different were the wisdom of a Golda Meir to prevail. In the early years of the modern state of Israel, the story is told, several rapes had been committed. At a cabinet meeting, one minister recommended that no woman be allowed out alone at night until the rapists were caught. Golda, from the depths of her great good sense, protested: "I don't understand. Men are committing the rapes. Men should not be allowed out at night."[6] Were so extraordinary and so simple an insight to gain sway, surely males outraged at loss of freedom of movement would take immediate, concerted action to prevent rape.

But as things actually stand, women of today who suffer rape and incest are still, as often as not, abandoned to cope as best they can with shattered lives. No matter how remarkable their adjustment, it is easy to imagine them praying, with Tamar, for a world of justice and safety:

Prayer

God our God, would that your spirit
were poured out upon everyone!
Then would good fortune be restored

---

3. Absalom may have provided a permanent home for his sister. Before his death, he also named his own daughter Tamar, apparently in her honor (2 Sam 14:27).

4. Emphasis added. *Megatrends for Women* (New York: Villard Books, 1992), 283.

5. Nancy Gibbs, "When Is It Rape?" *Time*, 3 June 1991, 51.

6. Joseph Telushkin, "Golda Meir (1898–1978)," *Jewish Literacy* (1991), 317.

and all people rejoice in your presence.
Then would right dwell in the desert,
equity abide in the groves.
All would live in secure dwelling places,
able to let their children wander freely.
God of peace, grant that such a world may come;
I know your rescue is near to all who turn to you.
In you I know that love and faithfulness *can* meet,
justice and peace embrace.
Faithfulness *can* spring from the earth,
justice look down from heaven.
God our God, give us what is good.
Let justice march before you, peace follow in your steps,
in an age of peace and justice you ordain.[7]

Connections

1. The more dysfunctional a family, the more the sins of parents seem to be visited upon successive generations. How are families of today that condone violence and incest similar to Tamar's family?

2. Write to Tamar the letter you would write to a friend who found herself in Tamar's situation.

3. Imagine a world in which Golda Meir's advice—to keep the men home at night—is enforced: What windows of experience open wide every evening to women of all ages? What are men doing, meanwhile, to change society in order to regain their own freedom of movement?

4. In society as it does exist, what is one practical step—however small—that you can take to work toward elimination of rape and incest?

For Further Reading

Alter, Robert, *The World of Biblical Literature* (1992), 114–17, 164–65.

Carmody, Denise Lardner, *Biblical Woman* (1989), 45–48.

Deen, Edith, *All of the Women of the Bible* (1955), 278, 296–97.

Nunnally-Cox, Janice, *Foremothers* (1981), 77–79.

Schaberg, Jane, *The Illegitimacy of Jesus* (1990), 72, 95.

Trible, Phyllis J., *Texts of Terror* (1984), 37–63.

7. Based on Num 11:29; Isa 32:16–20; and Ps 85:8–13.

18 Jezebel: Queen Condemned

1 Kings 16–21, 2 Kings 9–11

". . . no one will bury her."

Background

Jezebel was born a woman and she backed the wrong gods. These are the basic crimes that have earned her twenty-nine centuries of vilification. Otherwise, Jezebel behaved no worse than the men of her time. She lived about a century after David and Solomon, when David's kingdom had split into a northern section known as Israel and a southern section known as Judah. It was in the northern kingdom, Israel, that Jezebel exerted strong influence for thirty years— first as Ahab's queen, and then as queen mother after his death. Her influence extended into Judah, as well, through her daughter Athaliah—the only woman ever to exercise solo rule over either kingdom. Athaliah married a king of Judah, a worshipper of Yahweh, but followed her parents' worship of Baal and Asherah. On her husband's death, she secured the throne by massacring her own heirs. In the end, both Jezebel and Athaliah were executed during coups.

The story of Jezebel starkly illustrates two facts: that the Bible was written by proponents of Yahweh, and that it took centuries for worship of Yahweh alone to prevail. The Israelites were first admonished to destroy the altars and images of idols when they entered Canaan from the desert in the thirteenth century BCE. Yet three centuries later, King Solomon himself was still straying into worship of deities foreign to Yahweh. The problem grew even more acute when the nation split into two a century after David and Solomon. Even in the south, with the temple in Jerusalem as a point of focus, people still yearned for the old religions as late as the sixth century BCE: they protested to the prophet Jeremiah that disaster loomed not because they had strayed from Yahweh, but because they had abandoned the goddess (Jer 44:15–19; see also Mic 5:13–14).

The religious climate was even more volatile in the north. The diverse population there included large pockets of Canaanites who had never paid more than lip service to Yahweh, and even Israelites of the north tended to merge Yahweh with Baal and assign him a female partner. From the beginning, northern kings seem actively to have promoted worship of Baal and Asherah, while prophets of Yahweh mounted furious opposition.[1] But it

---

1. Forty Bible passages condemn the goddess Asherah; more denounce Baal. Besides temples and seals inscribed with sacred images, archaeologists have unearthed so many

is the monarchs of the north in Jezebel's time—the ninth century BCE—whose idolatry earns the most scathing contempt of the author of the books of Kings. These books follow a set formula. Whatever their secular achievements might have been, each king of Israel or Judah is introduced and then rated "good" or "bad" solely on the basis of devotion to Yahweh. Since Ahab, Jezebel, and three of their children who occupy thrones promote worship of Baal and Asherah, they are "bad."

History reveals that the family actually produced skillful monarchs. Known as the "House of Omri," the dynasty was established by Omri in 876 BCE through military coup. Omri inaugurated a vigorous program of building and fortification. He unified his kingdom by abandoning the old capital (Tirzah) and building a new one, Samaria—a city on a hill so high that from its citadel tower one could sometimes gaze twenty miles west to Mt. Carmel on the Mediterranean coast.[2] Omri also established cordial relations with Judah and Phoenicia as a defense against the rising power of Syria, and he merged politics with religion by arranging the marriage of his son, Ahab, to Jezebel, daughter of Ethbaal of Tyre: Ethbaal means "Baal's man"; he and his queen served also as high priest and priestess of Baal and Asherah.

Following his father Omri on the throne, Ahab proved an able economic and military leader for twenty years—an extremely long reign in an era marked by military coups. Despite ongoing problems with Syria, Ahab finished building the city of Samaria, where he erected an opulent two-story palace and a temple to Asherah and Baal. The palace became known as Ahab's "ivory house" because of its fine ivory furniture decorations and wall panels, imported through Tyre. It was large enough to accommodate the huge cadre of priests and priestesses Jezebel brought with her and housed at public expense. (Lack of any taxpayers' revolt at feeding them suggests that the people of Israel shared—or at least condoned—Jezebel's religious views.) The temple consisted of a walled court open to the sky and a small chapel. An eternal flame was kept burning in a dish-shaped brazier that rested on the altar.

Ahab also built a second royal residence in the valley city of Jezreel, about twenty miles due east of Mt. Carmel and about the same distance southeast of Samaria. It is in this villa at Jezreel that Jezebel plots a murder in order to obtain a vineyard Ahab covets, there that she holds court during the reigns of two of her sons, and there that she dies.

---

clay *asherah* figurines as to suggest that they were common household objects. Those from the era of Judges, Kings, and Prophets are never found intact, suggesting the kind of deliberate breakage that is reported in the Bible. Additionally, the *Harper Concise Atlas of the Bible* (1991, p. 68) reports "recent discoveries" at Kuntillet 'Ajrud that include inscriptions mentioning Baal and Asherah as well as Yahweh "and his consort."

2. Mt. Carmel, a steep promontory at modern Haifa, dominated the surrounding lowlands. It was considered sacred to Baal.

The Story of Jezebel as Told in 1 and 2 Kings

Elijah Challenges Ahab and Jezebel: *A Summary of 1 Kings 16:23–19:18*

When Ahab becomes king of Israel, he surpasses all his predecessors in idol worship. He marries Jezebel, daughter of the king of Tyre, and he erects a temple to Baal and a sacred pole to Asherah. Greatly provoked, Yahweh sends his prophet Elijah to tell Ahab that there will be "neither dew nor rain . . . unless I give the word." During the three years of drought that follow, Yahweh sends Elijah to live with a widow in Zarephath (in Phoenicia, modern Lebanon). Yahweh miraculously extends the widow's supply of flour and oil and restores the life of her sick son when he stops breathing. Then Yahweh directs Elijah to return to Israel and tell Ahab that rain is on the way.

Jezebel, meanwhile, has been murdering the prophets of Yahweh.[3] Only one hundred, hidden in caves by the king's chief officer, have survived. Ahab believes that the insolence of Yahweh's prophet, Elijah, has caused Baal to withhold the rain. So when Elijah approaches, Ahab calls out, "Is it you, you troubler of Israel?" Elijah retorts that Ahab is himself the troublemaker; he is responsible for the drought because he has turned his back on Yahweh. To convince Ahab he should return to Yahweh, Elijah urges him to set up a contest on Mt. Carmel between Yahweh and Baal. Intrigued, Ahab summons the people to Mt. Carmel, together with "the four hundred and fifty prophets of Baal and the four hundred prophets of the goddess Asherah . . . attached to Jezebel's household." The rules are that Jezebel's prophets will prepare a sacrifice and call upon Baal, and that Elijah will prepare a sacrifice and call upon Yahweh. The god who answers by fire is truly God. The crowd applauds the plan, and the prophets of Baal begin. All morning they invoke Baal and dance before his altar; all afternoon they cry out and hack themselves bloody. But Baal does not respond.

At last Elijah erects an altar, lays out his bull, and directs the people to drench it until the priceless water overflows into the trench he has dug around the altar. Elijah calls once upon Yahweh, and a bolt of fire streaks from the sky. It consumes the bull, the wood, and the altar stones; it even licks up the water in the trench. The people fall on their faces and cry out, "Yahweh is God! Yahweh is God!" At Elijah's command, they seize and kill all of the prophets of Baal. Later that evening the sky blackens with clouds, the wind rises, and a downpour commences. Elijah, filled with the power of Yahweh, hikes up his robe and races ahead of the chariot of Ahab all the way to Jezreel.[4]

When the soaked Ahab reports to Jezebel, she vows to avenge the death of her prophets with the death of Elijah. Elijah flees in terror to the Negev

3. These "prophets of Yahweh" may have been roving bands of ecstatic seers, or priests and prophets attached to shrines and households loyal to Yahweh.

4. Yahweh's manifestations at Carmel make him all but identical with Baal, but the story also demonstrates Yahweh's superiority to Baal even on Baal's own mountain in Baal's own country (Mt. Carmel, Phoenicia).

wilderness south of Beersheba. There he pauses and prays for death, but Yahweh's angels refresh him, and he journeys forty additional days and nights to Mt. Horeb (Mt. Sinai) on the Sinai peninsula. At that mountain Yahweh comes to him not in wind, earthquake, or fire, but in a faint murmuring sound. Yahweh commissions Elijah to return north and anoint Hazael as king of Syria, Jehu as king of Israel, and Elisha as prophet after himself.

The Story of Naboth's Vineyard: *A Summary of 1 Kings 21:1–29*

Meanwhile, Israel is at war with Syria. Ahab fights nobly and heeds the advice of the prophets of Yahweh. But then he sees a beautiful vineyard adjacent to his villa in Jezreel and covets it as his own. Naboth, the owner, refuses to sell at any price. He cites the long-standing legal right of a family to retain lands held since the Israelites entered Canaan, as long as heirs survive. Ahab goes home so depressed that he cannot eat. When Jezebel pries the story from him, she mocks his timid use of power and promises to make him a gift of the vineyard. She does so by arranging to have two men falsely accuse Naboth of cursing Yahweh and the king, a crime that constitutes treason. Naboth is tried in Samaria, he and his sons are stoned to death, and the property of the "traitor" reverts automatically to the king. For these crimes, Elijah delivers to Ahab a multi-pronged curse: "Where dogs licked the blood of Naboth, there dogs will lick your blood. . . . [Yahweh] shall sweep you away and destroy every mother's son of the house of Ahab. . . . Jezebel will be eaten by dogs near the rampart of Jezreel." The petrified Ahab humbles himself in repentance, and Yahweh promises to defer disaster until after his death.

Transitional Events: *Selected from 1 Kings 22–2 Kings 8*

For combined defense against Syria, Ahab allies himself with Judah by marrying his and Jezebel's daughter, Athaliah, to king Jehoshaphat of Judah. Jehoshaphat allows Athaliah to promote the idolatrous religious practices she brings with her from Israel. Later Ahab dies of battle wounds and is buried. His chariot is swilled out at a pool in Samaria, and dogs lick up the blood. His son Ahaziah succeeds him, but soon dies of injuries sustained in a fall from a window. Ahaziah is succeeded by his brother Jehoram (Joram). Elijah disappears, taken to heaven in a fiery chariot, and Elisha takes over as Yahweh's mouthpiece. Secretly, Elisha has the military commander Jehu anointed as the rightful king of Israel. Elisha commands Jehu to eliminate "every mother's son" of the house of Ahab. Jezebel, he says, "will be devoured by dogs, and no one will bury her."

Jehu's Coup d'État and the Deaths of Jezebel and Athaliah: *A Summary of 2 Kings 9–11*

War with Syria continues over many years. A son of Jehoshaphat and Athaliah succeeds his father as king of Judah. He is another Ahaziah, the nephew of king

Jehoram of Israel. Jehoram is recuperating from battle wounds at the villa in Jezreel, and Ahaziah comes to visit him. Seizing the chance for a double coup, Jehu drives his chariot furiously toward Jezreel. At his approach, kings Jehoram and Ahaziah mount their own chariots. They confront Jehu beside the plot of land that once belonged to Naboth. When Jehoram asks Jehu if he comes in peace, Jehu retorts, "Do you call it peace while your mother Jezebel keeps up her obscene idol-worship and monstrous sorceries?" Jehoram and Ahaziah wheel about in alarm, but Jehu's archers shoot Jehoram down. They later overtake and kill Ahaziah. Jehoram is tossed onto Naboth's land for the dogs, but Ahaziah—descended from David on his father's side—is given honorable burial.

When Jezebel hears that Jehu has killed her son, Jehoram, and her grandson, Ahaziah, she paints her eyes, adorns her hair, and stands looking down from a window of the villa. When Jehu enters the gates, she hails him as a murderer. Then she asks in sarcasm, "Is it peace?" Jehu calls for Jezebel's own eunuchs. When they appear at the window, he commands them, "Throw her down," and they do it. Her blood splashes onto the wall and the horses, and the horses trample her. After taking time to eat, Jehu orders Jezebel buried, "for she is a king's daughter." But the servants find only her skull, her feet, and the palms of her hands. Jehu recalls the prophecy that dogs would devour her, lest anyone be able to say, "Here lies Jezebel." Jehu next orders the elders of Samaria to kill the seventy sons of Ahab living in the capital and to send him their heads in baskets.[5] He consolidates his power by executing all other relatives of Ahab and prophets of Baal, burning the sacred pole of Asherah, and turning the temple of Baal into a latrine.

Meanwhile, in Jerusalem, Athaliah learns of the death of her son, Ahaziah, king of Judah. She too grasps power by ordering executions—death to all males of royal blood, her own sons and grandsons. But her stepdaughter, wife of the high priest of Yahweh, spirits away one infant, Joash, and hides him for six years. In the seventh year of Athaliah's reign, the backers of the boy take him to the temple and crown him king. Hearing shouts and trumpet fanfares, Athaliah rushes to the temple. She finds Joash standing in the spot reserved for the king. Though she tears her clothes and cries out "Treason," she is put to the sword. But lest the temple be desecrated, she is killed at the palace gate where horses enter. The people also demolish the temple and images of Baal and kill the priest of Baal. They escort Joash to the palace, and Jerusalem grows quiet.

Reflection

Today, few people remember Athaliah at all, and those who know something of her mother, Jezebel, may dimly recall a cruel woman who wore too much makeup. The Bible paints a broader portrait. Jezebel is fearless and forceful in

5. "Seventy," a multiple of seven, may be symbolic of the totality of Ahab's progeny.

taking on the powerful Elijah, she is loyal to her own gods to the end, and she is immensely courageous in the manner of her dying. Every inch a queen and astute enough to know she has no time to mourn her son and grandson, she arrays herself royally and seems not even to arch an eyebrow at the irony of being hurled to the ground by her own bodyguards. Even the rival religionist who tells her story never questions her fidelity to Ahab or suggests anything lurid about her sexual behavior; her use of expensive eye shadow is simply a sign of royal affluence.

It was only in sixteenth-century England, where women were suspected of loose morals if they wore "paint," that "jezebel" became a synonym for "shameless woman." The Bible condemns her on more serious grounds: murder, theft, and support of the wrong deities. Despite the secular successes of Ahab and Jezebel, these are the details that matter to the author of Kings. These sins make Ahab and Jezebel the very prototype of evil, exemplars of the kind of behavior that led to the downfall of both Israel and Judah.

But the author reserves his strongest condemnation for Jezebel, especially in the story of Naboth's vineyard. This story reduces the strong Ahab of history to a snivelling whiner, and it characterizes Jezebel as an unscrupulous foreigner. Ahab is depicted as still Jewish enough to accept Naboth's legal position, albeit with little grace, while Jezebel sneers at Jewish law. Her crime looms all the worse because she shows such mastery of that law: she knows the required number of witnesses; she knows exactly what crime to lay upon Naboth in order to ensure both his execution and reversion of his property to the king. The author positively relishes reporting that, in the aftermath, Jezebel suffers the wrath of Yahweh's prophets; and the ghostly memory of Naboth haunts the rest of the narrative until the moment Jezebel is flung from a window overlooking what used to be Naboth's property.

❖ ❖

Given her bloody deeds, no one is likely to deny that Jezebel merits censure. But why so much larger a share than her male counterparts? Reading her story impartially, it is difficult to distinguish between the slaughters ordered by Elijah and Jehu, and those ordered by Jezebel and Athaliah. Nevertheless, Jezebel's notoriety became so magnified in Christian times that by the fifteenth century, the Dominican Inquisitors who wrote the *Malleus Maleficarum,* "The Hammer of Witches," could cite in a matter-of-fact way "the accursed Jezebel, and her daughter Athaliah, queen of Judah" as examples of the malignant influence women have *always* exerted on "the kingdoms of the world."[6] In more modern times, even Elizabeth Cady Stanton, that staunch advocate of woman, viewed the life and death of Jezebel as tragedies of evil.

6. The full passage is presented in Joan Smith's *Misogynies* (1989), 68–69.

Considering Jezebel's actual story, even as it is reported by someone who hated her, one can only conclude that she looms more negatively than the men around her solely because of her gender. Out of sheer misogyny, she is, like Eve, denounced more bitterly than men for the same sins. Without intending to do so, her enemies very nearly grant her power equal to that of Yahweh: she is presented as constituting so great a threat to the fabric of history that, if she is not fought tooth and nail, the true God may vanish from people's minds. In a way, this is quite an accolade, for Jezebel the symbol.

Jezebel the person, however, gets lost in the rhetoric. It requires real effort to perceive her as a *woman*, a human being trapped in gender stereotyping. Only if we get beyond the stereotypes can we find the woman whom no one seems ever to have mourned, despite the cruelty of the death she suffered. Nor can that execution be dismissed as an example of some ancient savagery the world has outgrown. One need only consider families ravaged in fanatical cults, children obliterated by terrorist bombs, and countries so torn by religious-issue wars that, even today, families cannot always assemble the bodies of their dead. It is time to remember the child and the girl and the vibrant woman Jezebel was, and to grant her decent burial.

❖ ❖

The Book of Psalms contains only one love song. A nuptial ode, it is presented below as the Prayer. Jews apply this psalm to Solomon or to a future Messianic king. The Christian author of Heb 1:8–9 applies it to Christ and his church. But details within the poem call to mind Jezebel, princess of Tyre, and the "ivory house" of Ahab. Imagine the poem in terms of the wedding of Ahab and Jezebel. He is an Adonis, a young Henry VIII, and she is the archetypal beautiful princess. The promise represented by this dazzling couple moves the poet to extravagant flights of fancy. As Jezebel listens to the song, when does she turn an adoring gaze on Ahab? At what lines do her hackles rise? Does the song arouse in her any forebodings about her future?

Prayer

My heart is astir with a noble theme as I sing my ode to the king;
my tongue is as nimble as the pen of a skillful scribe.

Of all men you are most handsome, O king.
Gracious words flow from your lips, for God has blessed you forever.
Strap your sword upon your thigh, O warrior king;
in majesty and splendor ride on, ride on, in the cause of justice!
Your right hand will speed sharp arrows; nations will lie at your feet.
Your throne, O godlike one, will stand forever and ever.
Your royal sceptre is a tempered rod of equity.

You love right and hate wrong;
therefore, God, your God has anointed you
with the oil of gladness above all your rivals.
Your robes are fragrant with aloes and cassia;
from palaces panelled with ivory, string music brings you joy.
The daughters of kings attend you;
the queen takes her place at your right in gold from Ophir.

Listen, O daughter of Tyre; pay careful attention:
Forget your people and your ancestral home.
Let the king fall in love with your beauty.
He is your lord, now; do him obeisance.
The city of Tyre is here with gifts;
the richest in the land seek your favor.
You are decked in brocades woven with gold;
in the finest raiment you enter,
a train of bridesmaids as your escort.
Your retinue moves with resounding joy
as it enters the palace of the king.

Your children will occupy the thrones of their ancestors;
they will rule through all the land.
I shall immortalize your names,
and nations shall praise you forever.[7]

Connections

1. What was your previous image of Jezebel? How has reading her story influenced your ideas or feelings about her?

2. Can you offer any justification for Jezebel's views and actions? (Or for Athaliah's?)

3. How does the writer's slant resemble the approach of people who practice single-issue politics, or people who rigidly adhere to whatever views are currently considered politically correct?

4. Ancient Phoenicia, Jezebel's homeland, is today's Lebanon. A Lebanese official says of his country's five hostile religious and ethnic groups, "They hate each other more than they love their own children."[8] How does his remark connect with the stories of Jezebel or Athaliah?

---

7. An adaptation of Ps 45 based on several translations.
8. Joseph Telushkin, "Lebanese War," *Jewish Literacy* (1991), 331.

For Further Reading

Carmody, Denise Lardner, *Biblical Woman* (1989), 50–53.

Cartledge-Hayes, Mary, *To Love Delilah* (1990), 46–55.

Deen, Edith, *All of the Women of the Bible* (1955), 125–31, 140–42.

Gadon, Elinor W., *The Once and Future Goddess* (1989), 167–88.

Nunnally-Cox, Janice, *Foremothers* (1981), 85–88, 91–93.

Smith, Joan, *Misogynies* (1989), 68–69.

Stanton, Elizabeth Cady, *The Woman's Bible*, Part II, (1898), 74–81.

Telushkin, Joseph, *Jewish Literacy* (1991), 85–86.

19 The Prophet Huldah: Founder of Biblical Criticism

2 Kings 22:8–20 (2 Chronicles 34:14–28)

"Hilkiah the priest . . . went to Huldah the prophet . . ."

Background

Huldah is one of four Old Testament women identified by name as a prophet. Miriam and Deborah preceded her in time; Noadiah (mentioned below) followed her. These women and the male prophets whose names are used to title some biblical books did not arise from a vacuum. From very early times, Israel assumed that many were called to speak Yahweh's word. During the wilderness years after the Exodus (c. 1290 BCE), when a few Israelites complained that the gift of prophecy had been poured out too liberally, Moses responded, "Would that all the people of [Yahweh] were prophets! Would that [Yahweh] might bestow his spirit on them all!" (Num 11:29).

In the biblical world, Mesopotamia and Egypt had their seers and diviners; in fact, most cultures developed a professional class of sages entrusted with preserving the wisdom of their people and advising kings. Within Israel, in David's time, the "wise women" of Tekoa and Abel Beth Maacah offered counsel that, to some extent, prevented further bloodshed (2 Sam 14:1–24 and 20:15–22). It is possible that the word used in those stories—*hakamah*, variously translated as "quick-witted woman" or "wise woman"—constituted a professional title. In any case, additional sage advisors to kings are mentioned in Jer 8:8–9 and 18:18, and Isa 29:14.

In a development unique to Israel, however, the Hebrew people perceived prophets not merely as seers, diviners, or advisers to kings, but as women and men compelled to speak for God. Some prophets roamed the countryside in ecstatic bands, like a band happened upon by Saul, the first king of Israel. He joined them for a time in ecstatic frenzy (1 Sam 10:5–13). As a rule, however, Hebrew prophets did not constitute a separate profession, class, or caste. Prophecy was instead perceived as a call that might descend upon a person of any occupation—a judge like Deborah, a cowboy like Amos, a priest like Ezekiel. Although the call might concern matters of state, as in the books of Isaiah and Jeremiah or the stories of Elijah and Elisha, the task of the prophet might equally well lie in another area—anything from social justice to liturgical reform.

As late as the Babylonian Exile of the sixth century BCE, a follower of Isaiah continued to echo Moses in envisioning an outpouring of Spirit upon everyone (Isa 32:15 and 44:3). In the fifth century BCE, the prophet Joel also foretold an outpouring of Spirit upon women and men alike (2:28). From about that same time period, we encounter a complaint about false prophets. Perhaps referring to a group of political dissenters who opposed his rebuilding policies, Nehemiah, governor of Jerusalem, begged Yahweh to remember the evil done by the female prophet "Noadiah and all the other prophets who tried to intimidate me" (Neh 6:14). The tradition of male and female prophets extends into the New Testament in the stories of Elizabeth and Anna (Lk 1:39–45; 2:36–38) and in discussion of prophetic gifts within the early church (e.g., Acts 2:1–4; Rom 12:6; Eph 4:11).

Huldah, a prophet of the seventh century BCE in Jerusalem, lies midway in this continuous stream. Jeremiah and Zephaniah are her approximate contemporaries. Jezebel and Elijah have been dead two hundred years, and it has been nearly a century since Assyria conquered the northern kingdom, Israel. Babylon now threatens the southern kingdom, Judah. Reading the signs of impending disaster as indicative of Yahweh's displeasure, King Josiah of Judah (640–609 BCE) begins to institute religious reform. As the temple is being repaired, a previously unknown book of the Law is found. For verification of the book's authenticity and for Yahweh's word on its implications for the future of Judah, Josiah sends his priest Hilkiah to consult Huldah.

The Story of Huldah the Prophet as Told in 2 Kings

A Summary of 2 Kings 22:8–20 (2 Chronicles 34:14–28)

In the process of cleaning and restoring the temple, the high priest Hilkiah discovers a scroll of the Law. He gives the scroll to Shaphan, King Josiah's adjutant general, who reads the scroll aloud to the king. When Josiah hears what is written in the book of the Law, he tears his clothes and orders the priest Hilkiah to go and seek the guidance of Yahweh for himself, for the people, and for all Judah, with respect to the contents of this book. "Great must be the wrath of [Yahweh]," he says, "because our forefathers did not obey the commands in this scroll and do all that is laid on us."

Hilkiah and his entourage seek out the prophet Huldah, wife of Shallum, keeper of the king's wardrobe. They consult her at her home in the Second Quarter of Jerusalem.[1] She verifies the authenticity of the document: "This is the word of the Lord, the God of Israel." She directs Hilkiah to tell Josiah that Yahweh says, "I am about to bring disaster on this place and its inhabitants as foretold in the scroll which the king of Judah has read, because they have forsaken me and burnt sacrifices to other gods, provoking my anger with all the idols they have made with their own hands; for this my wrath is kindled against this place and will not be quenched." She further directs Hilkiah to tell

---

1. A section of the city northwest of the Jerusalem of David's time.

King Josiah that Yahweh has a personal message for him: "You have listened to my words and shown a willing heart . . . and have torn your clothes and wept before me. . . . Therefore . . . you will be gathered to your grave in peace; you will not live to see all the disaster which I am bringing on this place." Hilkiah and his aides bring all these words to the king.

Reflection

Although Huldah is married to a royal valet, she emerges from this brief story as far more than the appendage of a man. Clearly she pursues her own career. A century ago Elizabeth Cady Stanton wrote of her as a "statesman" able even to teach kings sound policy:

> While Huldah was pondering great questions of State and Ecclesiastical Law, her husband was probably arranging the royal buttons and buckles. . . . Marriage, in her case, does not appear to have been any obstacle in the way of individual freedom and dignity.[2]

It is possible that Huldah's career involved some sort of official position in the temple, since the Mishnah—a compilation of Jewish commentary and traditions completed in about 200 CE—states that the two southern gates to the Temple Mount were called the Huldah Gates.[3] But she seems especially to have merited renown as a scholar, for it is on that basis that the king and high priest seek her opinion on the authenticity of the newly discovered scroll. In support of such a reputation, one Jewish tradition holds that she publicly taught scripture to men; another holds that she taught only women, privately. The nature of her reputation seems all the more extraordinary when one realizes that Hilkiah immediately seeks her counsel, apparently never considering an approach to a male member of any school of priests, prophets, or sages.

It is in her second action—speaking the message of Yahweh—that Huldah most clearly functions as prophet. In her first action, however—authenticating the scroll—we might well revere her as the founder of professional Bible study. Biblical criticism has been defined as an "investigation of biblical writings that seeks to make discerning and discriminating judgments about these writings."[4] Scholars now believe that the "scroll of the Law" validated by Huldah contained the core chapters of Deuteronomy—a book that designates itself by the same expression (e.g., Deut 29:20 and 31:26). Today, of course, Bible study has branched into many specialties, and it is canonical criticism that seems particularly to echo the scope of Huldah's task: canonical critics seek to discern how a text authenticated as genuine addresses the faith community.

---

2. *The Woman's Bible,* Part II (1898), 82.
3. Middoth 1.3, cited in Miriam Therese Winter, *WomanWisdom* (1991), 336.
4. *Harper's Bible Dictionary* (1985), 129.

Huldah might thus serve specifically as patron saint of canonical critics, but also, more generally, as patron of all women theologians. In the past twenty-five years alone, what some call a "critical mass" of women—a number large enough to change the direction of a field—has emerged with advanced degrees in Scripture, theology, canon law, ethics, and liturgy. Some of these women have been ordained as ministers of Protestant churches, rabbis within Reform and Conservative Judaism, or priests of the Anglican communion. Ironically, however, the denial of ordination to Roman Catholic women has done more than anything else to advance theological study as woman's enterprise: The majority of professionally trained woman theologians of recent decades have been Roman Catholic, and the field known as feminist theology has been largely their project.

Many woman theologians, Catholic and otherwise, now teach in colleges, universities, and pastoral institutes; they find themselves educating significant numbers of male and female clerical and lay ministers. Their students—ministers in formation—often find themselves needing to reckon with the feminist method of inquiry. Some dismiss it as a fad, but many recognize it as a badly needed corrective to past views which, consciously or unconsciously, regarded man alone as the norm for humanity.

"Simply defined," writes Catherine Mowry LaCugna, "feminism is the belief that women and men are equal in dignity as human beings." Feminist theology in general and biblical criticism in particular, she continues, are therefore based on a "hermeneutics of suspicion." This methodology challenges whatever diminishes or distorts the full humanity of woman, viewing such things not as redemptive, but as flowing from historically conditioned male bias. It accepts whatever promotes the full humanity of women and men alike, such as the liberating message of Exodus, viewing these things as transmitting the revelatory word of God.[5]

Feminist biblical criticism allows women (and men) of today to reclaim and revitalize the role of women like Huldah. Many scriptural passages may be biased against women, and the policies of churches may be sexist, but women continue to feel called to follow in Huldah's footsteps, exploring and reshaping biblical theology. They feel this call because they find their own lives—not just the lives of men—affirmed within biblical religion. Whether Jewish or Christian, for them as for Huldah the Bible contains a Word worthy of praise:

Prayer

A lamp to my feet is your word, O God; a light to my path.
Grant me discernment that I may fathom your Law and cherish it.
Turn my heart to your word and not to love of gain;
let your decrees be my song

5. "Catholic Women as Ministers and Theologians," *America*, October 1992, 243. LaCugna is associate professor of systematic theology at the University of Notre Dame.

even when my views place me in exile.
Let your steadfast love come to me, O God,
liberation according to your promise.
I am friend to all who honor you and hold to your paths;
my eyes ache after your promise.
Though I be shriveled like a wineskin in the smoke,
I will never forget your word.
The arrogant may dig pits for me, but you give me life.
Your word endures forever,
a lamp for my steps, a light to my path.
Therefore my lips pour forth your praise
and my tongue exults in your steadfast love.[6]

Connections

1. The story of Huldah was probably written and certainly edited by men. If you had been there to write her story, what additional information about Huldah's life would you have included?

2. How has a dash of healthy skepticism, a methodology of "suspicion," enriched your reading of the Bible?

3. In what passages or themes of the Bible do you find liberation and affirmation?

4. Who are the prophets of your life? What is their message?

For Further Reading

Deen, Edith, *All of the Women of the Bible* (1955), 143–45.

Harkness, Georgia, *Women in Church and Society* (1972), 45–46.

LaCugna, Catherine Mowry, "Catholic Women as Ministers and Theologians." *America* 167, no. 10 (10 October 1992): 238–48.

Nunnally-Cox, Janice, *Foremothers* (1981), 93–95.

Stanton, Elizabeth Cady, *The Woman's Bible*, Part II, (1898), 81–83.

Winter, Miriam Therese, *WomanWisdom* (1991), 203–7, 335–39.

6. Based on verses from Ps 119.

20 Esther: Star of Justice

The Book of Esther

"If I perish, I perish!"

Background

The Book of Esther celebrates the overturning of a plot to exterminate Jews throughout the ancient Middle East. The time setting is the fifth century BCE—about one hundred years after the Babylonians conquered Judah. Jews have been dispersed throughout the Middle East, and the dominant world power is Persia. During the reign of King Ahasuerus of Persia, an orphaned Hebrew girl named Esther wins a beauty contest and becomes his queen. On the advice of her guardian, Mordecai, she does not reveal that she is Jewish. Meanwhile Haman, the king's prime minister, sets in motion a plan to kill Jews throughout the empire. Mordecai pleads with Esther to save her people, and she risks her life in order to secure the king's intervention. In a dramatic reversal, the story ends with the Jews slaying their enemies on the date Haman had set for their destruction.

These events are commemorated in the spring festival of Purim. Esther and Mordecai symbolize the powerless who vanquish their persecutors; Haman stands as the ultimate symbol of oppression. The story identifies him as belonging to the Agag family of the Amalekites—a desert tribe that harassed the Israelites at the time of the Exodus and later engaged in blood feuds with Saul and David. In time, "Amalek" and "Haman" alike came to mean anyone—like Adolf Hitler—bent upon destruction of Jews.

The feast of Purim probably originated as a secular Babylonian holiday, but the Book of Esther gives it a religious basis. Haman chooses the extermination date by *pur*—the casting of dice-like pebbles with designs carved or painted on them—and the word *Purim* is said to derive from *pur*. Today, when the scroll of Esther is read for the feast, listeners cheer the heroes, Esther and Mordecai, and boo the villain, Haman. Children clatter noisemakers as well. Since Jewish law requires that every word of the scroll be heard, cantors must often pause for the noise to subside. Remembering centuries of terrifying pogroms, however, the rowdiness offers immense emotional release, and no one cares how long it takes to read the scroll. As a Yiddish proverb puts it, "So many Hamans and only one Purim."[1]

---

1. Joseph Telushkin, *Jewish Literacy* (1991), 108.

Despite the emotional truth of the Book of Esther, the story itself is historical fiction. Except for King Ahasuerus (Xerxes I, 486–465 BCE), the characters appear in no other source, and even Ahasuerus was married to a different woman. Further, the ancient Persian empire consisted of 127 provinces that stretched westward from India to the Mediterranean and southward into Africa. Since all of these provinces were allowed their own religious practices, an empire-wide campaign against the Jews is highly unlikely. The story is probably based on a more localized act of oppression.

The book is nevertheless rich in historically accurate details. For example, eunuchs or castrated males, perceived as no threat to the king, were in great demand as royal guards and guardians of the king's harems. The author was also familiar with the audience hall of the king's winter capital at Susa or Shushan (on modern maps, in mid-Iran). The king sat in an inner throne room isolated, for security reasons, from the rest of the main hall. The hall was a richly decorated room 250 feet square. The author also knew the Persian bureaucracy so well he could satirize it. Legally, a king of Persia could issue a decree that affected the entire realm only after consulting his seven top officials. Such a decree could never be rescinded, though its effects might (rarely) be softened by a later edict. The author of the Book of Esther applies the cumbersome consultation process to a relatively trivial matter—the refusal of the king's first wife to obey him—yet later depicts the king as allowing decrees of great importance to be issued with no consultation at all.

The Book of Esther appears in different forms in Jewish, Catholic, and Protestant Bibles. The basic story was written in Hebrew in the fourth or third century BCE. Because these chapters never mention God, the book was accepted into the Jewish canon only after considerable debate. A century or two later, additional chapters of a more devotional nature were written in Greek. Jews assigned the new chapters to a category of apocryphal or "set aside" books; Protestants later did the same. Catholics, however, accept all of the chapters as canonical, because early Christians used both sets. The Story below summarizes the Hebrew chapters that are common to all traditions. The devotional Greek insertions are summarized in footnotes.

The Story of Esther as Told in the Book of Esther

The Cast in Order of Appearance:

Ahasuerus (ah • hahz' • yoo • air' • us): Xerxes I, King of Persia

Vashti (vahsh' • tē): Queen at the beginning of the story

Mordecai (mor' • duh • kī): Palace gatekeeper, foster father of Esther

Esther: Vashti's successor as queen

Haman (hã' • muhn): Grand Vizier or Prime Minister

Vashti Is Deposed at the Banquet of Ahasuerus: *A Summary of Esther 1*[2]

In the third year of his reign, King Ahasuerus of Persia presides over a six-month series of entertainments for the leading men of the provinces. The festivities conclude with a seven-day feast in the garden court for the officials and the men of Susa. Meanwhile, inside the palace, Queen Vashti hosts a feast for the women. On the seventh day, when the king is drunk, he orders Vashti to come and let him display her beauty to his guests. She refuses. Furious, Ahasuerus asks the advice of his seven chief officials. One of them says that when word of Vashti's conduct spreads, women will scorn their husbands "and there will be no end to the disrespect and the discord!" In order that men throughout the kingdom might remain masters of their own houses, Vashti must be deposed, and her place given to someone more worthy. Dispatches to this effect are rushed to every province in its own script and language.[3]

Esther Becomes Queen: *A Summary of Esther 2*

The king appoints commissioners to find the most beautiful unmarried girls of the entire empire. He will choose a queen from among them. The Jew Mordecai has a "beautiful and charming" cousin named Hadassah or Esther, an orphan he has raised. She is one of the girls selected. Her beauty and character so please the custodian of the royal harem that he gives her seven maids and the best accommodations. Every day Mordecai visits the harem courtyard to learn how Esther is faring. At his direction, she tells no one that she is Jewish. After twelve months of massages with oils and perfumes, each girl in turn goes to the king. The next morning she is taken to the harem of wives and concubines. She cannot return to the king unless he summons her by name. Esther's turn arrives four years after Vashti was deposed, in the seventh year of the king's reign. The king loves her more than any of the others. He places a royal diadem on her head and proclaims a holiday throughout the provinces. Mordecai, meanwhile, overhears two of the king's guards plotting to kill him. Mordecai tells Esther, who informs the king. The matter is investigated and verified, the eunuchs are hanged, and the details are recorded in the court chronicles.

Haman Plots Against the Jews: *A Summary of Esther 3*

The king promotes an Amalekite named Haman above all other officials. All royal servants are instructed to bow to him, but Mordecai refuses to do so.

---

2. Prologue from the Greek chapters: A Jew named Mordecai experiences a vivid dream. Amid great battles and turmoil on earth, the righteous who cry to God are ultimately exalted over their oppressors.—REB Apocrypha, chapter 11; NAB, chapter A.

3. The author satirizes Persian bureaucracy by giving a matter of no urgency the full treatment: translation into multiple scripts and languages (e.g., Aramaic, Babylonian), and delivery by rapid courier. Relay riders of the Persian "Pony Express" covered in a week or two a route that took the ordinary traveler three months.

Mordecai's behavior so enrages Haman that he seeks to kill not Mordecai alone, but all Jews. In late March[4] of the twelfth year of the king's reign, Haman conducts the casting of *pur* to select a date for exterminating the Jews. The lot falls on a day nearly a year distant, February 28. Haman then goes to Ahasuerus and tells him that a subversive people is spread throughout the realm. He offers to issue a decree for their destruction and to pay ten thousand silver talents into the royal treasury. Ahasuerus tells Haman to keep his money, gives him his royal signet ring, and tells him to deal with the people as he thinks best. At Haman's direction, royal scribes prepare a letter in all the proper scripts and languages and seal it with the king's ring: on February 28 all Jews are to be killed and their goods seized as spoils.[5] Couriers rush the letters to the provinces.

Mordecai Seeks Esther's Aid: *A Summary of Esther 4*

Jews everywhere weep and fast and beat their breasts. Mordecai appears at the palace gate in sackcloth and ashes. Since no one may enter the royal precincts dressed like that, Esther sends Mordecai some clothes, but he refuses to change. Instead he gives her eunuch a copy of the decree, tells him about the bribe Haman offered the king, and requests that Esther intercede with the king. Esther sends back a reply explaining that anyone who enters the king's inner court without a summons is put to death, unless the king extends his gold sceptre—and she hasn't been summoned for thirty days.[6] But Mordecai tells her not to imagine that even she would escape the death decree. It may even have been for such a time that she became queen. Finally Esther asks him to assemble the Jews of Susa to fast and pray on her behalf for three days and nights while she and her maids do the same. Thus prepared, she will go the king: "If I perish, I perish!"[7]

4. Literally, the thirteenth of Nisan. The story uses the Hebrew twelve-month lunar calendar that begins in spring with Nisan (March-April) and ends in late winter with Adar (February–March). Approximate Gregorian equivalents are used in these summaries.

5. The letter says that the Jews must be destroyed because they live by divergent laws that are inimical to the king's interests.—REB Apocrypha, chapter 13; NAB, chapter B.

6. No historical evidence supports the existence of this harsh penalty. The author seems to have invented it because the plot demands that Esther be placed in jeopardy.

7. In prayer, Mordecai asserts that he refuses to bow to Haman so as not to give him the honor that belongs to God. Esther sets aside her precious ointments and fine clothes, and covers her head with dung and ashes. She begs God to turn the counsel of evil men back upon them and to deliver her from her own fear. On the third day she bathes and replaces her penitential garb with royal raiment. She glows with beauty, though her heart shrinks with fear. Nearly fainting, she leans upon one of her serving girls for support.—REB Apocrypha, chapters 13–14; NAB, chapters C–D.

Esther Approaches the King: *A Summary of Esther 5*

Three days later, Esther arrays herself royally. She approaches the throne room and stands looking in. Seeing her, the king extends his sceptre. He asks, "What is it, Queen Esther? Whatever you request, up to half my kingdom, it shall be granted to you." She says that, for the moment, she requests only his company and that of Haman at dinner. That evening, over the wine, the king again asks what Esther wants. She says that if he and Haman come to dinner again the next night, she will then state her request. Haman leaves the palace in high spirits, but at the gate, Mordecai again refuses to honor him. Haman's rage is rekindled. He summons his wife and his friends, and complains that neither his riches nor his ten sons nor the honors bestowed upon him give him any satisfaction so long as Mordecai lives. So that he will be able to enjoy the second banquet, his wife and friends advise him immediately to set up a high gallows and ask the king to let him hang Mordecai on it. Haman has the gallows erected immediately.[8]

The King Rewards Mordecai: *A Summary of Esther 6*

Meanwhile, because sleep eludes him, the king orders the chronicle of notable events read to him. The passage about Mordecai's discovery of an assassination plot is read, and the king asks what was done to reward him. His attendants reply, "Nothing." At this point Haman arrives. The king asks him what he should do for a man he wishes to honor. Thinking the king means himself, Haman says that the man should be dressed in the king's robe, set upon the king's horse, and led through the city by a high official who keeps proclaiming that this is a man the king honors. The king directs Haman to take the robe and the horse and to do all he has described for Mordecai the Jew. Haman carries out the king's wishes, then slinks home with his head veiled in humiliation. When he tells his wife and friends what has happened, they say that his downfall has begun. Nothing he can do will avert it. While they are still talking, the king's eunuchs arrive to escort Haman to Esther's second banquet.

Esther Accuses Haman: *A Summary of Esther 7*

So Haman and King Ahasuerus dine a second time with Queen Esther. When the king again offers Esther nearly anything, she asks that her life and the lives of her people be spared. If it were merely a matter of enslavement, she says, she would have kept silent. But so vast an injustice as exterminating an entire people will do great harm to the king's reputation. When Ahasuerus demands to know who has dared plan such a thing, Esther answers, "A ruthless enemy—this wicked Haman!" Haman stands there aghast while the king

8. Despite use of the word "gallows," ancient Persian "hanging" of political prisoners differed from the hanging done in the Old West. The sharp end of a long pole was run through a man's body and the blunt end driven into the ground, thereby suspending or "hanging" him until he died.

storms into the garden in a rage against him. Then Haman throws himself on Esther's couch to plead for his life. Returning, the king exclaims, "Will he even assault the queen in the palace before my very eyes?" One of the king's eunuchs covers Haman's head in preparation for execution, and tells the king about the gallows Haman has erected for the very man who once saved the king. "Let Haman be hanged on it!" the king orders. And it is done.

A Second Decree Is Proclaimed: *A Summary of Esther 8*

That same day King Ahasuerus gives Queen Esther the property of Haman. He gives Mordecai the signet ring recovered from Haman. Later Esther asks that a decree be issued to correct the dispatch sent by Haman, and the king directs her and Mordecai to write it. Couriers mounted on the king's own horses distribute it posthaste. Thus the king grants permission to the Jews of every city to assemble in self-defense on February 28, to slay anyone who might attack them, and to seize their goods as spoils.[9] The city of Susa acclaims the Jews; in the provinces, many people profess Judaism out of terror.

The Jews Defeat Their Enemies: *A Summary of Esther 9–10*

Months later, the day arrives. Throughout the provinces of Persia, Jews assemble. Rulers and officials help them out of fear. The Jews slaughter thousands, including the ten sons of Haman, but they take no plunder. When Ahasuerus offers to grant Esther a further request, she asks that the Jews of Susa be permitted to fight the next day as well, and to hang Haman's sons upon his gallows. Thus the wicked plot of Haman recoils upon itself. Mordecai records all these things, and sends out a letter requiring Jews annually to call the dates Purim, from Pur, and to observe them "as days of feasting and joy, days for sending presents of food to one another and gifts to the poor."[10]

Reflection

Like the small David overcoming the gigantic Goliath, Esther and Mordecai emerge as classic examples of "little people" who turn the tables on the powerful. Whatever the historical basis of the story, it celebrates deliverance of all who suffer persecution (or the threat of persecution) on the basis of race, religion, or gender. Achieving such deliverance, the book suggests, requires the taking of personal responsibility for one's fate, not waiting for a miracle. Like Esther, one must abandon fear and defeatism and employ all available

9. The letter denounces Haman's edict as concocted by a despicable man who conspired against the king's benefactor Mordecai, the king's blameless consort Esther, and all their people. It also threatens with total destruction any city which fails to observe the new decree.—REB Apocrypha, another chapter 13; NAB, chapter E.

10. Epilogue: Mordecai recalls his dream of years earlier, and blesses the God who saved the Jews as his dream predicted.—REB Apocrypha, chapter 10; NAB, chapter F.

resources—everything from personal beauty to community solidarity in prayer and fasting. Ultimately, however, one must step alone into the unknown. Furthermore, the book reminds us, the process may require patience and persistence: months and years pass between scenes; Esther holds *two* banquets.

Like other Jewish literature of its time, the Book of Esther also deals with the issue of assimilation. Esther possesses a Hebrew name, Hadassah (based on *hadas* or myrtle—an evergreen shrub used as a symbol of peace and justice); but she goes by Esther or "star," a variant of Ishtar, name of the Babylonian goddess of love and war. As Rabbi Joseph Telushkin notes, it is as if an Orthodox Jew of today were to call herself Christine.[11] The heroine is thus a woman stretched between extremes. She is Hadassah, a woman in covenant with Yahweh; but she is also Esther, consort to a Persian king. Furthermore, she conceals her Jewish identity. Yet lest any sub-community ever write off anyone as hopelessly assimilated, the story shows that it is precisely Esther's willingness to appear assimilated that gives her access to the power to save her people.

To some extent, everyone faces Esther's conflict between inner person and public role. But women like Esther, who derive their status from their husband's position, find the conflict a constant companion. Still, in exchange for endless dinner parties and receiving lines, wives of public men often gain access to the power to influence their entire society. Like Esther, public women of today also owe debts to their predecessors. Had Vashti not defied Ahasuerus earlier, raising his consciousness, who knows how he might have responded to Esther's violation of custom? And finally, like Esther, public women gain from their own inner, private beliefs the strength to tackle the public issues that deeply concern them. Any woman, but especially women with access to power, might pray as Esther did before she approached the king:

Prayer

> Yahweh, you alone truly reign. Be with me, therefore,
> for my risk is great, and I have no help but yours.
> As a child I was taught how you made of us
> a special portion, your own everlasting possession.
> You fulfill your promises, but we too often stray,
> placing our faith in idols of wealth and comfort.
> Now the enemy threatens to destroy your heritage
> and close the mouths of those who praise you.
> Most High, do not yield your sceptre to these idols;
> let not our enemies gloat over our ruin.
> Reveal yourself by giving me and others courage to act;
> inspire my tongue as I enter the lion's den.

11. *Jewish Literacy* (1991), 108.

Save your people—and help me, your servant.
You know the straits in which I find myself—
the symbols of wealth and power I am forced to adopt,
the care I must take to be true to my beliefs.
Yet from the day of my preferment until now,
my greatest joy has rested in you.
Most High God, more powerful than all earthly forces,
hear the voice of your people.
Save us from the power of the wicked,
and deliver me from fear.[12]

Connections

1. What elements of the story of Esther did you especially enjoy? Which of these elements connect with your own life?

2. Both Vashti and Esther assert themselves in relation to the king, but their methods differ. What do you think of each woman's tactics?

3. How do you feel about the influence and power the public grants to female film stars and the wives of presidents? What do you perceive as the corresponding responsibilities of these women?

4. The Book of Esther offers no miracles. God remains hidden; people must act. How is this like our own times?

For Further Reading

Alter, Robert, *The World of Biblical Literature* (1992), 30–34, 78.

Carmody, Denise Lardner, *Biblical Woman* (1989), 55–59.

Deen, Edith, *All of the Women of the Bible* (1955), 146–52.

Heltzmer, Michael, "The Book of Esther—Where Does Fiction Start and History End?" *Bible Review* 8, no. 1 (February 1992): 24–30, 41.

Johnson, Ann, *Miryam of Nazareth* (1984), 41–48.

Sabua, Rachel, "The Hidden Hand of God," *Bible Review* 8, no. 1 (February 1992): 31–33.

Stanton, Elizabeth Cady, *The Woman's Bible*, Part II, (1898), 86–88.

Telushkin, Joseph, *Jewish Literacy* (1991), 107–8, 578–80.

Weems, Renita J., *Just a Sister Away* (1988), 98–110.

12. Based on the prayer of Esther, REB Apocrypha, chapter 14; NAB, chapter C.

21 Judith: Heroic Deliverer

The Book of Judith

"I will do something that will go down from generation to generation. . . ."

Background

Judith is a heroine on the grand scale. In her story, Assyria besieges Israel and endangers a key symbol of Jewish identity, the temple of Jerusalem. When the elders of Judith's town despair of blocking the Assyrian advance, Judith upbraids their lack of faith and places herself in God's hands. Using only guile and beauty, she then infiltrates the enemy camp, assassinates the commander-in-chief, and galvanizes her people to victory.

Judith's story offered hope to Jews persecuted under the Hellenistic king Antiochus IV Epiphanes. In 167 BCE he banned circumcision and sabbath observance, and made mere possession of Jewish scriptures a capital offense. A statue of Zeus that resembled Antiochus was erected in the temple of Jerusalem ("Epiphanes" means "God manifest"), and Jews were forced to sacrifice pigs to it. Finally the Maccabee family rose up in revolt, leading a rebellion that required two decades for achievement of victory. The Book of Judith, written during the turmoil of civil war, was designed to inspire hope and resistance. The book proclaims a God who delivers the oppressed, provided that the oppressed accompany their faith with action.

By thoroughly intermixing well-known names, times, and places, the author immediately alerts the reader that the story is fiction. In the very first line, the sixth-century BCE Nebuchadnezzar of *Babylon* is introduced as king of *Assyria* and is said to reign from Nineveh—an Assyrian city destroyed before the reign of the real Nebuchadnezzar. Further, this fictionized Nebuchadnezzar is given as his second-in-command a general from Persia—a nation not yet risen to prominence at the time. The Jews are said already to have returned from exile and rebuilt their temple, events of the fifth century BCE; and Jerusalem is said to be ruled by a high priest and senate—practices not known until the second century BCE. From the moment Judith's name is mentioned, it is also clear that she is a literary creation: Judith simply means "Jew," and her alleged pedigree is impossibly perfect.[1] Then, as the story progresses, she

---

1. Judith does not appear until halfway through the book. Since Jewish books were named by their first few words rather than by the name of the protagonist, the original readers would have enjoyed the surprise discovery that the hero was to be a woman.

proceeds to sum up in herself all previous heroes of her people. She renders judgment like Deborah, vanquishes the foe like Jael and David, sings like Deborah and Miriam, and even brings national liberation like Moses.

Overall, it is as if an American novelist were to interweave allusions to every war since 1776 in a suspense novel that introduces Adolf Hitler as Fuhrer of Iraq, names a certain Yassir Macarthur as his commander-in-chief, and depicts Iraqi forces as universally victorious until the day they come up against not some male superhero, but a woman named Americana—a woman who embodies the best of Mother Teresa, Sojourner Truth, Margaret Thatcher, and Sophia Loren.

The Book of Judith was composed too late for inclusion in the Jewish canon of scriptures, but because early Christians accepted it as scriptural, it appears in Catholic Bibles. (In the story below, direct quotes are taken from the Catholic *New American Bible* rather than the usual *New English Bible*.) Protestants have excluded it since Martin Luther placed it among the Apocrypha in his 1534 translation of the Bible. He said of the Apocrypha, "these are the books which are not held equal to the Sacred Scriptures and yet are useful and good for reading."[2]

The Story of Judith as Told in the Book of Judith

Nebuchadnezzar Devastates the West: *A Summary of Judith 1–3*

In the twelfth year of his reign [593 BCE], Nebuchadnezzar of Assyria demands that Persia and the lands of the West send him soldiers for a war against the Medes. But the rulers regard him as a mere mortal and dismiss his envoys. Declaring that he will destroy the defiant nations, Nebuchadnezzar swears, "What I have spoken I will accomplish."[3] As soon as Nebuchadnezzar wins his war against the Medes, he orders Holofernes, his second-in-command, to muster a huge supply train and thousands of chariots, infantry, and mounted archers. These picked troops are accompanied by an irregular force too huge to count, like a swarm of locusts. They devastate the West. Afflicted with dread, nations begin to welcome Holofernes with garlands and dancing. Even so, he demolishes their sanctuaries and cuts down their sacred groves so that every nation might invoke only Nebuchadnezzar as God. Finally he pauses in northern Israel for reprovisioning.

Israel Resists: *A Summary of Judith 4–7*

Having only recently returned from captivity and rededicated Yahweh's temple, the Israelites tremble for Jerusalem. Speeding warnings of Holofernes'

2. Quoted in *The New Jerome Biblical Commentary* (1990), 572.
3. Echoing passages like Isa 55:11, this is one of many instances in which Nebuchadnezzar assumes words or attributes Jewish tradition reserves to Yahweh alone.

arrival throughout the country, they occupy hilltops, fortify towns, store up their newly harvested spring grain, and block the mountain passes. In Jerusalem everyone fasts and prays. Even the animals are dressed in sackcloth. Enraged at Jewish resistance, Holofernes summons leaders from the surrounding regions and demands to know who those people think they are. Achior of Ammon speaks to the assembled leaders at length, recounting the great deeds the Israelites' God has performed for them from the people's origin right up to recent times. Achior contends that they are unbeatable unless they have sinned against their God; Holofernes must therefore try to verify such an offense.

Reacting to Achior's advice with scornful laughter, Holofernes vows to drench Israel in blood. Achior himself he binds in chains and dumps outside the town of Bethulia. The people of Bethulia rescue Achior and call a meeting to hear his story, even as Holofernes is spreading his terrifying forces across the plain. Holofernes next seizes all water sources and blocks all escape routes. After thirty-four days of siege, the cisterns of Bethulia are depleted and the parched citizens complain bitterly to the city elders. They believe that Yahweh is punishing them for their sins or the sins of their ancestors, and argue that it is better to live as slaves than to die of thirst. In response, Uzziah, one of the elders, proposes that they hold out five days longer. If Yahweh sends no help within that time, the elders will surrender the city.[4]

Judith Emerges: *A Summary of Judith 8*

News of Uzziah's ultimatum reaches Judith. She is a religious woman who has fasted and prayed in a small tent on the roof of her house since her husband Manasseh died of sunstroke three years and four months previously. Judith traces her family for sixteen generations, all the way to Israel (Jacob) himself, through his son Simeon. She has maintained the estate she inherited by appointing a maidservant as steward. Furthermore, she is gorgeous, and no one has a bad word to say about her. Judith sends her steward to summon Uzziah and the other city elders to her tent.

When they arrive, she upbraids them for putting Yahweh to the test by setting a time limit: protection or destruction will come at God's pleasure. She also tells them it was wrong to allow the people to believe that Yahweh is punishing them, when not a single clan worships idols any longer. They should have remembered how God tested Abraham and their ancestors, and been grateful for a similar challenge. Uzziah agrees that she makes sense, but points out that he has sworn an unbreakable oath. Though it is now midsummer and

---

4. The siege is reminiscent of the siege of Jerusalem by Sennacherib of Assyria, described in Isa 36–37 and memorialized in Byron's line, "The Assyrian came down like the wolf on the fold. . . ." (from "The Destruction of Sennacherib"). Yahweh ends that siege miraculously, sending an angel to strike down every Assyrian soldier.

rain can realistically be expected only in fall, he asks Judith to pray that Yahweh might send rain to fill up the cisterns, lest dehydration further weaken the people during the next five days.

In response to this idea, with its hint of little faith, Judith retorts, "Listen to me! I will do something that will go down from generation to generation." She says that if the elders allow her and her maid to pass through the city gate that night, Yahweh will rescue Israel by her hand within the time limit sworn by Uzziah. "You must not inquire into what I am doing," she adds, "for I will not tell you until my plan has been accomplished." Accepting these terms, Uzziah and the other elders depart.

Judith Sets Her Plan in Motion: *A Summary of Judith 9–10*

Alone again on her roof top, Judith prostrates herself in prayer. She addresses Yahweh as the God of her ancestor Simeon, whose sword avenged the rape of his sister Dinah. Surely the God who helped in ages past is also the God who designs the shape of the present and the future. The Assyrians may be a vast, proud force, but Yahweh's might lies not in numbers. Against all odds, Yahweh uplifts the oppressed, supports the weak, and saves the despairing. Judith asks, in particular, that her own guileful words be allowed to wound those who would profane Yahweh's temple. Her prayer finished, Judith descends into her house and removes her sackcloth and widow's garments. She washes, anoints herself with rich ointment, creates an elaborate hairdo, arrays herself in her finest clothes and jewels, and packs a bag of ritually clean food. She gives the bag to her maid to carry.

At the town gate, the elders gasp in awe at Judith's transformation. They watch as she and her maid disappear into the valley. When the women are questioned at an Assyrian outpost, Judith says that she has come because her people are about to fall into the hands of Holofernes. Dazed by her wondrous beauty, the soldiers tell her she has saved her life by coming.[5] All the way to Holofernes' tent, Assyrian soldiers gather to marvel at her beauty. If the Israelites can produce such women, they say, they had best not spare even one, for their women "could beguile the whole world." On his bed in an inner chamber, Holofernes is reclining under a fine purple canopy (a mosquito net) interwoven with gold and precious stones. He emerges, and Judith falls prostrate before him. His servants raise her to her feet.

Judith Defeats Holofernes: *A Summary of Judith 11–13*

Holofernes says to Judith, "Your life is spared tonight and for the future. No one at all will harm you." "I will tell no lie to my lord this night," Judith

---

5. Everything said in the Assyrian camp has a double meaning—the meaning the Assyrians understand, and the meaning Judith understands. The irony is especially strong in Judith's use of "my lord" in the next scene.

answers; "my lord will not fail in any of his undertakings." She says that Achior was correct in claiming that the Israelites lose only when they sin. But since hunger is about to drive them to eat even the first fruits of cattle and grain that are sacred to Yahweh, she has come to Holofernes. With him, she will perform deeds that astonish the world. But she needs permission to go into the valley each night to pray, so that God can tell her when the people sin. When they sin, she will help Holofernes advance into Jerusalem.

Holofernes' aides exclaim, "No other woman from one end of the world to the other looks so beautiful and speaks so wisely!" He himself adds, "[Your] God has done well in sending you ahead of your people." He offers Judith a meal, but she says that she must follow the dietary laws of her own people. The food she has brought along will suffice until "God accomplishes by my hand what he has purposed." She and her maid retire to the tent Holofernes assigns them. Before dawn, they go out to the valley for prayer and a ritual bath at the spring. They follow this routine for three nights.·

On the fourth day Holofernes throws a banquet for his household officials. He sends Bagoas, the eunuch in charge of his affairs, to persuade "the Hebrew woman" to join them, for he will lose face if he does not entice such a woman into bed. Agreeing to come, Judith affirms her pleasure at doing whatever pleases "my lord." Again she adorns herself. Her maid goes ahead to spread out Judith's food on the fleeces Bagoas gave her to recline upon at meals. When Judith enters, Holofernes burns to seduce her. At his urging she accepts some wine, saying that she has never "enjoyed life as much as . . . today." The enchanted Holofernes watches as she eats and drinks, and he drinks "more than he had ever drunk on one single day in his life." It grows late, and the servants leave. Judith tells Bagoas to allow her maid to wait outside, for they will pray before dawn as usual. Bagoas secures the tent, leaving Judith alone with Holofernes, who soon lies dead drunk on his bed. After a prayer for strength, Judith lifts Holofernes' sword from the bedpost, grasps his hair, and with two blows cuts off his head. She rolls the head in his fine canopy and takes it to her maid, who puts it in the food bag. They go off into the valley as usual, but this time they continue on to Bethulia.

As they approach the town, Judith calls out, "Open the gate! God, our God, is with us." Astonished at the women's return, the guards let them in, summon everyone, and build a fire for light. Only after praising God for shattering their enemies does Judith pull the package from her bag, saying, "Here is the head of Holofernes, . . . and here is the canopy under which he lay in his drunkenness. [Yahweh] struck him down by the hand of a woman." She swears that although her appearance seduced Holofernes to his ruin, he never sinned with her to her disgrace. The dazed Uzziah responds, "Blessed are you, daughter, by the Most High God, above all the women on earth"; and all the people cry, "Amen! Amen!"

Victory Is Made Total: *A Summary of Judith 14–16*

Summoned at Judith's command, Achior faints when he sees the head of Holofernes. For his sake, the entire story is retold, and Achior is circumcised and received into the house of Israel.[6] At Judith's direction, the head of Holofernes is hung on the city wall at daybreak, and the Israelite warriors pretend to advance on the enemy camp. An alarm spreads from sentries to captains to division leaders, until someone sends Bagoas to Holofernes' tent. He knocks politely on the frame of the inner chamber, thinking that Judith and Holofernes still lie asleep. When no one answers, he parts the curtains and discovers the headless corpse of his master. Howling and tearing his garments, he rushes out, screaming that a single Hebrew woman has brought disgrace on the house of King Nebuchadnezzar. "Here is Holofernes headless on the ground!" Wailing consumes the camp, the ranks scatter in all directions, and the fighters of Israel overwhelm them.

Messengers spread news of these events throughout Israel, and Israelites everywhere rise and slay their enemies. The citizens of Bethulia spend thirty days plundering the Assyrian camp, acquiring great riches. They give Judith the tent of Holofernes with all its silver, couches, dishes, and furniture. The high priest and elders come out from Jerusalem to meet and congratulate Judith. They bless her as "the glory of Jerusalem, the surpassing joy of Israel," and the people answer, "Amen!" The women gather to dance in her honor, and she hands out wreaths and olive branches and leads the dancing. Dressed in their armor the men of Israel follow, wearing olive garlands and singing. Then Judith leads a swelling song of thanksgiving.

Afterwards everyone goes up to Jerusalem to worship, and Judith donates to the temple all of the property of Holofernes that was given to her, together with the canopy she took. The celebration continues for three months, and then Judith returns home. She is famous for the rest of her life. Many suitors approach her, but she chooses none of them. Before she dies at the advanced age of 105, she grants her maid her freedom, and divides her estate among her relatives and in-laws. She is buried in her husband's tomb, and Israel mourns for seven days. No one dares to threaten Israel again during Judith's lifetime, nor indeed for a long time after her death.

Reflection

As a rule, the Old Testament does not examine too rigorously the character or methods of its heroes. When used in the service of Yahweh, even treachery and violence are admired or condoned. Jacob becomes the father of Israel through theft of his brother's birthright; David is recalled as the greatest king

---

6. Unlikely in real life, for Achior is an Ammonite, and Deut 23:3 decrees that no Ammonite or Moabite may ever be admitted into the community of Israel.

of Israel despite the lust that leads him to arrange a murder in order to acquire Bathsheba. Also as a rule, however, more is demanded of female heroes than of male. The daughter-sacrificing Jephthah is granted the title "judge" on the basis of military prowess alone; Deborah must demonstrate piety and wisdom as well as a gift for military strategy.

A similar pattern operates in the story of Judith. Not only does Judith possess the imagination, intelligence, and courage to conceive and execute a plan for the deliverance of Israel; she also possesses awesome physical beauty and depth of soul. In time of peace she withdraws for forty months to mourn the death of her husband, exploring through prayer and fasting the inner haunts of spirit. In time of peril she wades into action on behalf of her people. Calmly disregarding the male-oriented customs of her time, she has long since appointed a woman to administer her estate. Now, without even revealing her plan, she summons the town elders (instead of humbly approaching them), corrects their bad theology, and extracts their support. Later, while the warrior Achior faints at proof of her gory victory, she calmly assumes command of the ensuing military action. To top everything off, she continues to assert her full personhood by refusing to remarry.

This paragon is Yahweh's human representative. Against her, the would-be deity Nebuchadnezzar can field only Holofernes—a man blinded by his own arrogance and machismo. Holofernes cannot conceive a woman's posing a threat; he *assumes* that the poor thing seeks only to remain safe and warm. But Judith grasps the moment. Stepping into the torrent of history, she shatters with two blows other people's narrow concepts of divine and human roles.

❖ ❖

Today, some people question exalting Judith as a role model. After all, she employs sex and deceit in order to chop off a man's head; and then she *exults* in her bloody victory. Others, however, view her with an admiration as unqualified as that of the people she rescues. Judith's story offers authorization to fight all forms of victimization, stereotyping, and unjust use of brute force. To those suffering brutal victimization, the story of Judith validates the right to fight back. Rigoberta Menchu—Guatemalan Indian, Christian revolutionary, and recipient of the 1992 Nobel Peace Prize—testifies to the power of Judith's example:

> In the community we began to reflect together on what the Bible told us. The story of Judith, for example, impressed me very much: she beheaded the king to save her people. We too understood that faced with the violence of the rich, we have to respond with another kind of violence. The violence of justice.[7]

7. *We Continue Forever: Sorrow and Strength of Guatemalan Women* (International Resource Exchange, 1983), 18. Quoted in Schüssler Fiorenza, "The Will to Choose or Reject: Continuing Our Critical Work," *Feminist Interpretations of the Bible* (1985), 129.

For women in situations less drastic than that of Guatemalan women, admiration of Judith may focus more on qualities of soul than on tactics of action. Judith wastes no time in self-doubts or in concessions to male beliefs about women. Instead, from the depths of her own spiritual life she draws forth a vision of liberation and the courage to use every weapon she possesses. Judith's model—the discerning of a course of action through prayer and contemplation—is available to everyone: Should I run for political office, or work on someone else's campaign? Should I battle for human rights, or focus on my own lingering racial prejudice? Should I march on environmental issues, or do a better job of recycling in my own household?

In our perilous world, reflection that helps us answer questions like these may not result in contributions as dramatic as Judith's, but it will help clarify our personal path. Such reflecting will remind us that today, as in the second century BCE, Yahweh remains God of the lowly, helper of the oppressed, protector of the bereft, and savior of the hopeless (Jdt 9:11); and that Yahweh uses female power equally with male power to reveal "God with us" (Jdt 13:11). With Judith's people, we can pray:

Prayer

> Strike up a song to Yahweh with cymbals and tambourines;
> exalt the name of Yahweh who takes up camp among us.
> God, our God, you are glorious indeed!
> You speak and all things come to be;
> you send out your spirit and give them form.
> Mountains shake like water at your word, and rocks melt like wax.
> Yet the most fragrant sacrifices are to you but trifles;
> you count as great those who observe your ways.

> The Assyrian myriads choked the valleys and cloaked the hills;
> they threatened fiery devastation and death to infants.
> No man laid their champion low, no Titan struck him down:
> God thwarted him by the hand of a woman.
> Judith laid aside her widow's clothes, bound up her hair,
> anointed her face and chose a gown to beguile the enemy.
> Her beauty captivated his mind; her sword cut through his neck.
> Men shuddered at her daring; the weak shouted in triumph:
> Blessed be Judith beyond all women!
> She has brought us good, and her work pleases God.
> Let her trust in God pass not from human memory,
> but ever remind us of Yahweh, our Shield.[8]

---

8. Adapted from Jdt 13:18–20, 15:10, 16:1–17.

Connections

1. What do you enjoy or admire about Judith? Are there some areas in which you wish she had acted differently? Why?

2. To Judith and her people, the Assyrians embodied evil. To the author of Judith and his contemporaries, Antiochus Epiphanes seemed a devil incarnate. What dangers threaten your world? How does Judith's story energize you or offer you hope?

3. Judith dealt with her grief in a forty-month retreat before she rose to action on behalf of Israel. Do you ever grow impatient with the slow workings of spirit, and, rather than endure a period of discomfort or confusion, rush into action—*any* action?

For Further Reading

Great People of the Bible and How They Lived (1974), 284–95.

Johnson, Ann, *Miryam of Nazareth* (1984), 33–40.

Schüssler Fiorenza, Elisabeth, *In Memory of Her* (1983), 115–18.

Schüssler Fiorenza, Elisabeth, "The Will to Choose or Reject: Continuing Our Critical Work," in *Feminist Interpretation of the Bible* (1985), ed. Letty M. Russell, 129.

Women of the New Testament

22 Elizabeth and Anna: Prophets of the Age to Come

Luke 1 and 2

". . . filled with the Holy Spirit . . ."

Background

Elizabeth and Anna lived late in the reign of Herod the Great (37–4 BCE), a time when Israel was in ferment. Named King of Judea by the Roman Senate, Herod was Jewish by religion but Idumean (Edomite) in ethnic origins, and the people resented him. In an attempt to win them over, he rebuilt the temple. Through its cadres of priests, however, the temple came to constitute a vast commercial enterprise that maintained its power through cooperation with Rome. The Sadducees, a party of wealthy priests and community leaders, supported the temple establishment and cultivated good relationships with the imperial authorities. The Pharisees, a reform party consisting primarily of lay leaders, expressed dissatisfaction with Roman and temple authorities by shifting the focus of their religious life to family and synagogue. The Essenes, a party of priests and lay people, viewed themselves as the faithful remnant of Israel and retreated to the Judean desert. And a loose and shifting coalition of other groups, including the Zealots, actively resisted the Roman occupiers.

The one thing most of these groups shared was an expectation that Yahweh would send a deliverer, an "anointed one" (in Hebrew "Messiah," in Greek "Christ") who would bring order out of the chaos of Jewish life. Many expected a political agent, a king of the line of David. Others awaited a great prophet like Moses or a great priest like Aaron. Few, if any, identified the Messiah with the suffering servant of Yahweh described in Isa 52–53. Only after decades of reflection were Christian writers able to perceive the convergence of all of these images in Jesus. Both Elizabeth and Anna hail the infant Jesus as this promised personage. Even so, Luke, the only evangelist to tell their stories, does not explain what kind of deliverer they understood him to be. Their stories occur within that of Mary, the mother of Jesus. Mary visits Elizabeth, mother of John the Baptist, while both women are pregnant; Anna is present in the temple when Joseph and Mary present the infant Jesus there.

While Christian tradition has always regarded Elizabeth and Anna as historical people, the gospel of Luke assigns them symbolic functions as well. First, both exemplify the ancient prophetic tradition of Israel. Seized by the Spirit, they act as mouthpieces for God when they acclaim Jesus. Second,

Luke links Elizabeth with the priestly tradition of Israel. She comes from a priestly family and is married to Zechariah, priest of a line descended from Moses' brother Aaron. Third, by her barrenness, Elizabeth is connected with women like Sarah, Rachel, and Hannah, who also unexpectedly conceived sons destined for greatness. And fourth, Anna prefigures the class of widows of the early church. Like the widows described in 1 Tim 5, she was married only once, is older than sixty, and bears a reputation for prayer and good works. Metaphorically, Luke's portraits thus present Judaism and Christianity as one continuous tradition in which Yahweh particularly favors older women as channels of divine grace. Elizabeth and Anna may equally well be viewed as prophets of the Jewish tradition or as figures of a Christian church in which the Spirit is poured out upon a priestly, prophetic people.

The Stories of Elizabeth and Anna as Told in Luke

Elizabeth Is Promised a Son: *A Summary of Lk 1:5–22*

During the reign of Herod, there lives a priest named Zechariah of the Abijah division of the priesthood. His wife Elizabeth is also of priestly descent. They are devout people who blamelessly observe Yahweh's commands. Still, they are well along in years and Elizabeth is barren. On a day when Zechariah is serving in the temple in Jerusalem, an angel appears to him. He is struck with fear, but the angel bids him to fear not, for his prayers have been answered. Elizabeth will bear a son who is to be named John. "His birth will fill you with joy and delight, and will bring gladness to many; for he will be great in the eyes of [Yahweh]." Zechariah asks how this can happen, considering his and Elizabeth's age. The angel responds by identifying himself as Gabriel, who stands in God's very presence. For expressing doubt, Zechariah will lose all power of speech until the child is born. Meanwhile the people wonder what is detaining Zechariah. When he emerges from the sanctuary unable to speak, they realize that he has experienced a vision.

Elizabeth Bears a Son: *A Summary of Lk 1:23–47, 57–80*

After his period of duty, Zechariah returns home, and his wife Elizabeth conceives. For five months she lives in seclusion, pondering the fact that Yahweh has at last shown her favor and removed from her the disgrace of childlessness. In Elizabeth's sixth month, God sends the angel Gabriel to Nazareth in Galilee with a message for Mary, a girl betrothed to a man named Joseph, a descendant of David. The angel tells Mary that she will bear a child to be called Son of the Most High, and that her kinswoman Elizabeth has also conceived a son in her old age, for God's promise never fails. At this news, Mary sets out to visit Elizabeth in Judea. When Mary greets her, Elizabeth is filled with the Holy Spirit and exclaims in a loud voice, "God's blessing is on you above all women, and . . . on the fruit of your womb. Who am I, that the mother of my [God] should visit me? I tell you, when your greeting sounded in my ears, the baby in my womb leapt for joy. Happy is she who has had faith that [Yahweh's] promise to her would be fulfilled!" Mary responds in a song of praise: "My soul tells out the greatness of the Lord, my spirit has rejoiced in God my Savior. . . ."[1]

Mary stays with Elizabeth for three months and then returns home. Elizabeth's time comes, and she gives birth to a son. Her neighbors and relatives share her delight. When it is time to circumcise the child, they want to name him after his father. But Elizabeth speaks up. "No!" she says. "He is to be called John." Protesting that no one in the family has ever borne that name, they ask Zechariah what the boy should be called. To everyone's astonishment he writes, "His name is John." Immediately his tongue is freed. Filled with the Spirit, he praises Yahweh as the God who sends deliverance, and predicts that John will serve as Prophet of the Most High. All who hear these things are deeply impressed. They ask, "What will this child become?" For it is clear that the hand of Yahweh is upon him. Indeed, the child grows up strong in Spirit, and he lives in the wilderness until he is ready to appear publicly before Israel.

Mary Bears a Son: *A Summary of Lk 2:1–35*

After John is born, Elizabeth's kinswoman Mary gives birth to a son who is named Jesus, as the angel Gabriel commanded. He is born in Bethlehem, the city of David, where Mary and Joseph have traveled to register in accord with the census ordered by Caesar Augustus. Following the law of Israel, Mary and Joseph have the child circumcised on the eighth day. After Mary's period of purification,[2] they bring the child to Jerusalem to present him to Yahweh as their first-born. In the temple they encounter a devout old man named Simeon. He proclaims the child as Messiah, yet predicts that both the child and Mary will suffer.

The Prophet Anna Hails Jesus: *A Summary of Lk 2:36–40*

In the temple at that time there is also a prophet named Anna. She is a very old woman, who lived seven years with her husband after she was first married, and then alone as a widow to the age of eighty-four. She remains in the temple always, worshipping night and day in fasting and in prayer. Coming

---

1. Since Mary's words echo the song of a barren older woman of the Old Testament—Hannah, mother of Samuel—one tradition holds that Mary's song originally belonged to Elizabeth.

2. After giving birth, a woman remained ritually unclean for seven days after the birth of a son, fourteen after the birth of a daughter. A son was circumcised on the eighth day. The mother was then required to observe an additional purification period of thirty-three days for a son, sixty-six for a daughter (Lev 12:1–5).

up just after Simeon has spoken with Mary, Anna gives thanks to God. Then she begins to talk about the child to all who seek the liberation of Jerusalem. When Mary and Joseph have done everything prescribed in the law, they return to Galilee to their own town of Nazareth. The child grows big and strong and full of wisdom, and God's favor is upon him.

Reflection

Emptiness and fulfillment, mystery and revelation—these are motifs of the stories of Elizabeth and Anna. Each lives quietly, yet God notices and favors them. Elizabeth means "one to whom God has sworn"; Anna means "graced" one. In Elizabeth's story, it is Zechariah who receives the angel, but it is Elizabeth who carries the child in faith. It is Zechariah who subsides into silence; Elizabeth who hails Mary's child. Contrary to the custom by which fathers named children, it is also Elizabeth who announces her child's name. In Anna's story, it is Simeon who recognizes Jesus as Messiah, but it is Anna who proclaims his arrival to all who seek the liberation of Israel.

Although both Elizabeth and Anna lack the normal fulfillment of motherhood, each has achieved a degree of local prominence. As wife of a temple priest, Elizabeth knows that tongues wag about her barrenness, but she is old enough and secure enough to ignore them. As a long-term widow, Anna has moved from object of pity to the status of wise and holy elder. Both Elizabeth and Anna are women of experience and insight; both are women who ponder God's intentions in prayer. Each has learned to live with her personal expectations thwarted, as she turns her attention to a future larger than herself—that of her people, Israel.

Anna is suffused with joy at being able to serve as mother to Israel in a spiritual sense by announcing the arrival of the child of promise. Elizabeth, however, faces the confusion of a mixed blessing—a womb grown fertile long after she has grown resigned to sterility. How she must appreciate the coming of her kinswoman, Mary, who also bears within her womb a blessing she cannot explain. One wonders whether Elizabeth and Mary were able to continue comparing notes after their sons were born. Were they able, together, to ponder the pain and perplexities of rearing a child assigned a divine mission? Or did each need to learn, alone, that she was called to release her child in a way beyond that demanded of all mothers? Luke's Mary is a teenager; Elizabeth is menopausal—possibly as young as forty in her world. Was Elizabeth still available to Mary for consultation when the twelve-year-old Jesus remained behind in the temple? Did Elizabeth share with Mary her own confusion over the signs of divine call demonstrated even earlier by her son, John? The text cloaks that time in mystery: "As the child [John] grew up he became strong in spirit; he lived out in the wilderness until the day when he appeared publicly before Israel" (Lk 1:80). The Dead Sea Scrolls suggest that the boy could have survived in the Judean desert from very early childhood, because separatist communities that included women and children lived there. But could Elizabeth have let him go? We cannot know the answers to these questions, but we can deduce that Elizabeth and Mary, like the widowed Anna, surely experienced loss as well as fulfillment. It is no easy thing, serving as meeting point for God and humankind.

Echoes of the stories of Elizabeth and Anna reverberate today in the lives of women who experience unexpected callings late in life, whether in secular or religious arenas. Like Elizabeth and Anna, as mature women they are experienced enough and emotionally assured enough to cope with paradox and ambiguity. They can acknowledge the turmoil of their own era, yet believe in a better era to come. Thus they can devote their considerable talents to making at least bits of that future a reality in their own day. They might pray with Elizabeth and Anna:

Prayer

> Yahweh, you grant your servant peace,
> having shown mercy to Sarah and her children forever.
> You have raised up a deliverer
> from the house of David, your servant.
> Age after age your prophets proclaimed
> that you would set us free.
> Now we, a people living under the shadow of death,
> perceive the breaking of your new dawn.
>
> We see a light that brings
> revelation to those who do not know you,
> glory to those already your own.
> We see the coming of the servant you uphold,
> your beloved, in whom you delight.
> He comes not in violence, but in compassion;
> a bruised reed he shall not break.
> He shall not quench a smoldering wick
> until he establishes justice on the earth.
> The coasts and islands await his teaching,
> for he brings rescue:
> he guides our feet into the ways of peace.[3]

Connections

1. What uniquely feminine issues confronted Anna and Elizabeth? What parallels exist between their lives and your own?

---

3. Based on Lk 1:68–79 and 2:29–32; Isa 42:1–4; and Mt 12:18–21.

2. Within the limits of her society, the widow Anna forged a unique role for herself. What kind of life do you think she would adopt if she were transplanted to our time?

3. Luke says that Mary stays with Elizabeth three months, then leaves just before John is born. Do you consider this behavior likely? How do you think events unfolded?

4. Think about the roles assumed by older women today or assigned to them by society. Is this a time when age and gender discrimination stand in the way of older women, or a time of opportunity for them?

For Further Reading

Betz, Otto, "Was John the Baptist an Essene?" in *Understanding the Dead Sea Scrolls*, ed. Hershel Shanks (1992), 203–14.

Sleevi, Mary Lou, *Women of the Word* (1985), 33–36.

Tetlow, Elizabeth M., *Women and Ministry in the New Testament* (1980), 101–3.

Weems, Renita J., *Just a Sister Away* (1988), 112–25.

Winter, Miriam Therese, *WomanWord* (1990), 2–10, 40–43.

23 Mary, Mother of Jesus: Woman for All Seasons

Luke 1, 2, 11; Matthew 1, 2; Mark 3, 6; John 2, 19; Acts 1, 2

"Mary treasured up all these things and pondered over them."

Background

It is not surprising that most people's images of Mary derive more from art than from the Bible. Although New Testament writers *refer* to Mary many times, they *focus* on Jesus. Thus Paul, the earliest writer, mentions only "a woman" to whom Christ was born in the fullness of time (Gal 4:4). Mark, the next New Testament writer in time order, alludes to Jesus' mother and family mainly in passing. Only later writers spotlight Mary: Luke and Matthew in stories about the conception and birth of Jesus, and John, in reporting her role at the wedding of Cana and beneath the cross.

Together, however, the Gospels and Acts of the Apostles offer a number of details about Jesus' mother and family. Among them are these: Mary was pregnant with Jesus before she lived with Joseph; Joseph was the legal but not the biological father of Jesus; Joseph and Mary had other sons and daughters; the family lived in Nazareth and was well known there; the adult Jesus abandoned his family; Mary followed him; Mary and her other children joined the early Christian community.

Even that partial list suggests that Mary lived a long and varied life. She is most often recalled, however, as madonna, the young woman of the "Christmas stories" of Luke and Matthew—stories most probably never intended as literal fact. More likely, Luke and Matthew consciously employed *midrash*—a Hebrew literary form mixing fact and legend in order to communicate spiritual truth. In Jewish tradition God never physically fathered children, but sometimes aided natural conception (as in the story of Sarah), and a favored man (like David) could be called "God's son" without implying any conflict with normal conception. Thus Luke and Matthew probably used wondrous elements like angels and magi to convey that even though Jesus was fully human, he was also God's son to a unique degree. Gentile thinkers gradually lost the Jewish sense of metaphor, however, and most theologians of today take Luke and Matthew to mean that Jesus was conceived through a unique act of creation, with no human sperm involved.

The Gospels themselves never preclude Jesus' having had a human father. In fact, they hint at awareness of rumors that Jesus was the product of rape or seduction. In Mark, critics deride Jesus as "son of Mary" (6:3)—in a culture where men were called by their fathers' names even after the fathers' deaths, a usage equivalent to calling him a bastard.[1] In Luke and Matthew, oblique acknowledgement of the illegitimacy rumors may be implied by the authors' stress on the fact that Jesus is *legally* legitimate because Joseph accepts him. In John, critics of Jesus assert, "*We* are not illegitimate," implying their belief that Jesus is (8:41). For all of the Gospel writers, the issue pales to insignificance in the light of God's choice of Jesus as beloved son. For us, however, knowing about the traditions can at least alert us to the difficulties Mary may have faced.

Another detail affecting our view of Mary is every Gospel's matter-of-fact mention of the brothers or sisters of Jesus. Since there is nothing ambiguous about these words (and devout Jews like Joseph and Mary would have prized a large family), how did Christians come to regard Jesus as an only child? For that matter, how did they come to think of Joseph as an old man, the marriage as platonic, and Mary as a lifelong virgin? It seems that as the church grew more Gentile in membership, the notion that it was unseemly for Mary's womb to have hosted any other child gained currency. Once that idea gained wide acceptance, the siblings had to be explained away. The most popular solution proposed by non-biblical writings was that they were Joseph's children by a previous marriage. By the fifth century, such ideas had become so widespread that when Jerome translated the Bible from Greek to Latin, he consciously translated "brothers and sisters" with a more general word that could also mean "cousin." And his translation became the standard until quite recent times.

Over the centuries, evolving theological debate worsened matters by stressing Mary's *differences* from other human beings. To bridge the gaps left by the Bible and theology alike, believers developed extremely diverse devotional images of Mary, each new age apparently feeling compelled to create the Mary it needed. The challenge to us may be to weigh the images of Mary from every era, but to return our most intent focus to the gospels themselves, seeking the clues they do offer.

---

1. The custom was later specifically codified: "a man is illegitimate when he is called by his mother's name, for a bastard has no father" (Schaberg, *The Illegitimacy of Jesus*, 161). The illegitimacy rumor, with Mary always an unwilling victim, appeared in several non-biblical writings of the first two centuries CE, including *The Acts of Pilate, The Gospel of Thomas,* and Celsus' *True Doctrine* (discussed in Schaberg, 156–164). On both the illegitimacy tradition and the infancy narratives as midrash, see also the reading by Crouch, and a book by Episcopal bishop John Shelby Spong, *Born of a Woman: A Bishop Rethinks the Birth of Jesus* (HarperSan Francisco, 1992).

The Story of Mary as Told in the Gospels and Acts

Mary Is Chosen: *A Summary of Lk 1:26–38*

God sends the angel Gabriel to a girl of Nazareth in Galilee. Her name is Mary, and she is betrothed to a descendant of David named Joseph. The angel greets her as God's most favored one and tells her not to be afraid. She will conceive and bear a son who is to be named Jesus. God will give him the throne of his ancestor David, and his reign will never end. "How can this be?" Mary asks; "I am still a virgin." The angel says that the Holy Spirit will overshadow her, and her holy child will be called the Son of the Most High. Moreover, her relative Elizabeth has conceived a son in her old age, for nothing is impossible with God. "I am the Lord's servant," Mary says; "may it be as you have said." Then the angel leaves her.

Mary Celebrates with Elizabeth: *A Summary of Lk 1:39–80*

Mary hurries to Elizabeth's house in the hill country of Judea and greets her. At Mary's words, the baby leaps in Elizabeth's womb and Elizabeth is filled with the Spirit. She voices God's blessing upon Mary and upon her child: "Happy is she who has had faith that the Lord's promise to her would be fulfilled!" Mary responds with a poem that praises the God who reverses the fortunes of the lowly. She stays with Elizabeth for three months and then returns home.

Joseph Accepts Mary's Pregnancy: *A Summary of Mt 1:18–25*

Joseph is betrothed to Mary but has not yet brought her to live with him when he learns that she is pregnant. Although Joseph observes the religious laws of Israel, he is unwilling to expose Mary to public disgrace, so he decides to have the marriage contract quietly set aside. Then in a dream an angel directs him to take Mary as his wife. She has conceived "through the Holy Spirit," the angel says. She will bear a son Joseph is to call Jesus (meaning Savior), because "he will save his people from their sins." When Joseph awakens, he takes Mary home as his wife, but he does not have intercourse with her until her son is born. He names her child Jesus.

Mary Ponders the Visit of the Shepherds: *A Summary of Lk 2:1–20*

During the reign of King Herod the Great, Caesar Augustus orders a census of the empire. Being of David's line, Joseph takes his pregnant wife, Mary, south with him to register in Bethlehem, the ancestral city of David. There is no room for them in the inn. When Mary gives birth to a son, her firstborn, she wraps him in swaddling clothes and lays him in a manger. Nearby, an angel appears to shepherds who are tending their flocks. The angel proclaims the birth of their deliverer, whom they will find lying in a manger. A great throng of heavenly hosts joins the angel, singing praise to God. The shepherds hurry to Bethlehem and locate Mary, Joseph, and the baby. They tell what they saw and heard, and everyone marvels. Mary treasures up all these things and ponders them in her heart.

Mary Heeds Two Prophets: *A Summary of Lk 2:21–40*

In accord with the Law, the baby is circumcised eight days later. He is named Jesus. At the end of Mary's period of purification, she and Joseph take the baby to Jerusalem to present him to God as their firstborn. Living in Jerusalem at the time is a devout man named Simeon. God has told him he will see the Messiah before he dies. Guided by the Spirit, he enters the temple, takes Jesus into his arms, and acclaims him as a light of revelation to the Gentiles and glory to Israel. The child's parents marvel at his words. Simeon blesses them and tells Mary, "This child is destined to be a sign that will be rejected; and you too will be pierced to the heart." Also present in the temple is a prophet, an eighty-four-year-old widow named Anna. Coming up at that moment, she thanks God for this child, and begins to tell everyone who seeks the redemption of Israel about him. Having done everything the law prescribes, the child's parents return home to Nazareth. The child grows big and strong and wise, and God's favor is upon him.

Mary Experiences Exile: *A Summary of Mt 2:1–23*

Shortly after Jesus is born in Bethlehem, astrologers from the east arrive in Jerusalem. Having seen a star that heralds the birth of the "king of the Jews," they have come to pay him homage. Upset by their words, King Herod inquires where this king is to be born. His scholars say Bethlehem. Herod sends the astrologers there and requests that they report back to him. The star reappears and leads the astrologers directly to a house where they find the child with Mary, his mother. They bow to the child and present gifts of gold, frankincense, and myrrh. Then, warned in a dream not to go back to Herod, they return to their country by another route. Meanwhile, in another dream, Joseph is directed to take the child and his mother and escape into Egypt. Joseph gets up and flees with them by night. Realizing that the astrologers have tricked him, the enraged Herod orders the massacre of all boys under two years of age in the entire Bethlehem area. After Herod dies, an angel again appears in a dream to Joseph and tells him it is safe to return home. Joseph takes his family and settles in the Galilean town of Nazareth.

Mary Ponders Her Son's Behavior: *A Summary of Lk 2:41–52*

When Jesus is twelve years old, Joseph and Mary make their usual pilgrimage to Jerusalem for the Passover festival. Afterwards, the boy remains behind. Assuming he is in the caravan, his parents seek him among their friends and relatives only at the end of the day. Unable to find him, they return to Jerusalem. Three days later they find him sitting in the temple surrounded by teachers, listening to them and asking them questions. Everyone is amazed at his intelligence and his answers. Mary asks him, "My son, why have you treated us like this? Your father and I have been anxiously searching for you." He answers, "Did you not know that I was bound to be in my Father's house?" They do not understand what he means. He goes back with them to Nazareth, and continues to live under their authority. Mary stores all these things in her heart.

Mary Calls upon Jesus to Act: *A Summary of Jn 2:1–12*

A wedding is held at Cana in Galilee. Jesus, his disciples, and his mother are among the guests. When the wine gives out, Jesus' mother tells him, "They have no wine left." Although he says that that is no concern of his, his mother tells the servants to do whatever he asks. At his word they fill six huge jars with water to the brim, draw off a sample, and take it to the master of the feast. The master tastes the beverage, hails the bridegroom, and says, "Everyone else serves the best wine first, and the poorer only when the guests have drunk freely; but you have kept the best wine till now." So Jesus performs in Cana the first sign revealing his glory. Afterwards he spends a few days in Capernaum with his mother, his family, and his disciples.[2]

Mary Follows Jesus: *A Summary of Passages from Mark, Luke, and John*

One day Jesus visits his home town. So great a throng surrounds the house he enters that he cannot even eat. When his relatives hear about his activities they say, "He is out of his mind." They set out to take charge of him, but the crowd is so great that his mother, his brothers, and his sisters cannot reach him. They send in word that they want to see him. Looking around the circle, Jesus asks, "Who are my mother and my brothers? . . . Whoever does the will of God is my brother and sister and mother."—*Mk 3:20–21, 31–34 (See also Mt 12:46–50 and Lk 8:19–21.)*

Jesus goes to his home town another time, accompanied by his disciples. On the sabbath, he gets up to teach in the synagogue. The large congregation asks in amazement, "What is this wisdom he has been given? How does he perform such miracles? Is he not the carpenter, the son of Mary, the brother of James and Joses and Judas and Simon? Are not his sisters here with us?" They turn against him, and he is unable to do any miracle there, apart from curing a few sick people.—*Mk 6:1–6 (See also Mt 13:54–58, Lk 4:16–30, and Jn 6:42.)*

On yet another occasion, when the crowds are swarming around Jesus, a woman calls out, "Happy the womb that carried you and the breasts that suckled you!" He replies, "No, happy are those who hear the word of God and keep it."—*Lk 11:27–28*

At length, when Jesus is condemned to die on a cross according to the Roman manner of criminal execution, Mary continues to follow him. She

---

2. In John, this story is positioned to present Mary as the first to believe in Jesus. In contrast, Mark's Gospel (cited next) implies that she at first fails to understand Jesus.

stands near his cross with her sister; Mary, the wife of Clopas; and Mary Magdalene. Seeing her standing there next to the beloved disciple, Jesus says to her, "Mother, there is your son." To the disciple, he says, "There is your mother." From that moment she becomes part of the disciple's family circle.—*Jn 19:25–27*

Mary Mothers the Church: *A Summary of Acts 1:1–5,12–14 and 2:1–4*

During the forty days following his death, the risen Jesus shows himself to his followers many times. Because he directs them to stay in Jerusalem to await the baptism of the Holy Spirit, they gather in the upstairs room where they have been lodging. With one accord, they pray together constantly. Among them are the mother and family of Jesus and a group of women. On Pentecost, the sound of a strong, driving wind comes suddenly from the sky. The noise fills the whole house. Flames like tongues of fire come to rest upon each person present, and all are filled with the Holy Spirit.

Reflection

Women in general have not fared well in comparison with Mary. Because they were not conceived immaculately, John Chrysostom (347–407) abhorred them as "whited sepulchers" from birth.[3] Historically, a great many male theologians have dismissed women as base, uppity, *messy* creatures afflicted with the need to menstruate. Such evidence of human gender was carefully stripped from Mary. In the medieval Litany of the Blessed Virgin Mary, she became the physically inviolate Tower of Ivory; the asexual, divinely fertilized Mother Undefiled.

The actual Gospel stories seem to have little in common with such thinking. In the Gospels we meet a teenager who faces scandal and ignominy as an unwed mother. We meet a young mother forced to flee into exile carrying an infant. We meet a woman struggling to understand a son who not only deserts his family, but urges others to abandon theirs and follow him—and this in a culture where any tie might be broken for a good reason *except* ties of family. We meet a woman whose son's activities are construed by some as subversive zealotry. We meet a mother whose son is condemned and executed as a criminal. And finally we meet a woman who discovers, beyond that tragedy, a new coming of the Spirit. *This* Mary, the Mary of the Gospels, is a woman intimately acquainted with prejudice, pain, and poverty. She is a woman of earth who needs God; she is a woman for all times and seasons.

If the illegitimacy tradition is correct, Matthew's genealogy of Jesus (1:1–17) and Luke's Magnificat (1:46–55) add to these images. In his genealogy, Matthew adopts the unheard-of practice of including five women. They

---

3. Much quoted; see, for example, Mary Jo Weaver, *New Catholic Women* (1985), 202, and Leonard Swidler, *Biblical Affirmations of Woman* (1979), 343.

are Tamar, daughter-in-law of Judah; Rahab the prostitute; Ruth, a Moabite widow; Bathsheba, the wife of Uriah whom David forced into adultery; and Mary. The first four are women wronged or disappointed by the male world, women who need men to legitimize their marginal social position. A virginal Mary does not belong on this list; a Mary understood as impregnated against her will suddenly fits. Luke's Magnificat hides a similar theme. In it, the phrase usually translated "the lowly" actually means "the abased" or "the humiliated." A Mary intimately acquainted with the degradation of rape could sing that phrase.

And what if the angels and the magi and the shining star were fictional elements created by Matthew and Luke to dramatize the meaning of God's design? For one thing, it explains Luke's and Matthew's discrepancies regarding times and places. For another, it becomes clear why Mary and Joseph can be surprised by Jesus; why Mary needs to ponder things; why Jesus' siblings think he has lost his mind when he goes off preaching. Understanding the wonders as poetry also suggests what a remarkable man Joseph must have been. He could have used the law to push an uncomfortable reality out of sight; he could even have had Mary stoned as an adulteress. Yet he quietly takes as his wife a pregnant woman whose child is not his. The absence of cosmic signs makes Mary and Joseph more like us—flesh-and-blood people who do not know their children's future, flesh-and-blood people surprised by events that call into question their most cherished values and attitudes.

Great value remains in the elements of wonder, however, whether they represent stone-cold reporting or poetic metaphor. Gabriel's words, for example, "God is with you." Those words make explicit the faith-foundation that enables Mary to face all challenges—the certainty that God indeed is with her, no matter how she is judged. And Mary's unqualified "yes" in response to Gabriel suggests the faith-stance needed by anyone who faces a future pregnant with unplanned possibilities. Mary's song, too, like the annunciation story, reminds us one more time that Yahweh is a God of the unexpected:

Prayer

My being proclaims your greatness, O God;
my heart rejoices in you, my Savior.
You give meaning to the humiliation of your servant;
future generations will understand how blessed I am.
You, the Almighty, have done great things for me;
holy is your name!
Age after age, you extend your faithful love
to all who hold you in awe.
You rout the arrogant with your might;
you topple princes and lift up the lowly.
You fill those who hunger with all that is good,

and let the self-satisfied cling to their emptiness.
Mindful of your steadfast love,
you fulfill your promises to our ancestors—
to Sarah and her children forever.
My being proclaims your greatness, O God;
my heart rejoices in you, my Savior![4]

Connections

1. What images of Mary do you find most meaningful? Are these the same images you found meaningful ten years ago? In childhood?

2. When you ponder the various phases of Mary's life, where do you find connections with your own experience?

3. How are Mary and Elizabeth similar to Ruth and Naomi?

4. If you were to write a litany of Mary, what phrases would you use to address her?

For Further Reading

Crouch, James E., "How Early Christians Viewed the Birth of Jesus," *Bible Review* (October 1991): 34–38.

Deen, Edith, *All of the Women of the Bible* (1955), 156–67.

Johnson, Ann, *Miryam of Nazareth* (1984), 26–28.

Moloney, Francis J., *Woman: First Among the Faithful* (1986), 43–66.

Moltmann-Wendel, Elisabeth, *A Land Flowing with Milk and Honey* (1988), 193–94.

Ostling, Richard N., "Handmaid or Feminist?" *Time*, 30 December 1991, 62–66.

Schaberg, Jane, *The Illegitimacy of Jesus* (1990), entire book.

Sleevi, Mary Lou, *Women of the Word* (1989), 33–36, 75–78.

Smith, Joan, *Misogynies* (1989), 55–59.

Swidler, Leonard, *Biblical Affirmations of Woman* (1979), 176–79, 241, 244–47, 264–71.

Tetlow, Elizabeth M., *Women and Ministry in the New Testament* (1980), 103, 109–10.

Warner, Marina, *Alone of All Her Sex* (1976), 3–49, 342–45.

Weaver, Mary Jo, *New Catholic Women* (1985), 201–9.

Winter, Miriam Therese, *WomanWord* (1990), 11–38.

---

4. Based on Lk 1:46–55.

24 Peter's Mother-in-Law and the Crippled Woman: Women Set Free

Mark 1:29–31 (Matthew 8:14–15; Luke 4:38–39) and

Luke 13:10–17

"He approached . . . he called. . . ."

Background

Throughout the ministry of Jesus, his miracles demonstrate his inclusion of both women and men in the personal commission he adopts from Isaiah: release of captives from their bonds (Lk 4:16–20). On the very first day of his ministry in Galilee, Jesus frees Peter's mother-in-law of a fever. Near the end of his ministry, when the authorities are seeking a pretext to execute him, he heals a crippled woman on the sabbath. In both cases, it is Jesus who seeks out the woman.

The story of Peter's mother-in-law occupies three verses in Mark's Gospel, only two in the later Gospels of Matthew and Luke. The sheer physical impact of Mark's scene is caught in a line drawing by the seventeenth-century Dutch artist, Rembrandt: bending to grasp the hands of a woman lying on a mat, Jesus strains to help her rise. In Mt 8:14–15, the miracle no longer requires lifting; Jesus need merely touch the woman's hand. And in Lk 4:38–39 Jesus need not touch her at all: he simply stands over her and rebukes the fever.

Despite this progressive spiritualizing of the story, all three Gospels agree that the healed woman immediately begins to tend to the needs of Jesus and his companions. The writers' intention is to illustrate how immediately and completely she has been cured; she needs no period of recuperation. Her rush to serve the men also suggests freedom from legalistic restrictions. Just as a first-century Jewish teacher never touched a woman, so he would not usually allow a woman to serve him. As a rabbi of the next century expressed the custom, by then rigidified, "One must under no circumstances be served by a woman, be she adult or child."[1] In Mark's vision of the life of Jesus, the very first day of Jesus' public life is thus highlighted not only by Jesus' extraordinary healing of a woman, but also by his freeing of that woman from gender customs.

The later cure, that of the crippled or bent woman, is reported by Luke alone, although three Gospels report Jesus' having healed men on the

---

1. Francis J. Moloney, *Woman: First Among the Faithful* (1986), 20.

sabbath.[2] Luke so clumsily inserts the story into a section made up of teaching material that scholars believe he considered it of great importance. They see him as willing to abandon his usual concern for literary structure in order to make the point that the woman, who begins to praise God the moment she is cured, is truly religious, while the synagogue president who objects to the cure has succumbed to legalism. Jesus teaches by action that people matter more than regulations. He reinforces action by calling the woman "daughter of Abraham"—a title that appears nowhere else in the New Testament, even though "son" or "children" of Abraham is sometimes applied to a Jewish man or to the people of Israel. Jesus thus makes it clear that women are full-fledged participants in the covenant established by Yahweh.

By curing the woman on the sabbath, Jesus also restores the ancient meaning of the sabbath as a time for celebrating the creative and liberating power of God (Ex 31:17, Deut 5:15). By Jesus' time, observance of the sabbath had sometimes become an end in itself. Recalling such texts as Num 15:32–34, where a man is sentenced to death for gathering sticks on the sabbath, the most strictly religious Jews kept the sabbath by observing a myriad of restrictions. They kindled no fires, walked no more than 1,000 yards (a "sabbath day's journey"), and performed no manual labor, cooking, or household work. Jesus' sabbath cures reinforce sayings that appear elsewhere in the Gospels: the sabbath is made for human beings, not the reverse (Mk 2:27), and Jesus is lord even of the sabbath (Mk 2:28; Lk 6:5).

The Story of Peter's Mother-In-Law as Told in Mark

A Paraphrase of Mk 1:29–31

On leaving the synagogue of Capernaum, Jesus enters the house of Simon Peter and Andrew, together with James and John. Peter's mother-in-law lies sick with a fever, and Jesus is immediately told about her. He approaches her, grasps her hand, and helps her rise. The fever leaves her, and she waits on Jesus and his companions.

The Story of the Crippled Woman as Told in Luke

A Paraphrase of Lk 13:10–17

Jesus is teaching in a synagogue on the sabbath. A woman is present who has been crippled by a spirit for eighteen years. She is bent over, completely incapable of standing erect. When Jesus sees the woman he says to her, "You

---

2. Matthew's and Mark's parallel to the cure of the crippled woman is the cure of a man with a withered hand (Mt 12:9–14; Mk 3:1–6). Luke also reports sabbath cures of two men, one possessed by a demon (4:31–37) and one suffering from dropsy (14:1–6).

are rid of your trouble." He lays his hands upon her. She stands up straight at once, and glorifies God. The president of the synagogue is indignant that Jesus has cured someone on the sabbath. He says to the crowd, "There are six working days: come and be cured on one of them, and not on the sabbath." Jesus replies, "What hypocrites you are! Is there a single one of you who does not loose his ox or his donkey from its stall and take it out to water on the sabbath? And here is this woman, a daughter of Abraham, who has been bound by Satan for eighteen long years: was it not right for her to be loosed from her bonds on the sabbath?" At these words his adversaries are humiliated, and the mass of the people rejoice at the wonders Jesus performs.

Reflection

Peter's mother-in-law, like her daughter, Peter's wife, is one of the many nameless women of the Bible. She may be a widow, for the story suggests that she lives in Peter's household rather than with her husband. Her daughter is mentioned one other time: Paul says in 1 Cor 9:5 that she accompanies Peter on his missionary journeys. But of Peter's mother-in-law, the Gospels report only this cure. The miracle occurs in early afternoon, a time when fevers often rise. She is confined to bed with what may be a recurrent bout of malaria. In Luke's telling of the story, his stress on her "high" fever suggests that she may be suffering from delirium as well, a condition terrifying to people of the first century CE.

One wonders whether the woman's daughter, Peter's wife, was present that day. Does the sick woman feel indignant about a son-in-law who has abandoned his livelihood to follow an unknown visionary? Is she fearful for her own future as well as that of her daughter? Does she resent Peter for his casual attitude toward showing up for meals? Are her fever dreams accompanied by white-hot anger toward a man who seems to have abandoned all sense of responsibility for his family? If any of these things is true, she is healed of that concern as well as her fever, for she feels rejuvenated enough immediately to serve Jesus, Peter, and their companions. And, like Jesus, she immediately places a higher priority on service than on blind obedience to custom. Having given her a sense of her own wholeness, Jesus has freed her to serve anyone.

The crippled woman, too, is nameless. In her own story, she is shuffled to the periphery. She is treated like an object, useful only insofar as her existence provides an occasion for theological debate. Since her story occurs late in Jesus' ministry, she may well have heard of his extraordinary works and attitudes. But she remains so conditioned to the idea that no public religious figure would speak with a woman that it never occurs to her to ask him for help: Jesus seeks *her*. Noticing her on the fringes of the crowd, he either goes to her or calls her to himself—either way, an extraordinary act for a male religious leader of his time.

To everyone else the crippled woman is, at best, a pathetic figure to be avoided. Not troubled merely with a case of gout or a mild form of arthritis, she seems to suffer from the results of a serious accident, or from the effects of a severely crippling form of arthritis. She has been doubled over, totally unable to lift her head or walk upright, for eighteen years. So severe is her disfigurement that the authorities say she is bound by Satan—a condition rendering her, like a menstruating woman, ritually unclean. Ostracized and bent double for nearly two decades, she has lived in a world of earth and feet and paving stones. Has she forgotten the beauty of moon and stars? When has she last seen a human smile?

Yet this deformed woman spends her sabbaths at the synagogue. She may be broken in body, but Jesus himself recognizes her wholeness of spirit. *Before* he touches her, he tells her that she is set free. Then, at his electrifying touch, she stretches herself upright and praises the God who heals. The crowd breaks into delighted approval of Jesus' "tricks"; but she, a true daughter of Abraham, glorifies God.

❖ ❖

The evangelists say so little about Peter's mother-in-law that it is difficult to recognize her parallels today. She could be a mother who believes her daughter has married beneath her, a mother afire with rage at the man who seems to treat her daughter with cavalier disregard. Or perhaps she is a mother who resents what she perceives as the loss of a child to a religious calling. Certainly she could be anyone who discovers how difficult it is to pray in a body wracked with illness.

On a literal level, the crippled woman can stand for all whose faith never wavers, despite their inability to comprehend the misfortune that has befallen them. But it is on a metaphoric level that her story has captured the imagination of Gospel readers. For scriptural theologian Elisabeth Schüssler Fiorenza, her story is "a paradigm for [both] the oppression and [the] liberation which women experience in biblical religion."[3] For suffragist Elizabeth Cady Stanton, "The condition of the woman in this parable, bowed to the earth with all her disabilities, well represents the degraded condition of the sex under every form of government and of religion the world over."[4] For biblical commentator Francis Moloney, hers is a story whose implications cry for redress: "All the legal and cultural conditioning that surrounds womanhood must be eliminated, as she is just as important as man in being a hearer of the word, a companion of Jesus on his way, and the recipient of his powerful, . . . curing presence."[5]

3. "Lk 13:10–17: Interpretation for Liberation and Transformation," *Theology Digest* 36, 4 (Winter 1989), 303–4.

4. *The Woman's Bible*, Part II (1898), 136.

5. *Woman: First Among the Faithful* (1986), 73.

The crippled woman of today may be a single head of household imprisoned in the desperation of poverty. She may be a victim of abuse or rape, locked for years in crippling fear and anxiety. She may be a career woman hemmed in by invisible barriers that prevent her from realizing her goals and expectations. She may be a woman who has successfully completed pastoral or seminary training, only to discover that she cannot find church employment, or can find it only at a wage that leaves her in poverty. Whoever Peter's mother-in-law and the crippled woman may now be, they might pray with the women Jesus freed:

Prayer

Peter's Mother-in-Law:
>You took pity on me, O God, when I was in trouble.
>Fire consumed my eyes, my throat;
>my bones burned within me.
>Those who came to see me relished my bad fortune
>and spread the news about me everywhere.
>They tormented me, adding to my pain,
>for I seemed a mystery to them.
>In my distress I sought you.
>By night when nothing would cool me,
>when my body blazed with despair,
>I stretched my hands to you.
>I pleaded for your help, and you answered me;
>you did not hide your face from me.
>Through your servant, Jesus, you blessed me
>with the cooling touch of life.
>Forever will I praise your faithfulness,
>O Holy One of Israel.

The Crippled Woman:
>In your goodness, O God, you turned to me;
>my crushed bones dance for joy!
>Sacrifices give you no pleasure;
>had I offered a holocaust, you would have refused it.
>My sacrifice, for eighteen years,
>was a body wrenched and a spirit wracked with pain.
>I had become loathsome to my neighbors,
>to my friends a thing of fear.
>Those who saw me in the street hurried past me;
>I was dead in their hearts, a thing discarded.
>But in you I trusted, and you smiled upon me;
>you saved me in your love.

Open my lips, Most High,
that my tongue may proclaim your glory!
For today I lift my head high;
I plant my foot upon level ground.
In the assemblies will I bless you always,
singing and making melody to you.[6]

Connections

1. With whom do you identify most strongly—Peter's mother-in-law, Jesus, the crippled woman, or the synagogue official? Why?

2. What effect can recurrent illness or pain have on a person's spiritual, emotional, and social life? Is there someone whose "fever" you can help to dispel, someone whom you can empower to "stand upright"?

3. Is there something in your own life that causes you to burn with rage or to feel twisted out of shape? How can you find release?

4. Jesus taught that people take priority over regulations. To what extent do you see his attitude lived out in churches and other organizations of your experience?

For Further Reading

Deen, Edith, *All of the Women of the Bible* (1955), 181–84.

Moloney, Francis J., *Woman: First Among the Faithful* (1986), 19–20, 72–73.

Moltmann-Wendel, Elisabeth, *The Women Around Jesus* (1987), 143–44.

Moltmann-Wendel, Elisabeth, *A Land Flowing with Milk and Honey* (1988), 125, 136.

Nunnally-Cox, Janice, *Foremothers* (1981), 107–9.

Schüssler Fiorenza, Elisabeth, *In Memory of Her* (1983), 125–26.

Schüssler Fiorenza, Elisabeth, "Lk 13:10–17: Interpretation for Liberation and Transformation," *Theology Digest* 36, 4 (Winter 1989): 303–19.

Sleevi, Mary Lou, *Women of the Word* (1989), 50–54.

Stanton, Elizabeth Cady, *The Woman's Bible*, Part II (1898), 136.

Winter, Miriam Therese, *WomanWord* (1990), 75–79.

Yamasaki, April, *Remember Lot's Wife* (1991), 67–68, 87–88.

6. Based on Ps 31, 38, 41, and 77.

25 The Daughter of Jairus and the Woman with a Flow of Blood: Women Dead to their Worlds

Mark 5:21–43 (Luke 8:41–56; Matthew 9:18–26)

"... I shall be healed."

Background

The story of the twelve-year-old daughter of Jairus serves as a frame around that of a woman healed of a twelve-year menstrual flow. At Capernaum, Jairus begs Jesus to come and heal his daughter. As Jesus sets out to do so, the hemorrhaging woman touches his cloak and is healed. While Jesus speaks with the woman, a messenger reports that Jairus' daughter has died. Jesus nevertheless continues on to Jairus' house, where he dismisses the mourners and restores the girl to life.

Both Luke and Matthew retell Mark's story. Luke, who is thought to have been a physician and whose Gentile community included prominent women, varies Mark's story in two details. Where Mark implies that doctors have victimized the bleeding woman, Luke softens the judgment to "nobody had been able to cure her" (8:43). Where Mark depicts the woman as conversing with Jesus alone, Luke gives her a role in proclaiming the wonder: "Before all the people she explained why she had touched him and how she had been cured instantly" (8:47). Matthew, who places less stress than Mark and Luke on stories of women, presents a highly condensed summary of the story.

Although the first writer, Mark, spliced the two stories together from different sources, they nevertheless form a thematic unit: symbolically and then literally, Jesus raises women from the dead. Further, by what he does and by what he omits, Jesus welcomes women to a life of freedom in which taboos of the past are canceled. These taboos included the custom forbidding Jewish men to address or touch any woman in public—especially a girl of marriageable age. Second, Lev 15:25–30 decreed that a prolonged menstrual flow rendered not only the woman unclean, but also any man she touched. He was required to bathe, wash his clothes, and isolate himself until evening. Even when prolonged discharge ceased, the woman herself remained unclean another week. She was then required to have a priest offer two turtle doves or pigeons of purification in her name. Third, Num 19:11–15 decreed that anyone who touched a dead body or entered a place where death had just occurred became ritually unclean for seven days. If such a person failed to perform a purification ritual on the third and seventh days, he or she was to be "cut off from Israel."

Jesus, however, neither observes any purification rituals himself nor requires anyone else to do so. Far from cringing in horror at the presence of the woman newly cured of her flow of blood, he seeks her out, commends her faith, calls her the affectionate "Daughter" rather than the formal "Woman," and sends her off "healed" (the same word that was used in the early church to mean "saved"). Instead of standing outside Jairus' house to offer empty condolences, he enters the very chamber of death, addresses a girl of marriageable age with the warm Aramaic expression, "My dearest little one," and takes her by the hand. These were eloquent, ambiguous gestures for a man of religion, and the early church considered them significant enough to merit preservation in three Gospels.

One of the attitudes Jesus repudiated has nevertheless endured for centuries—that of viewing menstruating women as "unclean." The endurance of this attitude can be attributed to the fact that *all* ancient patriarchal societies enforced it. For example, in the fourth century BCE, the Greek philosopher Aristotle wrote that the presence of a menstruating woman could cause a mirror to turn "bloody-dark, like a cloud." By the first century CE, Pliny the Elder, a Roman authority on natural science, had further asserted that contact with menstrual blood rusted bronze and iron, dulled steel blades, destroyed crops, and turned new wine sour.[1] Medieval Christian women who were menstruating were barred from entering churches, and to this day Orthodox Jewish women are required to perform a ritual bath of cleansing after their menstrual periods. And many commentators cite unconscious remnants of this fear of contamination as the real basis for male reluctance to allow Christian women to enter church sanctuaries.

The Story of the Daughter of Jairus and the Woman with a Flow of Blood as Told in Mark

A Paraphrase of Mk 5:21–43

While Jesus is at the lake side, a synagogue president named Jairus throws himself down at Jesus' feet. "My little daughter is at death's door," he says. "I beg you to come and lay your hands on her so that her life may be saved." Jesus goes with him, and a great crowd presses around him. In its midst is a woman who has suffered from hemorrhages for twelve years. She has spent everything she had on long treatment by many doctors, but has become worse rather than better. She has heard about Jesus, and comes up behind

---

1. Aristotle and Pliny are quoted in Anderson and Zinsser, *A History of Their Own* (1988), 28.

him in the crowd to touch his cloak. She tells herself, "If I touch even his clothes, I shall be healed." The moment she touches his cloak, her flow of blood dries up and she knows within herself that she is cured.

Aware at once that power has gone out from him, Jesus turns around in the densely packed crowd and asks, "Who touched my clothes?" His disciples respond, "You see the crowd pressing around you and yet you ask, 'Who touched me?'" But he keeps looking around to see who it was. Then the woman, trembling with fear because she knows what has happened to her, falls at his feet and tells him the truth. He says to her, "Daughter, your faith has healed you. Go in peace, free from your affliction."

While Jesus is still speaking with the woman, Jairus receives a message: "Your daughter has died; why trouble the teacher any more?" Jesus overhears and says to Jairus, "Do not be afraid; simply have faith." He allows only Peter, James, and John to accompany him to Jairus' house, where they find great lamentation occurring. Jesus enters the house and says to the mourners, "Why this crying and commotion? The child is not dead: she is asleep." The mourners laugh with scorn, but Jesus turns them out of the house. He takes only the child's parents and his own companions into the girl's room. She is twelve years old. Taking hold of her hand, Jesus says to her, "Talitha cum"—"Get up, dearest little one." Immediately she gets up and walks about. Everyone present is overcome with amazement. Jesus gives them strict instructions not to publicize what he has done, and tells them to give the girl something to eat.

Reflection

This story is a natural for today's tabloids: *PROMINENT OFFICIAL AND WOMAN IMPOVERISHED BY MEDICAL ESTABLISHMENT TURN TO FAITH HEALER!* Nor was the account any less sensational in Jesus' time. In a world where girls were chattels and where menstruating women were forbidden access to the well and the marketplace, Jesus matter-of-fact-ly summons two "dead" women to fullness of life.

Unlike the ostracized bleeding woman, Jairus' daughter may have enjoyed a small degree of status as the daughter of a synagogue president, the layman who made all the arrangements for Sabbath worship. She would have overheard conversations that revealed both the growing popularity of Jesus and the skepticism with which some of the religious authorities viewed him. While such stories may have intrigued her, she would have known she was unlikely to meet Jesus. After all, her life lay entirely in the hands of her father. As a minor she was his legal possession; prior to the age of twelve she could even have been sold as a slave. Up to the age of twelve and a half, she was required to marry any man her father chose. Only beyond twelve and a half could she refuse a prospective mate, and the man she accepted paid a marriage price not to her but to her father.

It is unlikely, however, that a man willing to forsake all dignity and fling himself at the feet of Jesus would have forced an undesirable partner on his daughter. In the love Jairus shows for his daughter and the faith he places in Jesus, he contrasts sharply with the scoffing mourners. It is therefore no surprise that Jairus and the girl's mother are invited to enter that calm center where Jesus grants life and freedom to a person technically rated of little account—a girl not yet alive to adult legal rights. Her story celebrates restoration to normal life as symbolized by the ability simply to walk around and to eat—the physical bases for ability even to imagine a future.

During the years the daughter of Jairus has been bound by the rules of childhood, another woman has become bound by her people's belief that her very presence constitutes pollution. Suffering from a prolonged menstrual flow, for twelve long years she has been barred from all association with God's people. By the time Jesus appears on the streets of Capernaum, she has already risked medical incompetence and financial ruin in order to regain health, cultic purity, and restoration to community life.

While her actions demonstrate initiative, they also reveal her desperation and the degree to which she has internalized her cultural conditioning. Having heard stories of Jesus, she has come to view his mysterious power as her last hope. Yet she dare not contaminate a man of God. Shielded by the anonymity of the crowd, she manages instead the merest brush against the fringes of his cloak. Even when a jolt of well-being electrifies her, she rigidly suppresses any spontaneous whoop of joy. Indeed, when the eyes of Jesus insistently seek her out, she drops before him, trembling with fear. One wonders what reactions from other religious figures taught her such terror.

But Jesus is no ordinary teacher: he overwhelms her with gentleness. Knowing she needs a restoration that extends beyond physical health, he breaches custom to converse with her. Treating her as a daughter of God and a full member of society, he neither recoils from her nor regards himself as contaminated. He says nothing about the woman's segregating herself yet another week. He even takes pains to locate the source of the healing not within himself, but within the woman: "*Your faith* has healed you." Her courage in breaking through the conditioning of a lifetime has brought her a condition she can barely remember: *shalom*—peace and well-being.

❖ ❖

Every woman of today is, to some extent, the daughter of Jairus or the woman with a prolonged flow of blood. In today's churches, women's voices often remain unheard or heard only with skepticism, however vehemently male authorities may deny charges of sexism. Given, however, the flimsy reasons placed on the table for barring Orthodox Jewish women from the rabbinate and Roman Catholic women from the priesthood, it is difficult *not* to conclude that church officials still believe—consciously or unconsciously—that women's natural processes bar them from intimacy with God.

Even outside houses of worship, women remain stigmatized as secondary human beings whose biology renders them "dirty" and whose medical problems merit little attention. Some marketers urge women to wear pads all the time, suggesting that they are permanently "unclean." (Women's internalization of that message is evidenced by the acute embarrassment they suffer when an accident reveals them to be menstruating.) In medicine, only recently has women's activism begun to moderate the number of mutilating hysterectomies and mastectomies performed when less invasive treatment would suffice. Only in the last decade has PMS gained recognition as a physiological condition. Despite women's long lives, menopause constitutes a nearly unstudied area, and problems related to osteoporosis—problems that kill as many women every year as breast cancer does—have been little investigated. Most AIDS studies focus on men, even though heterosexual transmission is on the rise, and a healthy woman who has sex with an infected man is fourteen times more likely to contract the virus than if the situation were reversed.[2]

In fact, even though many conditions know no gender bias, medical researchers often explicitly ignore women, arguing that female hormones "complicate" their work. In 1988, researchers reported that aspirin reduces the risk of heart attacks: they had studied 22,071 men. In 1990, researchers found that heavy coffee-drinking does not increase the incidence of heart attacks or strokes: they had studied 45,589 men. Heart attacks kill women and men in almost equal numbers, yet the applicability to women of conclusions such as these remains largely unexamined.[3]

❖ ❖

Unlike the daughter of Jairus and the woman with the prolonged menstrual flow, women of today cannot physically touch Jesus. But inspired by touching Jesus spiritually, they can insist on better medical research and treatment, and on equality in the classroom, work place, and political office. They can become educated in theology. They can invade church chancels; they can walk out when subjected to the reading of repressive passages or demeaning sermons. Like the woman who dared, despite her conditioning, to clutch the cloak of Jesus, they can refuse to hold back out of false shame and guilt.

2. Katrine Ames and others, "Our Bodies, Their Selves: A bias against women in health research," *Newsweek*, 17 December 1990, 60.

3. Ames, 60. See also "Medical sleuths study older women—at last," *AARP Bulletin* 34, no. 6 (June 1993): 1, 4. The AARP news story reports that in Fall 1993 the National Institutes of Health will begin a fifteen-year clinical investigation "that will probe the causes of disease and death in midlife and older women."

They can reject the "unclean" role. The process will be but little easier for them, however, than for the rule-bound daughter of Jairus or the woman made a pariah by her flow of blood. Like them, women of today might be moved to pray:

Prayer

God of healing, I have had my fill of woe.
Failings ascribed to me tower above my head;
they form a heavier load than I can bear.
All day long I go about as if in mourning,
my very body derided as loathsome.
Friends shun me, my relatives disown me.
I have nowhere to turn.
Outrage threatens to burst my heart.
God of tender touch,
my longing lies open before you;
wipe away my tears.
Bring to life in me your new heaven and earth,
your holy realm of freedom and grace.
Grant me in this world a glimpse
of your New Jerusalem, that holy city where
the old order has passed utterly away.[4]

Connections

1. Imagine the joy of the daughter of Jairus and the woman healed of her prolonged flow of blood. What great blessings have, as it were, restored you to life? How does your own sense of wonder make you a wellspring of life to others?

2. In what ways do you find bias against women still operative in your world? How can you, like the hemorrhaging woman, tap into a power that works toward peace, equality, and freedom?

3. The woman with the flow of blood had internalized what society told her about her worthlessness. What false messages have you internalized? What can you do to replace them with truths that affirm your worth?

For Further Reading

Anderson, Bonnie S., and Judith P. Zinsser, *A History of Their Own*, Vol. I (1988), 28–29.

Carmody, Denise Lardner, *Biblical Woman* (1980), 16–20.

4. Based on Ps 38 and 88 and Rev 21.

Deen, Edith, *All of the Women of the Bible* (1955), 182–83.

Mollenkott, Virginia Ramey, *Women, Men, and the Bible* (1988), 4–6.

Moloney, Francis J., *Woman: First Among the Faithful* (1986), 20–22.

Nunnally-Cox, Janice, *Foremothers* (1981), 102–3.

Schüssler Fiorenza, Elisabeth, *In Memory of Her* (1983), 124.

Tappa, Louise, "The Christ-Event: A Protestant Perspective" in *With Passion and Compassion* (1988), ed. Virginia Fabella and Mercy Amba Oduyoye, 32–33.

Tetlow, Elizabeth M., *Women and Ministry in the New Testament* (1980), 95, 99, 104.

Wahlberg, Rachel Conrad, *Jesus According to a Woman* (1975), 35–45.

Winter, Miriam Therese, *WomanWord* (1990), 57–65.

Yamasaki, April, *Remember Lot's Wife* (1991), 69–72.

26 The Canaanite Woman: An Assertive Gentile

Mark 7:24–30; Matthew 15:21–28

"For saying that, go . . ."

Background

The story of the Canaanite woman appears in the Gospels of Mark and Matthew. It occurs during a brief journey into Phoenicia (today's Lebanon). Near Tyre he is accosted by a woman who begs him to cure her young daughter of possession by a demon.[1] With uncharacteristic curtness, Jesus informs her that his mission is to "the children," not to "dogs." By "children," Jesus means his own people, the Jews. By "dogs" he means non-Jews, Gentiles. Because Jews regarded both pigs and wild dogs as unclean, their everyday slang had come to include derision of Gentiles as "swine" or "dogs." Some interpreters of the story argue that Jesus meant to be playful, since the original Greek of both Gospels employs a diminutive form connoting "house puppies" or "little lapdogs." In context, however, both Jesus and the woman take "dogs" as a slur, and it seems more reasonable to read the insult as demonstrating the genuine humanity of Jesus: Like anyone else, he could have a bad day; he could be caught in an unguarded moment.

As the dialog between Jesus and the woman progresses, Jesus also emerges as someone who can learn new facets of his own mission. The woman educates him by pointing out that even dogs eat the children's table scraps. Jesus' response to this sally differs in Mark and in Matthew, because the writers' views of Jesus differ. Mark sees Jesus as a young man in a hurry, a man much affected by his own emotions and senses. His thoroughly human Jesus so enjoys the woman's topping his remark that he tells her her daughter is cured because of her *wit*. Matthew, on the other hand, views Jesus as an elevated personage, a new Moses and great teacher. His more lofty Messiah rewards the *faith* he discerns in the woman's response.

The fact that Mark and Matthew also intended their Gospels for different audiences affects the way they identify the woman. Keeping in mind the thought categories of Gentile Christians in Rome, Mark first identifies her as

---

1. In the first century CE, demonic possession was the universally accepted label for any alarming psychological disorder (such as schizophrenia) or any baffling physical condition (such as epilepsy). The exact nature of the girl's illness is unknown.

a "Gentile" ("Greek" in the original)—someone whose cultural attitudes are Hellenistic and who speaks Greek, the everyday language of the empire. He further identifies her as "Phoenician," a native of a small coastal country west of Galilee whose people had always focused outward into the Mediterranean. (Ethnically the Phoenicians were Canaanites, a Semitic people distantly related to Jews, but their active seaports such as Tyre and Sidon made them the most cosmopolitan people of the Semitic world.) Finally, Mark adds that she is "of Syria," the name of the Roman geopolitical province within which Phoenicia was located.[2]

Matthew, on the other hand, who addresses a Jewish audience, identifies the woman as "Canaanite." Already an archaic scriptural term in Matthew's day, "Canaanite" was as derogatory as "dog," since Jews traditionally regarded Canaanites and Samaritans as unclean from birth. Matthew, however, writing at a time when the early church was struggling to define the breadth of Jesus' mission, probably intended his readers to recall that he opened his Gospel with a genealogy of Jesus that included two respected Canaanite women, Tamar (daughter-in-law of Judah) and Rahab. Both were regarded as foremothers of King David, and, therefore, of Jesus (Mt 1:3–5). Lest his point prove too subtle, Matthew stresses it by placing a most unlikely title on the lips of this non-Jewish woman; she addresses Jesus as "Son of David."

In one area, however, both sets of readers would have responded much the same. They would have recognized the relevance of the story to an emotion-charged issue of their own day: could Gentile "dogs" who embraced Christianity immediately share the eucharistic table with Jewish Christians? Or must they become "children"—adopt Judaism—before sharing in the Eucharist? Both Mark and Matthew teach that Gentiles, as they are, may share the banquet: Jesus breaches all cultural barriers.

To demonstrate the language differences between the two writers, both Mark's and Matthew's versions of the story of the Canaanite woman follow, presented in the REB translation instead of paraphrase.

The Story of the Gentile Woman as Told in Mark 7:24–30

Jesus moved on from [Galilee] into the territory of Tyre. He found a house to stay in, and would have liked to remain unrecognized, but that was impossible. Almost at once a woman whose small daughter was possessed by an unclean spirit heard of him and came and fell at his feet. (The woman was a Gentile, a Phoenician of Syria by nationality.) She begged him to drive the demon out of her daughter. He said to her, "Let the children be satisfied first; it is not right to take the children's bread and throw it to the dogs." "Sir," she

2. In some translations, such as *The New American Bible,* "Phoenician" and "of Syria" are combined into the descriptive identifier, "Syrophoenician" or "Syro-phoenician."

replied, "even the dogs under the table eat the children's scraps." He said to her, "For saying that, go, and you will find the demon has left your daughter." And when she returned home, she found the child lying in bed; the demon had left her.

The Story of the Canaanite Woman as Told in Matthew 15:21–28

Jesus then withdrew [from Galilee] to the region of Tyre and Sidon. And a Canaanite woman from those parts came to meet him crying, "Son of David! Have pity on me; my daughter is tormented by a devil." But he said not a word in reply. His disciples came and urged him: "Send her away! See how she comes shouting after us." Jesus replied, "I was sent to the lost sheep of the house of Israel, and to them alone." But the woman came and fell at his feet and cried, "Help me, sir." Jesus replied, "It is not right to take the children's bread and throw it to the dogs." "True, sir," she answered, "and yet the dogs eat the scraps that fall from their master's table." Hearing this Jesus replied, "What faith you have! Let it be as you wish!" And from that moment her daughter was restored to health.

Reflection

This woman qualifies to teach seminars in assertiveness training. She recognizes the power of a sense of humor; she is determined and intelligent; she is both bold and humble. She sets a goal and lets nothing deter her from it—not her own lack of status, not the attitudes of the aides protecting the visiting wonder-worker, not even the insults of the prophet himself.

Yet her story raises many questions that are never answered: Has her daughter been ill from birth, or is the illness recent? Where is the girl's father, the woman's husband? Is he dead? Will no other man assume responsibility for the child? How does the woman support herself? By now, does her entire life revolve around her daughter? Has she exhausted herself, hauling her child from one doctor to another? Has she tried her own country's ancient religion, making offerings to Asherah and Baal that she can ill afford? And considering the status of woman, only marginally better in her Hellenistic culture than in the Jewish, why does she care so much about a girl child? Does the daughter represent a future marriage and thus, for the woman, a secure, respectable old age? Or—more likely—does this story present a case of parental love so strong that a mother throws aside all caution to find relief for her child?

None of these questions can be answered with certainty. Yet the woman's desperation suggests her situation, for in her world the social differences between Jew and Greek were so vast as never to be lightly breached. She must have been a woman alone, a woman with no man, no influential relatives to help her. Furthermore, in a world where women did not publicly accost even men of their own society, she demanded the attention of a man of another society. She could only expect a Jewish male to dismiss her as worthless: if not as a woman or as a Gentile, then surely as a despicable Canaanite. But even if our questions cannot be answered, we can still imagine some of what it may have been like for her. . . .

❖ ❖

That she hears about Jesus is no surprise. The traders who move constantly in and out of Tyre are as famous for the tales they carry as for their goods. Perhaps it is a neighbor, or a gossip come home from the marketplace, who first alerts her to the reputation of Jesus. What she learns is that all Galilee, to the east, throbs with news of a prophet who casts out demons and cleanses lepers. He flouts customary restrictions, too, speaking even with social outcasts. They say that he actually *touched* a woman rendered taboo for years by an endless menstrual flow. "Wherever he goes," they report, "to village or town or farm, they fill the place with the sick. And he heals them all!"

At first she finds such stories a mere diversion. After all, care of her daughter binds her to her home; she cannot travel to Galilee to locate this Jesus. But the wonder of him keeps invading her thoughts. When the news breaks that he is coming to Tyre, she begins cautiously to think that she could speak to him about her daughter. "Should I?" she wonders. "Why not? What do I have to lose?" Planning an approach, discarding scheme after scheme, she opts finally to drop all subtlety. She will simply shout until he listens. He need only speak, even just look at her, and she will know what to say next.

The day finally arrives; Jesus enters Tyre. Her neighbors warn her that she is building a tower of hope on shifting sands, but they do at least agree to watch her child. Rushing to join the throng surging around Jesus, she abandons all reserve and elbows her way forward until she reaches the group of aides who form a sort of shield around Jesus. Repeatedly she screams for pity, until even these men, in disgust, shrink back just enough to open up a small space.

She hurls herself at Jesus' feet; she looks up into his face. All sights, sounds, and smells fade to a distant blur. It is as if a clear glass globe encloses the two of them alone. But his words startle her. How can a man with eyes so warm call her a dog and claim to have come only for his own people? Unspoken responses flash through her mind: "Why are you in Tyre, then?— Power like yours must not be hoarded!—If you really believe I'm a little dog, why are you talking to me?" She grasps instead at that merest hint of play in Jesus' tone, that smallest of loopholes in his argument. "Even puppies get to eat the table scraps!" she shoots back.

And his reaction astonishes her. His face lights up as if she had given him something precious. Has no one ever challenged him before? Most wonderful of all, he responds, "For saying that, go. You will find that the demon has left your daughter."

She believes him. She believes *in* him. Oblivious to the dust, oblivious to the people stumbling over her, she sits back on her heels, smiling. When she reaches home to find her neighbors agog with the news of her daughter's health, she will not need to shriek for joy. Here, now, she *knows*. And it does not matter whether the words of Jesus cured her daughter, or whether he simply knew, somehow, that the girl had grown better. Either way, Jesus is something—some*one*—entirely new in her experience. "I won the debate," she thinks, "but he wins me."

❖ ❖

In her powerlessness, the Canaanite woman was granted a way to power. In her willingness to settle for scraps, she was given a place of honor at the banquet. She was the first Gentile to come to faith, the foremother of all Gentile Christians. In fact, she might have been the actual foremother of a Christian community at Tyre. Thirty years later, when Paul and a companion journey there, an already existing community of believers hosts them for a week. Acts 21:2–6 reports the visit and the send-off provided by the women, children, and men of Tyre. Yet on the day the Canaanite woman first encountered Jesus, her prayer might have been one of wonder and of searching:

Prayer

God of Jesus—Yahweh, they call you—
your name falls strangely upon my tongue.
The Jews of Tyre say you always hear the cry of the hungry,
that for the high and mighty you show no special regard,
that you consider rich and poor alike your creatures.
But that you would listen to me,
one they call a dog, an alien to your ways!
Though I do my best, I make no secret of my faults;
and I could not help but wonder whether something I had done
had brought such pain upon my child.
Then you gave me the bread to end my famine.
Only yesterday we were slaves, my daughter and I;
today, through your prophet Jesus, you set us free.
In my deepest being I bow to you, my Hope.
In you who answer, I fix my heart.
Through the Holy One you have sent,
help me to find my way to you.[3]

3. Based on Ps 38:15–18 and Job 34:19–20, 28.

Connections

1. Today a girl may be tormented by an intractable "demon" such as anorexia nervosa or bulimia. What other demons torment young women you know? What need for healing do they and their mothers experience?

2. Like the Canaanite woman, many people serve as sole caretakers of seriously handicapped or chronically ill friends or relatives—a person with AIDS, for example, or Alzheimer's disease. Has such an issue touched you? How did it affect you socially, emotionally, or spiritually?

3. When people in need work up the courage to seek help, they often experience the dispiriting game of agency tag. One office refers them to another, and another, and another. Have you ever had this experience? How does the example of the Canaanite woman give you hope?

4. Does a Canaanite woman already exist within you, or do you need to allow her to come to life in some area? Do you need, for example, her mothering instinct, her assertiveness, or her courage to go to any length for help?

For Further Reading

Deen, Edith, *All of the Women of the Bible* (1955), 189–92.

Moloney, Francis J., *Woman: First Among the Faithful* (1986), 22–23.

Nunnally-Cox, Janice, *Foremothers* (1981), 103–4.

Schüssler Fiorenza, Elisabeth, *In Memory of Her* (1983), 137–38.

Tetlow, Elizabeth M., *Women and Ministry in the New Testament* (1980), 95, 99.

Wahlberg, Rachel Conrad, *Jesus According to a Woman* (1975), 13–18.

Winter, Miriam Therese, *WomanWord* (1990), 84–87.

27 The Widow of Nain and the Poor Widow: Focus of Divine Concern

Luke 7:11–17; Mark 12:41–44, and Luke 21:1–4

". . . his heart went out to her. . . ."

Background

Jesus exemplifies the traditional Jewish awareness of and concern for widows. He uses the story of Elijah, fed by a Phoenician widow, to illustrate how a prophet may be rejected by his own people (Lk 4:25–27); he uses the image of a persistent widow to illustrate the need for perseverance in prayer (Lk 18:1–8); from his cross, he provides for the care of his own widowed mother (Jn 19:25–27); and he personally helps one widow and praises another. One is the widow from Nain, whose only son Jesus restores to life. The other is a poor widow whose tiny financial contribution to the temple Jesus praises as surpassing the philanthropy of the rich—a woman whose story is often called that of the "widow's mite."

Jesus' concern for widows demonstrated his absorption of key values of his own culture. In ancient Israel, three kinds of people—the alien, the widow, and the orphan—were especially vulnerable. For that very reason, Yahweh was said to love them and to visit wrath upon all who oppressed them (Ex 22:20–23; Deut 10:18, 24:17, 27:19). The plight of a widow was a special matter of concern, because the concept of "independent woman" simply did not exist. Strong widows like Tamar (daughter-in-law of Judah) and Ruth were the exception. By New Testament times, a widow might be protected by a financial settlement specified in a *ketuba* (a marriage contract), or she could sue her husband's estate to recover part of her dowry. But as a rule, a woman depended upon a father, husband, or son. A widow did not inherit when her husband died; his estate passed to their children or, if the couple was childless, to his nearest male relative. A childless young widow might remarry or return to her father's house; the future of an older widow was more precarious. A brother or close male relative of her husband might honor the levirate customs of Israel by marrying her, but he could refuse to do so (Deut 25:9–10; Ruth 4:6). Thus an older widow who had no children could be left penniless and open to victimization by creditors, judges, or anyone with a modicum of power.

Theoretically, widows were granted a share in tithes given the priests and in the sacrificial offerings on major feast days (Deut 14:28, 16:11, 14). They were also permitted to glean behind harvesters (Deut 24:19–21). But like the general prohibition of injustice toward widows, these laws lacked specifics for enforcement; the laws had no teeth. Thus it is no surprise that the prophets repeatedly upbraided Israel for oppression of widows (Isa 1:17; Jer 7:6; Ezek 22:7; Zech 7:10). Ps 94:6 even speaks of those who *murder* widows—not quite the poetic exaggeration it seems, since ill treatment could reduce a widow to starvation. By Jesus' time, even if a widow was protected by a *ketuba*, lawyers and scribes could gain a share in her property by administering it for her. Since widows would be attracted toward those legal experts who were known to be religiously observant, Jesus reserves harsh castigation for any scribe who prayed ostentatiously while simultaneously "devouring the houses" of widows—cheating them (Mk 12:38–40 and Lk 20:45–47).

The story of the widow of Nain, which appears only in the Gospel of Luke, occurs early in Jesus' ministry, in Galilee. This widow faced a dire situation. It was bad enough that she had lost her husband and her only son, but social attitudes made matters worse: custom attributed the death of a young person to some sin of the parent. Thus the very crowd that had gathered to comfort the widow would also have been speculating as to the nature of her sin. Jesus grasps all of this at a glance. Moved by pity, he demonstrates that divine compassion assigns no blame and recognizes no limits. He violates custom by speaking to the woman on a public street; and, then, in order to restore a life, he breaks the laws of ritual purity by touching the corpse (Num 19:11,16).

The story of the widow of Nain closely echoes an episode from 1 Kings 17:17–24 in which the prophet Elijah revives the only son of the widow from Zarephath. It also evokes a story from 2 Kings 4:8–37 in which the prophet Elisha revives the son of a woman from Shunem. As in the Old Testament stories, Luke's widow is nameless, that namelessness reflecting her lack of power. Jesus, in contrast, is presented as a mighty prophet like Elijah and Elisha, a man through whom divine power comes to brilliant focus on behalf of the dispossessed.

The story of the "widow's mite" appears in both Mark and Luke just after Jesus' condemnation of the "devouring" scribes. "Mite" comes from the King James translation of the word *lepton*, the name of the smallest copper coin then circulating in Jerusalem. A lepton was smaller than a U.S. dime. Two lepta together were worth about 1/64 the daily wage paid an unskilled laborer. Parallels to Mark's and Luke's tellings of the story occur in other Jewish and world literature, including Buddhist writings. In fact, the ending of the story resembles a Buddhist koan, a paradox that requires explanation: The woman's action in giving all she has to a corrupt religious institution accomplishes exactly what Jesus has just denounced unscrupulous advisers for doing—it destroys her estate. Given the literary parallels, some scholars suspect that the story originated as a parable or as a lament of Jesus on the fate of widows, and that Mark (and Luke after him) turned it into an actual event in order to make a point.

Both Mark and Luke sharply contrast the false religiosity of unjust scribes with the true devotion of the widow. Mark may also have been warning Christian leaders of his own day to be careful how they administered the property turned over to their care by members of the community. And Luke, who often speaks of the financial contributions of women, may have been trying to influence wealthy widows among his Gentile readership toward even greater generosity.[1] At yet another level, it should be noted that both evangelists place the story of the poor widow at the end of Jesus' ministry. The incident occurs during Passover week, just before Jesus enters upon his Passion. In this context, the widow who gives her all prefigures Jesus, who offers himself in equally total, generous sacrifice.

The early church continued the Jewish concern for widows exemplified by Jesus (Acts 6:1). In fact, James 1:27 lists care of widows and orphans as a sign of genuine religion. According to 1 Timothy 5:3–16, there also existed a specific order of widows, women who received fixed support in exchange for devoting their lives to prayer and good works. To qualify, a widow had to be sixty or older and totally devoid of family and resources.[2] Nonbiblical writings of the first centuries CE demonstrate the continued existence of this order of widows, and the esteem in which the women were held.

The Story of the Widow of Nain as Told in Luke

A Paraphrase of Lk 7:11–17

Accompanied by his disciples, Jesus goes to a town called Nain.[3] As he approaches the town gate, he meets a funeral procession. The man who died was the only son of his mother, a widow, and many of the townspeople accompany her. When Jesus sees her, his heart goes out to her. "Do not weep," he says to her. He steps forward and lays his hands on the stretcher, and the bearers halt. "Young man," he says, "I tell you to get up." He sits up and begins to speak, and Jesus gives him back to his mother. Everyone is filled

---

1. Although Luke's gospel contains many stories of women, he often subtly downplays women's value except as aides. This pattern leads New Testament scholar Elizabeth M. Tetlow to comment on this story, "The one role of women which Luke could affirm without qualification was that of giving alms." (*Women and Ministry in the New Testament*, 105.)

2. The writer shows such animosity toward younger widows that one can only assume he expected destitute younger women to remarry. In fact, his anxiety that such women might become gadabouts and busybodies suggests that they were, at the time, serving as "the church's principal pastors to and among women" (L. William Countryman, *Dirt, Greed, and Sex* [1988], 226). See also Bonnie Bowman Thurston, *The Widows* (1989), 40–44.

3. A Galilean town about six miles southeast of Nazareth, identified with today's Nein. Ancient rock-cut tombs still exist outside Nein.

with awe and praises God. "A great prophet has arisen among us," they say. The story of what Jesus did spreads from Galilee through the whole of Judea.

The Story of the Poor Widow as Told in Mark and Luke

A Paraphrase of Mk 12:41–44 and Lk 21:1–4

As Jesus sits in Jerusalem across from the temple treasury, he watches the people dropping their gifts into the chest. Many rich people put in large amounts. Presently there comes along a destitute widow. She drops in two tiny copper coins, together worth about a penny. Jesus calls his disciples to him and says, "Truly I tell you: this poor widow has given more than any of them, for those others . . . had more than enough, but she, with less than enough, has given all she had to live on."

Reflection

The widows of Jesus' time would have known the stories of the widows of Zarephath and Shunem, whose sons were restored nine centuries earlier by the prophets Elijah and Elisha. Perhaps they looked back upon that day with nostalgia, idly wishing that God would once again send a prophet of such power. The widow of Nain may even have heard rumors of the wonders recently attributed to a new preacher, a local man named Jesus, the son of Joseph and Mary of Nazareth. But she has not heard enough to create in her heart even a spark of hope; it is only after Jesus revives her son that she and the people of Nain recognize him as a prophet of the ancient mold.

Since the destitute widow of Jerusalem appears late in Jesus' ministry, she probably knew more about Jesus. But she may never have known that she was the object of his praise and compassion, and we do not know whether or not her situation ever improved. Still, Jesus' words and his restoration of one woman's son—like Yahweh's reviving of the sons of widows in the past—show that God's concern goes beyond words. God does not desire that widows be offered comfort only; God desires that they be provided with sustenance.

The needs of all widows, ancient and modern, evoke yet another Old Testament story, this one from 2 Kings 4:1–7. A newly widowed mother begs the prophet Elisha for help. She is reduced to a single jug of oil, and her husband's creditors are pressuring her to sell her children into slavery to pay his debts. Elisha tells her to borrow all the vessels she can from her neighbors and to pour oil into them from her jug. She immediately collects the vessels, and she and her children form an assembly line to fill them. The oil lasts until she runs out of vessels. Then she sells the oil, making enough to pay the debts and to put her household on a solid foundation.

Where are God's miracles of justice for the poor today? They most often lie, as in the story of the miraculous oil, in the marshalling of ordinary efforts to bring about extraordinary results. The miracle of the oil depended on the number of containers the woman borrowed, her neighbors' willingness to lend them, her family's work to fill the vessels, and her efforts to sell the oil. Who would have thought that a single donated vessel could do much good? Who, then, can dismiss as wasted effort the giving of a single rain poncho to a homeless man, on the basis that it does not solve the problem of homelessness? Who is to say that a word spoken in kindness may not bear extraordinary results? Small efforts joined together have built shelters, fed the hungry, changed laws.

Similarly, some may have laughed at the paltry contribution the poor widow made to the temple treasury. How much could two lepta affect the temple's overall financial picture? A day laborer earned as much in fifteen minutes. Some may have gone even further and denounced the woman's effort as *totally* wasted, shoring up, as it were, a decaying institution. Yet Jesus praises something about her action that goes beyond the money itself. Who, then, is to say that women who still form altar guilds and work on worship committees and teach Sunday school are wasting their time by serving flawed institutions?

The stories of widows thus take us in many directions. By reminding us that God, source of all power, nevertheless requires our oil and our work, they lead us to evaluate our stewardship of time and ability and money. The stories further remind us not to discount any contribution we are able to make as too insignificant to matter. And they remind us to persevere in working toward reformation of laws and institutions, for the way a society treats its weakest members serves as an accurate gauge of its moral fibre.

❖ ❖

Of the many ways in which the Bible makes it clear that Christianity arose as a strand within Judaism, concern for the dispossessed is among the clearest. The widow of Nain and the poor widow may have known and drawn strength from Yahweh's words, and they may later have pondered similar words spoken by Jesus. God speaks today in those same words:

Prayer

*Yahweh:*This is the fasting I want from you:
     releasing those bound unjustly,
     untying the thongs of the yoke;
     setting free the oppressed, breaking every yoke;
     sharing your bread with the hungry,
     sheltering the oppressed and the homeless;
     clothing the naked when you see them,
     and not turning your back on your own.
     Then shall your light break forth like the dawn,
     and your own wounds quickly be healed.

Jesus: When I come in glory I will say to you,
          Come, you blessed ones.
          Inherit the kingdom prepared for you
          from the foundation of the world.
          For I was hungry and you gave me drink,
          a stranger and you welcomed me,
          naked and you clothed me,
          ill and you cared for me,
          in prison and you visited me.
          Whatever you did for one of my
          least brothers and sisters,
          you did it for me.[4]

Connections

1. What similarities do you perceive between the fate of biblical widows and widows of today? What differences do you notice?

2. A phrase often heard is "the feminization of poverty." Why does poverty continue to be a state more often suffered by women and children than by men? How can a woman help herself?

3. Consider the case of the poor widow who gives her all to a male-dominated religious institution and receives no obvious recompense. Why might she have found it important to support the temple? Why do women still support religious institutions that may fail to treat them well?

For Further Reading

Countryman, L. William, *Dirt, Greed, and Sex* (1988), 226.

Deen, Edith, *All of the Women of the Bible* (1955), 351–53.

Moloney, Francis J., *Woman: First Among the Faithful* (1986), 24, 66–67.

Telushkin, Joseph, *Jewish Literacy* (1991), 503–4.

Tetlow, Elizabeth M., *Women and Ministry in the New Testament* (1980), 95–96, 105.

Thurston, Bonnie Bowman, *The Widows* (1989), 7–17, 21–44.

Winter, Miriam Therese, *WomanWisdom* (1991), 248–51, 313–21.

Yamasaki, April, *Remember Lot's Wife* (1991), 37–40, 73–74, 79–80.

4. Based on Isa 58:6–8 and Mt 25:31, 34–36,40.

28 The Trapped Adulterer: A Woman None Dare Condemn

John 7:53–8:11

"Neither do I condemn you."

Background

The story of "the *woman* caught in adultery" strikes many readers as absurd: by definition, adultery takes two. As religious writer Rachel Conrad Wahlberg observes, "To 'catch' one person is like saying one person was caught playing tennis."[1] The story was absurd within its own cultural setting as well, since Lev 20:10 and Deut 22:22–23 assigned the death penalty to *both* parties in cases of adultery. Given the risk of pregnancy, however, a woman was more likely to be caught—and punished—than a man. Adultery was defined as a man's having intercourse with a woman betrothed or married to another man, or, conversely, as a betrothed or married woman's having intercourse with any man other than her husband. Like all regulations concerning unlawful intercourse, adultery law rested on economic concepts. It required execution of the man as a thief who had stolen or depreciated a woman who was another man's property, and execution of the woman as irreparably damaged goods.

Stoning was the usual form of execution prescribed in Leviticus and Deuteronomy, but lesser punishments seem to have been the norm. The man seems either to have suffered a beating or paid the wronged husband a fine (Prov 6:32–35). The woman seems to have been quietly divorced by her husband (Jer 3:8, Mt 1:19), or divorced after having been stripped and paraded in front of her children, her lover, and the community (Hos 2:3, 10; Jer 13:26; Ezek 16:36–39, 23:29). The story of the woman caught in adultery offers no proof that the death penalty was ever enforced, but it does demonstrate that women, at least, could still be threatened with death in the first century of the Common Era.[2]

By bringing to Jesus the woman alone, the scribes and Pharisees were nonetheless disregarding the letter of the Law to which they had dedicated

---

1. *Jesus According to a Woman* (1990), 19.

2. Other Jewish writings do, however, report the burning to death of an adulterous woman c. 62 CE, as prescribed in Lev 21:9 for the daughter of a priest.—*Mishnah Sanhedrin 7, 3*, cited in Swidler, *Biblical Affirmations of Woman* (1979), 142–43.

their lives. But then, neither morality nor law was the true concern of these particular men. According to Jn 18:31, the Romans had denied Jews the right to exact the death penalty even when their own law required it. The woman's accusers therefore hoped to trap Jesus into speaking against either the law of Israel or that of Rome. Jesus, however, sidestepped the legal issues and concerned himself with human beings. By implication, he asked the scribes and Pharisees to hold themselves to the same standard they wished to apply to woman when he asked that the man without sin cast the first stone. Then he waited, writing on the ground, until all of the accusers departed, leaving the woman behind.

Jesus' allusion to the right to cast the first stone demonstrates his awareness of the nuances of Hebrew law. Deut 17:6–7 asserts that no one must be put to death on the testimony of a single witness, and that the witnesses must throw the first stones. As for why Jesus writes on the ground, no one is sure. Commentators of the first few centuries CE believed he was imputing guilt to the accusers—men well versed in the Hebrew scriptures—by giving them a visual reminder of Jer 17:13, "Those who forsake [God] will be inscribed in the dust, for they have rejected [Yahweh]." Others have suggested that he was writing down the accusers' sins.

The story is, in some ways, a subversive one, and that fact may explain why it occupied no fixed place in gospel manuscripts until the third century CE The story is subversive in that it depicts Jesus as calmly forgiving a sin considered unpardonable by a patriarchal society—the sin of a woman's acting as if she were as free as a man, sexually and economically. What would happen to society if wives were allowed to act like husbands? What would happen if other judges felt free to dismiss legitimate indictments? Yet the tale remained well-loved in the early church, and its survival suggests that it may reflect not a parable, but an actual event in the life of Jesus.

Because of the story's late inclusion in Gospel manuscripts, its placement varied. Sometimes it appeared in Luke. Placement there was appropriate because Luke, like the writer of this story, depicts Jesus as praying on the Mount of Olives and teaching in the temple. But the story was most often inserted after the seventh chapter of John. There it anticipates Jn 8:15, "You judge by worldly standards; I pass judgment on no one."

The Story of the Trapped Adulterer as Told in John

A Paraphrase of Jn 7:53–8:11

The crowd Jesus is teaching goes home, and he retires to the Mount of Olives. At daybreak he returns to the temple, and the people again gather around him. He has taken his seat and is engaged in teaching when the scribes and Pharisees bring in a woman caught committing adultery. Making her stand in the middle, they say to him, "Teacher, this woman was caught in the very act of adultery. In the law Moses has laid down that such women are to be stoned. What do you say about it?" They are posing the question as a test, hoping that his answer will enable them to frame a charge against him.

Jesus bends down and begins to write on the ground with his finger. When the accusers continue to press their question, he sits up straight and says, "Let whichever of you is free from sin throw the first stone at her." Again he bends down and writes on the ground. Hearing what Jesus said, the accusers slip away one by one, beginning with the elders. Jesus is left alone with the woman standing before him. He sits up and asks her, "Where are they? Has no one condemned you?" She answers, "No one, sir." "Neither do I condemn you," he says. "Go; do not sin again."

Reflection

Imagine a quiet morning in Jerusalem. Dawn has broken; the city is beginning to stir. In recent weeks the Jewish authorities have begun to harass Jesus, whom they perceive as a threat. But in the early morning, people can still gather unmolested to hear him teach in an area of the temple grounds accessible both to women and to men. This day the peace is shattered, first by raucous voices shouting for blood and then by a bustling band of scribes and Pharisees who drag to the feet of Jesus a frightened, disheveled woman. They present her in grim triumph: "We caught her in the very act of adultery! What do you have to say about that?"

One wonders about the man in whose house the requisite number of male witnesses had been lurking. Was the householder the adulterer? Was the adulterer someone paid to tackle and rape a woman chosen at random? Was the adulterer a petty criminal blackmailed into helping to set the trap in exchange for the quiet dropping of charges against him? Was he a man of substance who had long conducted what he believed to be a discreet affair? One wonders, too, about the woman. Had she been innocently going to the well for water? Was she so stunned and shamed by sudden assault that she held her silence instead of shouting for help as the law prescribed? Was she a woman so battered by life that she believed she loved any man who welcomed her to his bed? Was she a willing participant in either a one-night stand or a long-term affair?

Whoever the man and the woman were, and whatever their relationship or lack of one was, the hidden officials must nearly have chortled aloud at the brilliance of their trap for that champion of women, that rabble-rouser, that Jesus. Pruriently they peered from behind a curtain; callously they shattered the most intimate moment of intercourse with rough, grasping hands and voices raised in savage, righteous wrath. By the time they had hauled the woman all the way to the temple they had attracted a crowd, for mobs have always succumbed to the delicious delight of hurling abuse at someone *else* guilty of scandalous behavior, someone else *caught* doing wrong.

The woman herself maintains a resigned silence. She knows that she possesses no defense; legally, "mitigating circumstances" simply do not exist. Her accusers may merely intend to use her as an object of debate, but she braces herself for physical pain. Battered women of today can imagine the barbarity she dreads, the impact of stone on face and breasts and limbs, shattering bone and making her body run with blood.

Imagine her relief when nothing happens. Jesus bends down, but not to pick up a stone. Sinners neither threaten nor shock him; they challenge his ability to lead them to deeper self-awareness. From the depths of his own wholeness, he finds a way to reach both the calculating men and the woman they have victimized. To Jesus, the men are as guilty of sin as she is, and the woman herself is no object, but a valuable human being. He condemns neither the men nor the woman—she has been shamed enough—but neither does he condone sin. He forgives her and directs her to change her ways. The very fact of such total acceptance by the one sinless man in the whole crowd may have been all she needed to transform her life.

❖ ❖

Christian preachers have long focused on one line from this story: "Sin no more." They miss the words "Neither do I condemn you." Official Christianity seems unable to believe that Jesus did not consider sexual transgressions the most heinous of sins; official Christianity finds such an attitude too permissive—for women, anyway; no one comments on Jesus' dismissal of the lascivious men. Yet surely the attitude of a God who passionately courts people just as the prophet Hosea pursued and forgave his faithless wife is better represented by Jesus than by churchmen obsessed with cataloging every possible nuance of illicit intercourse.

Nor do people in general find it any easier than their religious leaders to live Jesus' message, stated more broadly in his words, "Stop judging, that you may not be judged" (Mt 7:1). Many working and middle-class people find it easy to condemn all recipients of public assistance. Many of the poor and those with modest incomes believe that all who are rich ought to be relieved of their money. Members of one racial group condemn members of another on the basis of sheer stereotypes.

And women of all social classes and ethnic backgrounds still find themselves fighting a male-female double standard. Employed women must be twice as competent as men to be considered for the same promotions. The American Association of University Women cites "compelling evidence that girls are not receiving the same quality, or even quantity, of education as their brothers."[3] Prostitutes are harassed while the men who hire them go free.

3. Richard N. Ostling, "Is School Unfair to Girls?," *Time*, 24 February 1992, 62.

Women victimized by sexual assault find themselves raped again, *their* lives dissected, in court. According to the Senate Judiciary Committee (June 1990), between three and four million American women are beaten each year, one million severely enough to seek medical help; and more than half of all homeless women are fleeing domestic violence.[4]

Given these conditions in a supposedly developed nation, any woman can find her heart resonating with that of the woman caught in adultery. As she stood in the temple precincts dumb with terror, she might have prayed:

Prayer

O God, rebuke me not in your anger
nor chastise me in your wrath.
I confess my iniquity; I am sorry for my sin,
but be gracious to me, for I am weak.
Reach from on high to defend me;
deliver me from those who hate me.
They came upon me when I was down,
but you are my support.
Save my life for the sake of your steadfast love.

I stand dumb and silent, I refrain from speech,
but my heart throbs violently within me.
Trembling assails me, terror of death overwhelms me.
Oh God, rescue me!
I have slipped into deep water; waves pound over me.
I wallow in quicksand with no foothold for safety.
The very hairs of my head seem fewer
than the number of those who revile me.
Holy One, you know I have been a fool;
I cannot hide my faults from you.
But in your abundant love, rescue me from this swamp;
let me sink no further. O God, do not delay![5]

Connections

1. This woman's story may be about forgiveness, but it is also about justice. How does it proclaim a word of hope for all who are victims of discrimination?

Hope lies

4. Katha Pollitt, "Georgie Porgie Is a Bully," *Time* (Fall 1990 Special Issue, "Women: The Road Ahead"), 24.

5. Based on Ps 6, 38, 39, and 69.

2. Imagine yourself writing a sermon based on this story. What would you title it? What points would you make?

3. How can women and men work for the elimination of sexual harassment and other forms of the sexual double standard?

For Further Reading

Deen, Edith, *All of the Women of the Bible* (1955), 373.

Eisler, Riane, *The Chalice and the Blade* (1987), 97.

Greeley, Andrew M. and Jacob Neusner, *The Bible and Us* (1990), 154–55, 184–85.

Lefebure, Leo, *Life Transformed* (Chicago: ACTA Publications, 1989), 103–4.

Mollenkott, Virginia Ramey, *Women, Men, and the Bible* (1988), 6–10.

Moloney, Francis J., *Woman: First Among the Faithful* (1986), 25–26.

Nunnally-Cox, Janice, *Foremothers* (1981), 111–13.

Wahlberg, Rachel Conrad, *Jesus According to a Woman* (1975), 19–26.

Winter, Miriam Therese, *WomanWord* (1990), 48–50.

Yamasaki, April, *Remember Lot's Wife* (1991), 99–100.

29 The Samaritan Woman at the Well: Missionary

John 4:4–42

Many come to believe because of her word.

Background

The story of the woman at the well, found only in the Gospel of John, contains the longest conversation on record between Jesus and anyone—and the person so honored is a non-Jew and a woman. Traveling from Judea to Galilee, Jesus chooses the direct route through Samaria, even though most Jews detoured to the route along the far bank of the Jordan. In the noonday heat, he rests at Jacob's well. The well lies near Mount Gerizim, the focal point of Samaritan worship. While the disciples go into town to buy food, Jesus violates custom not only by speaking with a woman in public, but also by asking to share the drinking jug of an "unclean" Samaritan. The woman questions these breaches of custom, and by the time the disciples return, the ensuing theological debate has culminated in Jesus' proclamation of himself as Messiah. The woman then evangelizes her entire town, leading many to believe in him.

The story reflects tensions between Jews and Samaritans that extended centuries into the past. In the era of the divided kingdoms, Samaria was the name of the capital city of the northern kingdom, Israel. Samaria and other cities were destroyed when Assyria conquered Israel in 722 BCE and exiled most of its people into Assyria and Mesopotamia (today's Syria and Iraq). According to 2 Kings 17:24–25, the conquerors then transported ethnically varied settlers into Israel. Because these settlers sought to know the god of the Israelites who had escaped deportation, an Israelite priest was sent back from Babylon to instruct them in worship of Yahweh. The intermixed population of aliens and Israelites became known as Samaritans. They came to view themselves, not the Jews to the south, as the true preservers of the Torah. They focussed especially on Deut 11:26–29 and 18:15–20, passages that proclaimed a blessing on Mount Gerizim and promised the coming of a Messiah who would be a prophet like Moses.

Meanwhile, in 586 BCE, the kingdom to the south—Judah—suffered conquest by Babylonia. When Jewish exiles began returning to Jerusalem a few decades later, the Samaritans offered to help rebuild their temple and join them in worship. The offer was rebuffed, setting in train centuries of antagonism marked by recurrent bloodshed and acts of vandalism. Under Alexander the Great, the Samaritans were allowed to build their own temple on the peak of Mount Gerizim, and to rebuild the city of Shechem at its base (c. 350 BCE). Mount Gerizim rivaled Jerusalem as a sanctuary of Yahweh by the time the throne of Judah was assumed by John Hyrcanus (c. 175–104 BCE)—a Maccabean king who nurtured an especially virulent hatred of Samaria. At his command, Jewish forces marched on Mount Gerizim and destroyed both town and temple.[1] By Jesus' time, only the village of Sychar occupied the site, and Jews regularly denounced Samaritans as "menstruants from the cradle"—that is, as ritually unclean from birth.

Against the backdrop of this history, the author of the fourth Gospel presents a story that can almost be described as romantic, evoking, as it does, the courtships of Rebekah and Rachel that occurred at a well like the one where Jesus and the Samaritan woman converse. Theologically, these "well stories" recount the meetings of future spouses who then play an important role in salvation history. In the story of Jesus and the Samaritan woman, he is the Bridegroom of Israel, and she represents Samaria as an integral part of the renewed Israel, the Christian community.

Some scholars question whether the conversation ever occurred. No other Gospel reports Jesus' having converted a Samaritan town, and the earliest Gospel—Mark—never mentions Samaria. Luke does tell the parable of the Good Samaritan (10:29–37), and he mentions a Samaritan leper who returns to give thanks (17:11–19). But Luke also reports that Jesus and his disciples turned away from a hostile Samaritan village (9:51–56), and Matthew quotes Jesus as directing the Twelve, on their first mission, to avoid Samaritan towns (10:5–6).

Whether or not the incident actually occurred, it represents the strong belief of the Johannine community in the validity of the Samaritan faith tradition. By the time the story was included in the fourth Gospel, it was presented in a way that combines characteristic attitudes and actions of Jesus with the atmosphere of later events such as those recorded in Acts 8–9. Acts 8:4–8 reports the warm reception Philip receives on a mission to Samaria; Acts 8:14–15 reports confirmation of Philip's work by Peter and John; and Acts 9:31 states that the church is growing peacefully throughout Judea, Galilee, and Samaria. Language such as Jesus' harvest dialogue with his disciples is also more appropriate to reflections from later times on the manner in which faith develops; and the townspeople hail Jesus as "savior," a non-Jewish usage of the first century CE applied to deities and kings. (The title "savior of the world," used specifically of the Roman emperor, became a common title for Jesus only late in the first century.)

Specific language choices within the story demonstrate the esteem the Johannine community rendered its women leaders, an esteem evident also in

---

1. Excavations since 1984 show that up to 10,000 people may have lived in Shechem before Hyrcanus leveled it.

the Johannine conversation between Jesus and Martha (Jn 11:20–27). The Samaritan woman's true missionary status is established by Jesus' implication that the technical verb "I send you" (*apostellein*) applies to her as well as to male disciples; the writer also says that the townspeople believe "through her word." This phrase recurs in Jesus' prayer for the disciples gathered at the last supper: "I pray not only for them, but also for those who will believe in me through their word" (17:20, NAB).

Whatever its origins, the story is beautifully constructed. The first long scene presents a dramatic debate in which the Samaritan woman moves from awareness of Jesus as a Jewish male to acceptance of him as "I Am"—a Messiah identified with Yahweh. In scene two the woman evangelizes her people while Jesus discusses missionary work with his disciples. In scene three an entire town experiences Jesus as savior. Further, by its placement within the Gospel of John, the story belongs to a series that illuminates stages of faith and the spread of the gospel. The stages encompassed are the unconditional faith of Mary at the wedding in Cana; the active disbelief of hostile listeners in Jerusalem; the hesitant initial queries of Nicodemus, a prominent Jew; the gradual illumination of the Samaritan woman; and, finally, another example of unconditional faith, the Gentile royal official from Cana. The story of the Samaritan woman is of special note in that, by itself, it recapitulates an entire journey in faith. For this reason, in churches where different cycles of readings are proclaimed over a three-year period, communities that include catechumens proclaim the story of Jesus and the Samaritan woman every year.

The Story of the Samaritan Woman at the Well as Told in John

A Paraphrase of Jn 4:4–42

As Jesus is passing through Samaria, he comes to the site of Jacob's well. In the noon heat, Jesus is tired and thirsty. He sits down beside the well while his disciples go into the village of Sychar to buy food. When a Samaritan woman comes to draw water, Jesus asks her for a drink. She reminds him that Jewish men neither speak with women nor share utensils with Samaritans. Jesus replies, "If only you knew what God gives, and who is asking you for a drink, you would have asked him and he would have given you living water." The woman points out that the well is deep, and Jesus does not even have a bucket. "So where can you get 'living water'? Are you greater than Jacob, our ancestor, who gave us the well and drank from it?" Jesus replies that the water he offers will cancel all thirst; it will become a spring of inner water, welling up into eternal life. The woman responds, "Sir, give me this water, and then I shall not be thirsty, nor have to come all this way to draw water."

"Go and call your husband," Jesus says, "and come back here." She replies that she has no husband, and Jesus says she is right: she has had five husbands, and her current partner is not her husband. His knowledge leads the woman to recognize Jesus as a prophet, and she initiates a theological discussion about the proper place to worship: Is it the Samaritans' Mount Gerizim, or the Jews' temple in Jerusalem? Jesus replies that a time is coming—indeed, is already at hand—when people will worship in neither place, but "in spirit and in truth." The woman cautiously responds, "I know that the Messiah is coming. When he comes he will make everything clear to us." Jesus replies, "I am he, I who am speaking to you."

At this point the disciples return. Although they are shocked to find Jesus talking with a woman, no one challenges either of them. The woman leaves her water jar behind and hurries into the town to invite everyone to come and meet a man "who has told me everything I ever did. Could this be the Messiah?" The disciples, meanwhile, urge Jesus to eat. He tells them that for him "it is meat and drink" to do the will of the One who sent him. "Look around at the fields," he says; "they are already white, ripe for harvesting. I sent you to reap a crop for which you have not labored. Others labored and you have come in for the harvest of their labor."

Then the Samaritans of that town, many of whom have already come to believe in Jesus on the basis of the woman's word, approach Jesus. They press him to remain with them, and he stays for two days. Many more come to believe in him because of his own word, and they tell the woman that their faith no longer depends on her. "We have heard him ourselves, and we are convinced that he is the savior of the world."

Reflection

In the highly symbolic fourth Gospel, both Jesus and the woman emerge as more human than usual. Jesus is tired enough to rest at a well, thirsty enough to share a Samaritan's drinking cup. The woman is skeptical, intelligent, irrepressible. Though alienated from Jesus by race, gender, and life style, she cannot easily be pressed into service or conformity. Neither she nor Jesus shows any hesitation; at times they seem amused or even flirtatious. She delights in him; he openly enjoys teaching her.

Only three of thirty-nine verses actually deal with the woman's questionable marriage, yet some readers of the story make much of her dubious past—as if repentance, not evangelization, were the theme of the story. Focusing on the woman as disreputable strays from the overall context of the story—its use of the "courtship" motif to evoke God's century-long wooing of chosen people. In context, the discussion of husbands serves as a reminder of the way the prophets had repeatedly used sexual metaphors to describe true and false worship.[2] The woman herself immediately recognizes Jesus' declaration that she—

2. See the discussion of whoring after false gods in chapter 10, Rahab, page 87.

Samaria—currently has "no husband" not as a call to repentance, but as a call to true worship. In other words, the exchange about husbands is not biographical, but a highly symbolic element within the theological discussion.

Even if the exchange is taken literally, however, it is clear that the woman's faith and the known reliability of her word matter far more than her past. Such a view is presented by Teresa of Avila, a sixteenth-century Spanish mystic who was declared a doctor of the Catholic Church in 1970:

> Indeed she was very humble because when the Lord told her faults to her she didn't become offended (as the world does now, for the truth is hard to bear), but she told Him that He must be a prophet. In sum, the people believed her; and a large crowd, on her word alone, went out of the city to meet the Lord.[3]

Similarly, sixteenth-century Reform theologian John Calvin notes in his *Commentaries* that the woman's "earnestness and promptitude" merit attention; "scarcely had she tasted Christ when she spread his fame throughout the whole city."[4]

In the end, what matters is that Jesus respects a Samaritan woman enough to fill her with the living water of faith. What matters, that is to say, is what scriptural theologian Sandra Schneiders calls the "astonishing, even shocking, inclusiveness" of Jesus' covenant.[5] When God's kingdom breaks into the world, the most despised are welcome, and a messy personal life bars no one from spreading the gospel. The Samaritan woman does not wait for education or ordination; she does not sit back while her community establishes a committee to evaluate the degree of local need. She simply drops her jar and begins to preach the *euangelion*, the "good news" of Jesus. As religious writer Rachel Conrad Wahlberg puts it, "Her culturally assigned status gave way to her Jesus-assigned status—one who is worthy to go and tell."[6]

❖ ❖

The woman of Samaria is a good model for all believers. Though she belongs to no establishment, she neither apologizes for herself nor goes about with downcast eyes. In her approach to Jesus, she implicitly asks the question pivotal to all spiritual growth: "Who *are* you, anyway?" Through his responses, Jesus slakes her thirst of spirit. Similar critical junctures—similar wells of meeting—occur in every life.

For women, however, the Samaritan woman is an especially potent model. It is impossible to believe that Jesus chose this bright, assertive messenger by

3. *The Collected Works of St. Teresa of Avila*, Vol. 2, translated by Kieran Kavanaugh and Otilio Rodriguez (Washington DC: ICS Publications, 1980), 258–59.

4. Quoted in Wahlberg, *Jesus According to a Woman* (1975), 90.

5. *The Revelatory Text* (1991), 196.

6. *Jesus According to a Woman*, 90.

chance, when he could so easily have chosen a man. Somehow, in spite of all the negatives of her situation, he saw in her exactly the person needed to bring the kingdom to Sychar. Would that Christian churches were equally quick to perceive women as people called to the same vocations as men.

❖ ❖

As the woman of Samaria trudged to the well that day, attempting to conserve her energy in the heat, perhaps she glanced up at Mount Gerizim and wished for the restoration of its temple. As she shaded her eyes and made out in the distance the distinctive garb of a Jewish man, perhaps an entire history of hostile encounters flashed through her mind. Surely she anticipated the pleasure of descending the long cool steps down into the earth to the well itself, in order that its bubbling waters might slake a thirst she could not fully define. Perhaps she prayed:

Prayer

How lovely was your dwelling place, O Lord of hosts!
As a deer longs for flowing waters, so my soul yearns for your courts.
Even the sparrow finds a home, and the swallow a nest for her young—
your altars, my savior and my God!
Happy were those who dwelt in your service, singing your praise;
happy, even now, those whose hearts are set upon pilgrimage.
They go from strength to strength as they seek you
on your holy mountain.
When they pass through the heat-baked valley,
you make a spring of it.

I know that when your Messiah comes,
justice will well up from the earth.
Deserts will burst with streams, the wilderness with rivers.
Burning sands will become pools; thirsty ground, springs;
and we will flourish in your sight.

Yet within me my soul is downcast:
steadfastness renew within me.
As deep calls unto deep in the roar of your cataracts,
so let your breakers and billows gush over me.
Immerse me that I may spring to new life in your presence.
Hear my prayer, O God of hosts; hearken, God of Jacob!
Let me see the face of your anointed;
let my mouth proclaim his praise.[7]

7. Based on Isa 35:5–7 and on verses from Ps 42, 51, 84, and 85.

Connections

1. Imagine that you are the woman of this story. How would you feel when a man from a social group that despised your people approached you as an equal? How would you interpret his offer of "living water"?

2. Everyone seeks to quench inner longings. But the waters chosen—alcohol, drugs, shopping, clothes, relationships—may fail to satisfy. What things have you found insufficient to satisfy your thirst?

3. The Samaritan woman leaves her jar behind in order to go and spread word about Jesus. What must you set aside in order to reach a deeper level of commitment in some area of your life?

4. Jesus recognized and touched a dream hidden deep within the heart of the Samaritan woman. What dream within you awaits recognition and release?

For Further Reading

Carmody, Denise Larder, *Biblical Woman* (1989), 102–7.

Crown, Alan D., "The Abisha Scroll—3,000 Years Old?" *Bible Review* 7, no. 5 (October 1991): 13–21, 39.

Dunning, James B., "Scrutinizing the Samaritan Woman," *Catechumenate* (January 1993), 27–30.

Moloney, Francis J., *Woman: First Among the Faithful* (1986), 84–86.

Nunnally-Cox, Janice, *Foremothers* (1981), 109–11.

Pummer, Reinhard, "The Samaritans—A Jewish Offshoot or a Pagan Cult?" *Bible Review* 7, no. 5 (October 1991): 22–29, 40.

Schneiders, Sandra M., *The Revelatory Text* (1991), 180–199.

Sleevi, Mary Lou, *Women of the Word* (1985), 45–48.

Tetlow, Elizabeth M., *Women and Ministry in the New Testament* (1980), 111.

Wahlberg, Rachel Conrad, *Jesus According to a Woman* (1975), 85–97.

Yamasaki, April, *Remember Lot's Wife* (1991), 97–98.

30 Martha and Mary: Friends of Jesus

Luke 10:38–42; John 11:1–45, 12:1–8

"... he loved Martha and her sister ..."

Background

Three stories of Martha and Mary appear in the Gospels—one in Luke, two in John. Although Luke places the sisters in a village near Jericho, along the route from Galilee to Jerusalem, tradition follows the other Gospels in identifying the village of Martha, Mary, and Lazarus as Bethany (today's El-Azarieh), located on the southeastern slope of the Mount of Olives near Jerusalem. In Luke's story, Martha complains about Mary's sitting at Jesus' feet rather than helping with the cooking. Jesus chides her and commends Mary. In the first of John's two stories, Martha and Mary summon Jesus because their brother Lazarus is ill. All three siblings are identified as known friends of Jesus. Finding Lazarus dead on his arrival, Jesus converses with each of the sisters and then restores their brother to life. In John's second story, Jesus and Lazarus attend a dinner, during which Martha serves; and Mary anoints Jesus' feet with nard and dries them with her hair.

Mark and Matthew indirectly confirm Jesus' friendship with the family by reporting that he spends his nights in Bethany the week before his death, but no Gospel mentions the parents of Martha, Mary, and Lazarus. Since the three appear to practice no trade, yet can afford luxuries like imported nard, scholars speculate that their parents died and left them a sizeable inheritance. Because no spouses are mentioned either, it is thought that Lazarus and Mary may have been in their early teens, not yet betrothed to anyone. Martha—in keeping with a name derived from the Aramaic *martā*, "lady" or "mistress"—appears to manage the estate and to be the oldest.

Both Luke and John present Jesus, the other major character of the stories, as a self-confident man who feels no need to enforce the strictest gender-role customs of his time. He spends time alone with women who are not his relatives, allows women intellectual discourse with a religious teacher, and ignores the fact that women are not supposed to serve men at table or even to enter the dining area.[1]

As for the sisters, Luke depicts them as one-dimensional—the active Martha, the passive Mary. John develops richer characterizations. In the

---

1. Only male slaves tended the needs of the reclining male guests. They sometimes also served their master by letting him wipe his greasy hands in their hair.

Lazarus story, John's Martha possesses a mature, well-integrated personality that balances activism with spiritual perception. In the anointing story, John's Mary demonstrates her spiritual richness in action by anointing Jesus' feet with nard and drying them with her hair.

The stories of both writers contain reminders that the Gospels were written on at least two levels. In presenting events of Jesus' life, they also comment on practices of the early church. Both Luke and John knew a Christianity in which women as well as men functioned as deacons, eucharistic presiders, and preachers of the gospel. Writing c. 80–85 CE, Luke ministered to Hellenistic Christians in whose culture women enjoyed greater autonomy than within Judaism. His church would have been unimaginable without wealthy women who hosted the comradeship of the eucharistic table in their homes. But Luke rarely depicts women as proclaiming the gospel, and his picture of Jesus rebuking Martha while affirming the silent Mary may reflect the bias of some Christian men, themselves indoctrinated from birth in male-dominant attitudes, toward subordinating women despite the example of Jesus.

By the time the Gospel of John was written (c. 100 CE), the trend hinted at in Luke—the limiting of official roles to men—had strengthened. But in contrast with Luke, the Gospel of John strongly reasserts Jesus' treatment of women as equal with men. In the anointing story, set on a Sunday (the day of eucharistic celebration in the early church), Mary becomes the active heroine and Martha "serves." "Serves" is a form of the Greek *diakonein*, the technical term of the early church for the service of deacons. Even more significantly, in the Lazarus story the author places on Martha's lips a profession of faith in Jesus as Messiah that Mk 8:29 assigns to Peter—and Peter's is a profession of faith to which Popes still relate his primacy, and their own. For the Johannine community, Martha is thus identified as holding no less than apostolic authority.

Ancient tradition places both Martha and Mary at the cross of Jesus, and sometimes also in the Garden of Gethsemane. As late as the fifteenth century, in a painting by Fra Angelico, Jesus prays while his men sleep. But the alert Mary reads a book and the watchful Martha prays, like Jesus, with hands uplifted. Other medieval art confused Mary of Bethany with Mary Magdalene,[2] but expanded Martha's identity to mythic proportions. She was often depicted as *magna mater*, a great mother whose outstretched cloak variously sheltered groups of monks or children, or whole churches. And she was repeatedly portrayed, in the paintings, statues, and stained glass windows

---

2. Confusion arose because many New Testament women are called Mary and because all four Gospels relate an anointing story. Luke's anonymous anointer became identified with Mary Magdalene, and it took but one more step to confuse Luke's Mary Magdalene with John's Mary of Bethany.

of the churches of Switzerland, France, and Italy, as the tamer of a dragon—sometimes a literal river monster; always the figurative equivalent of the ancient serpent who caused such grief in the traditions of patriarchal cultures.

The Story of Martha and Mary as Told in Luke and John

A Paraphrase of Lk 10:38–42

Jesus and his followers come to a village where a woman named Martha welcomes them. She has a sister, Mary, who seats herself at Jesus' feet and stays there listening to his words. Distracted by her many tasks, Martha complains to Jesus, "Lord, do you not care that my sister has left me to get on with the work by myself? Tell her to come and give me a hand." He answers, "Martha, Martha, you are fretting and fussing about so many things; only one thing is necessary. Mary has chosen what is best; it shall not be taken away from her."

A Paraphrase of Jn 11:1–45 and 12:1–8

A man named Lazarus falls ill. He lives in Bethany with his sisters, Mary and Martha. The sisters send a message to Jesus: "Sir, you should know that your friend lies ill." Hearing this, Jesus remarks to his disciples, "This illness is not to end in death; through it God's glory is to be revealed and the Son of God glorified." Therefore, though he loves Martha and Mary and Lazarus, he stays where he is on the other side of the Jordan for two more days. Then he says to his followers, "Let us go back to Judea. . . . Our friend Lazarus has fallen asleep, but I shall go and wake him." Thinking Jesus is referring to natural sleep, the disciples respond, "Master, if he is sleeping he will recover." Jesus then speaks plainly. "Lazarus is dead. I am glad for your sake that I was not there; for it will lead you to believe. But let us go to him."

On arriving near Bethany, Jesus learns that Lazarus has already been in the tomb four days. The village is not far from Jerusalem—just under two miles—and many people have come out from the city to console Martha and Mary. When Martha hears that Jesus is on his way, she goes out to meet him, leaving Mary at home. Martha says to him, "Lord, if you had been here my brother would not have died. Even now I know that God will grant you whatever you ask of him." Jesus responds, "Your brother will rise again." "I know that he will rise again," Martha says, "at the resurrection on the last day." Jesus replies, "I am the resurrection and the life. Whoever has faith in me shall live, even though [that one] dies; and no one who lives and has faith in me shall ever die. Do you believe this?" "I do, Lord," Martha says; "I believe that you are the Messiah, the Son of God who was to come into the world."

After saying this, Martha goes to her sister Mary, takes her aside and tells her, "The Master is here and is asking for you." Mary immediately gets up and goes out to him, for Jesus has not yet entered the village, but has remained at the place where Martha met him. The comforters see Mary leave and follow her, assuming she is going to the tomb to weep there. When Mary reaches Jesus, she falls at his feet and says, "Lord, if you had been here my brother would not have died." She is weeping. When Jesus sees her tears and those of the other mourners, he is deeply distressed. "Where have you laid him?" he asks. They reply, "Come and see." Jesus, too, begins to weep. This causes some to remark, "How dearly he must have loved him!" But others say, "Could not this man, who opened the blind man's eyes, have done something to keep Lazarus from dying?"

Again deeply moved, Jesus approaches the tomb. It is a cave with a stone placed against it. "Take away the stone," he says. Martha objects. "Sir, by now there will be a stench; he has been there four days." Jesus says to her, "Did I not tell you that if you have faith you will see the glory of God?" Then they remove the stone. Though Jesus knows that God always hears him, he looks upward and prays aloud for the sake of the crowd. Then he lifts his voice in a great cry: "Lazarus, come out!" The dead man comes out, his hands and feet bound with linen strips and his head wrapped in a cloth. "Loose him; let him go," Jesus says. This event causes many of the people who had come to visit Martha and Mary, and who saw what Jesus did, to put their faith in him.

❖ ❖

Six days before the Passover festival, Jesus comes to Bethany to the home of Lazarus, the man he raised from death. A supper is given in Jesus' honor. Martha serves, and Lazarus is among the guests. Then Mary brings in a pound of costly perfume, pure oil of nard. She anoints Jesus' feet and wipes them with her hair, and the whole house is filled with the fragrance. At this, Judas Iscariot—the disciple who was to betray Jesus—protests. "Could not this perfume have been sold for three hundred denarii and the money given to the poor?"[3] Judas speaks not out of true concern for the poor, but because he manages the common purse and used to pilfer money from it. "Leave her alone," Jesus tells him. "Let her keep it for the day of my burial. The poor you have always among you, but you will not always have me."

Reflection

Relaxed human fellowship pervades these stories. Jesus is a man who eats and rests and weeps with his good friends of Bethany. The feeling of intimacy triumphs even over the crowds milling in the background. In Luke, Jesus arrives at Martha's house with his disciples in tow (perhaps a dozen men and

3. The silver denarius was a Roman coin. One denarius represented the daily wage of an unskilled laborer. Thus the imported nard or spikenard (derived from the roots of a plant grown in the mountains of northern India) is valued at nearly a year's wages.

an equal number of women); and John's stories are replete with mourners, neighbors, onlookers, and dinner guests. Yet in all of the tableaus, three figures glow: Jesus, Martha, and Mary.

In the Lazarus story, both sisters freely complain to Jesus, a freedom that must have arisen from many nights of friendly intimacy in which Jesus became both mentor and friend. Yet in Luke's story, the two women are poles apart in temperament. Luke's Mary expresses her love by lounging at Jesus' feet, while Martha expresses hers by chopping vegetables in the kitchen. Seeing Mary neglecting her usual share in the duties of hospitality, Martha turns not to Lazarus—even as a youngster, the male and thus the titular head of the family—but to her substitute big brother, Jesus. Jesus rebukes Martha, but perhaps his tone makes it clear that he objects not to necessary chores (someone must cook), but to obsession with them. Mary may feel smug at Jesus' commendation (someone must also pay attention to the guest), but perhaps remorse overcomes her when she catches sight of Martha's face. Since Luke never finishes the story, it is tempting to imagine that Jesus adjourns to the kitchen with both women, where all three can converse while three pairs of hands make light of the work.

In the Lazarus story, John adds a spiritual, questing dimension to Luke's portrait of Martha. The rules of hospitality called for awaiting a guest at one's home, but she rushes to meet Jesus on the road. Then she boldly initiates the conversation, even though, elsewhere in John, Jesus always speaks first. To this woman, this homemaker, Jesus reveals his mysterious identity. Well in advance of witnessing the raising of Lazarus, she responds by professing faith in him as Messiah—an insight Luke's story might have led us to expect of Mary. Martha then goes off to share her joy with Mary, like Andrew and Philip who called their brothers (Jn 1) and the Samaritan woman who recruited an entire town (Jn 4).

As for Mary, might not her Lucan "laziness" suggest an adolescent crush on Jesus? The fourteenth-century Dominican mystic, Meister Eckhart, theorizes that she sat before him for the sheer pleasure of his company. If so, why not? Did he not charm women by allowing them to touch him? Did he not speak to women without the slightest trace of condescension? But Mary has matured by the time Jesus attends a banquet with the revived Lazarus. Showing a sensitive insight into the increasing opposition of the authorities, she deduces both the dark future Jesus faces and his need for comfort. Abandoning her usual reserve, she makes a lavish gesture, and again Jesus says, "Let her be." Mary's intentions contrast sharply with those of the false disciple, Judas. He will soon betray Jesus for thirty pieces of silver, a price some estimate as equal to one-third the value of Mary's ointment. He may claim to know the value of money, but it is Mary and Jesus who recognize that the necessity of helping the poor does not cancel the human need for an occasional extravagance that fills a house—or a liturgy—with its fragrance.

❖ ❖

Considering the fullness of character John ascribes to both Martha and Mary, development of a destructive tradition based solely on Luke's stereotypes must originally have required concerted effort. But the effort succeeded. For centuries, Luke's story has been used to polarize women into no-win situations. "Marthas" have been criticized for their mundane busy-ness, while studious or professional "Marys" have been condemned for unnatural disregard of family or usurpation of male roles. Among Roman Catholics, single and married Marthas once felt stigmatized as worth less than the Marys who joined religious orders. Feminists of the 1970s succumbed to a similar polarization when they discounted home-making Marthas and elevated career Marys.

Today the stories challenge churches, especially, but also society as a whole to recall *both* Martha's and Mary's evident fitness for friendship with Jesus. Instead of affirming dichotomies, the stories present differences in personality as complementary. The friendship that both sisters found with Jesus also offers an image for prayer—an image not freighted with the issues of dominance that cloud metaphors of God as "master," "Lord," "father," or even "mother." The image of friendship is, in fact, Jesus' own choice for describing his relationship with his followers: "No longer do I call you servants. . . . I have called you friends" (Jn 15:15). With Mary, Martha, and Lazarus, women and men of today can therefore pray:

Prayer

> Jesus, brother and friend,
> before you came we squabbled like children,
> but you have taught us to set childish ways aside.
> Who now is brother, sister, mother, or father to us?
> Those who do the will of the One who sent you.
> You fill us not with the world's spirit,
> but with your Spirit,
> that we may recognize our different gifts
> as building one body in you.
> No eye has seen, no ear has heard,
> nor had it so much as dawned on us
> the sharing you had planned for those who love you.
> You are the way to God and the truth of who God is;
> you are resurrection and life.
> You live in us as we serve one another,
> exploring your word, sharing your cup,
> and breaking, in your name, the bread of friendship.
> May we celebrate you always until you return in glory![4]

4. Based on Lk 11:28, Jn 11:25 and 14:6, and verses from 1 Cor 2, 12, and 13.

Connections

1. How would you characterize Martha? Mary? How can you integrate the best qualities of both women within your own personality?

2. Even on the basis of Luke, Martha and Mary seem usually to have worked together. In the raising of Lazarus story, their friendship with each other is suggested by their smooth interplay—the ease with which they trade off the role of on-duty hostess. How can their relationship serve as a model for friendships among women of differing types and backgrounds?

3. As Martha once sought freedom from drudgery and Mary sought freedom for theology, what broader freedom do you seek?

4. Many Protestant denominations ordain women; some parts of Judaism admit women to the rabbinate. What are the pluses and minuses of ordaining women to clerical rank in denominations that do not yet ordain them?

For Further Reading

Carmody, Denise Lardner, *Biblical Woman* (1989), 108–13.

Deen, Edith, *All of the Women of the Bible* (1955), 176–81.

Greeley, Andrew M. and Jacob Neusner, *The Bible and Us* (1990), 204–7.

Kirk, Martha Ann, "A Story of Martha and the Women of the Early Church," *God of Our Mothers* (1985), audiocassette.

Mollenkott, Virginia Ramey, *Women, Men, and the Bible* (1988), 9.

Moloney, Francis J., *Woman: First Among the Faithful* (1986), 71–72, 87–90.

Moltmann-Wendel, Elisabeth, *The Women Around Jesus* (1987), 15–58.

Nunnally-Cox, Janice, *Foremothers* (1981), 105–6.

Schüssler Fiorenza, Elisabeth, *In Memory of Her* (1983), 165.

Sleevi, Mary Lou, *Women of the Word* (1989), 39–42, 57–60.

Tepedino, Ana Maria, "The Fruit of Passion and Compassion," in *With Passion and Compassion*, ed. Virginia Fabella and Mercy Amba Oduyoye (1988), 168–72.

Tetlow, Elizabeth M., *Women and Ministry in the New Testament* (1980), 104, 111–13.

Wahlberg, Rachel Conrad, *Jesus According to a Woman* (1986), 73–84.

Weems, Renita J., *Just a Sister Away* (1988), 39–50.

Winter, Miriam Therese, *WomanWord* (1990), 125–34.

31 The Woman Who Anointed Jesus: Herald of the Reign of God

Mark 14:1–9; Matthew 26:3–13; Luke 7:36–50; John 12:1–8

". . . what she has done will . . . be told in memory of her."

Background

All four Gospels speak of a woman who interrupts a private dinner to anoint Jesus with costly ointment. Setting the story at Passover time, Mark places the event within a section about the Jewish authorities' search for a way to destroy Jesus. When the woman anoints the head of Jesus, the male guests object to her extravagance, but Jesus praises her for recognizing his impending death and burial. Matthew's account—an abbreviation of Mark's—is sandwiched between the plotting of priests and Judas Iscariot's offer to turn Jesus over to them for a price. In both Mark and Matthew, Jesus declares that wherever the gospel spreads, the woman's action will be reported in memory of her.

John's and Luke's versions of the story appear to derive from somewhat different traditions. John identifies the house as that of Lazarus and the anointer as Lazarus' sister, Mary. She anoints Jesus' feet instead of his head, and Judas Iscariot is the one who objects to her wasteful use of nard. Luke alone of the four evangelists shifts the time to Jesus' earlier ministry in Galilee; Luke alone shifts the focus to repentance. Luke identifies his woman as a known sinner[1] who, like John's Mary, anoints the feet of Jesus. When the host, a Pharisee named Simon, wonders why Jesus allows such a woman to touch him, Jesus contrasts her attentions with Simon's lapses of hospitality. He tells the woman her sins are forgiven because of her great love,[2] and bids her go in peace.

In all four Gospels, the basic plot nevertheless remains the same: A woman anoints Jesus, male diners object, and Jesus praises her. Preservation of the story in varying traditions argues strongly for the actual occurrence of at least one anointing, and possibly as many as three: the one reported by

1. No basis exists for identifying her with Mary Magdalene, whom Luke introduces in the next chapter.

2. A problem in the Greek verb tense in Luke's story causes translations to vary. The original does not make clear whether the woman is forgiven because she loves much, or loves because she is forgiven much. Both interpretations work.

Mark and Matthew, the one reported by John, and the one reported by Luke. Because John's story (12:1–8) has already been presented in the chapter on Martha and Mary of Bethany, the rest of this chapter focuses on the account by Mark and Matthew (taking them as the same account) and the account by Luke.

Anointing carried various meanings in the cultures of biblical times. Hosts anointed guests and the wealthy used fragrant oils after bathing for purposes of refreshment. In lieu of embalming, bodies were anointed with aromatic oils before they were wrapped for burial. Mark's and Matthew's account more strongly reflects a third use of oil, its symbolic use to invest a man with power or consecrate him to a sacred purpose. Jews called their king "the Lord's anointed"—a phrase which developed into the Hebrew *Messiah* and the Greek *Christos*, meaning the king who would rule in the end times. While the woman who anointed Jesus understood that his kingship would entail suffering and death, her anointing of his head paralleled the anointing of the heads of Jewish kings by male Old Testament prophets. Mark's and Matthew's anointer thus acts prophetically: by her action, she acclaims Jesus as Messiah; she dares to choose the king.

In contrast, Luke's anointing story draws attention to the hospitable, refreshing purposes of anointing. Luke may have characterized his woman as a notorious sinner for any one of a number of reasons: because his Gospel stresses repentance as a major theme, because he wished deliberately to avoid treating a woman as bestower of a prophetic action, or because he was recording a different event. In the other versions of the story, no theme of sin or repentance obscures the woman's prophetic role. Yet Luke's describing her as a loving, repentant sinner actually serves to complement Mark's and Matthew's depiction of the woman as prophet-anointer. Remembering her as a sinner whose love surpassed that of the righteous celebrated the shocking inclusiveness of Jesus's concept of the reign of God. Remembering her as prophet-anointer did the same by implying that women ranked equally with men in God's realm. And perhaps it was precisely the subversiveness of this notion of women's equality, one biblical theologian theorizes, that caused even the evangelists who memorialized the woman to forget her name.[3]

The Story of the Prophetic Woman Who Anoints the Head of Jesus

A Paraphrase of Mk 14:1–9 and Mt 26:3–13

Two days before Passover, when the chief priests and elders are scheming to seize Jesus, he reclines at table in Bethany at the house of Simon the leper.[4] A

---

3. Elisabeth Schüssler Fiorenza, *In Memory of Her* (1983), xiv, 128–29.

4. Probably a label lingering from past disease, to distinguish him from other Simons.

woman enters, carrying an alabaster jar of pure, costly nard. She breaks the jar and begins to pour the nard on Jesus' head. Jesus' disciples protest that the perfume could have been sold for more than three hundred denarii and the money given to the poor.[5] They begin to scold the woman, but Jesus says, "Let her alone! Why are you bothering her? She has done me a courtesy. Remember, there will always be poor around, and whenever you want you can do good for them, but I won't always be around.[6] She did what she could—she anticipates in anointing my body for burial. So help me, wherever the good news is announced in all the world, what she has done will also be told in memory of her!"[7]

The Story of the Loving Woman Who Anoints the Feet of Jesus

A Paraphrase of Lk 7:36–50

Jesus reclines at dinner in the home of Simon, a Pharisee. Learning that Jesus is there, a local woman known as a sinner enters the house with an alabaster jar of myrrh. She takes up a position behind Jesus, moistening his feet with her tears.[8] She dries his feet with her hair, kisses them, and anoints them with the myrrh. Simon thinks to himself, "If this man were a real prophet, he would know who this woman is who is touching him, and what a bad character she is." Jesus challenges his host with a brief parable about two men in debt to a moneylender. Seeing that they cannot pay, the moneylender cancels both debts. Asked which man will love the moneylender more, Simon responds, "I should think the one that was let off more." Jesus tells him that he is correct. Then he says, "You see this woman? I came to your house: you provided no water for my feet, but this woman has made my feet wet with her tears and wiped them with her hair. You gave me no kiss, but she has been kissing my feet ever since I came in. You did not anoint my head with oil, but she has anointed my feet with myrrh. So, I tell you, her great love proves that her many sins have been forgiven; where little has been forgiven, little love is shown." To the woman herself he says, "Your sins are forgiven." The other guests begin to ask themselves who Jesus is, that he can forgive sins. Jesus says further to the woman, "Your faith has saved you; go in peace."

5. The amount the woman uses would cost a laborer nearly a year's income, since one denarius (a silver Roman coin) represented a day's wage.

6. Far from suggesting that the poor may be ignored, Jesus reminds his listeners to heed Deut 15:11: "The poor will always be with you in your land, and that is why I command you to be open-handed towards any . . . who are in . . . need."

7. Jesus' words are here quoted not from the usual REB, but from *The Complete Gospels: Annotated Scholars Version* (Sonoma, Calif.: Polebridge Press, 1992), 46.

8. At dinners held in the Greek or Hellenistic style, guests removed their sandals and reclined at table, their feet stretching away behind them.

Reflection

Although the prophetic anointer of Mark and Matthew and the loving anointer of Luke may have been two different women, it is easier to reflect upon them as if they were one. Imagine the scene. In the Palestine of Jesus' time, private dinners do not necessarily exclude uninvited guests. Visitors walk in and out, interacting with the reclining diners. Observers stand along the walls, relishing the chance later to report that they shared a room with the famous guest of honor. Male slaves move steadily throughout the room, serving the guests. Perhaps the woman who anoints Jesus hopes to slip into this scene unnoticed (or at least ignored), perform her act of devotion quietly, and slip silently away. But the setting is hostile to women; women are welcome neither as guests nor to serve guests, and her presence is protested.

Who would take upon herself the potential for such embarrassment? Several elements of the stories suggest that the woman is no casual bystander, emotionally moved to perform a single flamboyant act, but a long-term disciple of Jesus. First of all, she knows who Jesus is and where to find him. Second, she senses that the identity and mission of Jesus so deeply affront those in power that he walks in mortal danger. Third, she plans her action: no one just happens to carry around a heavy jar of expensive ointment. And fourth, since the stories themselves (and Lk 8:1–3) suggest that Jesus' followers pooled their resources to support his ministry, even the protests that her oil should have been sold for the sake of the poor suggest that she travels among Jesus' companions: the disciples would have had no reason to level this particular criticism on an outsider.[9]

If the woman is, indeed, a long-time follower of Jesus, her courageous violation of ingrained custom reflects, further, deep absorption of the message of Jesus. She would often have witnessed Jesus' healing of women and men alike. She would have heard him addressing parables to women as well as men. She would have noted his disregard for regulations prohibiting speaking with women in public, teaching them, touching them, and allowing them and the unclean to touch him. She would have learned to the depths of her soul that whatever the men around her might think, she was welcome in the kingdom Jesus proclaimed.

Thus can love of Jesus overcome her every fear. She can enter a dining room reserved for men, she can touch the prophet himself, she can even let down her hair in public—in her culture, so scandalous a breach of propriety as to constitute grounds for divorce.[10] She dares even to take upon herself a

---

9. Rachel Conrad Wahlberg adds another observation. No male authority has ever called the gifts of the three Wise Men "wasteful." It appears to be all right for men to offer lavish gifts, she concludes, but not women.—*Jesus According to a Woman* (1975), 56.

10. Neal F. Fisher, *The Parables of Jesus* (1990), 76–77.

role of prophetic and political leadership. Going beyond merely anointing Jesus for burial, she prophetically marks this man as the messianic king her people have long awaited.

In all versions of the anointing story, Jesus remains essentially passive. It is the woman who initiates events, the male guests who object. Only then does Jesus respond. The righteous Simons of that world view the woman "through a dirty filter of sin/sex/woman/Eve."[11] The disciples raise an uproar over a side issue that is none of their business—the proper use of the woman's money. The woman, in contrast, embodies all of the liberating qualities of devotion, generosity, compassion and courage that Jesus proclaims, and he accepts her. He perceives a person, not a stereotype.

In defending the woman, Jesus speaks for all whose focus on the needs of real human beings occasions the condemnation of those who insist on rigid adherence to regulations. Far from dismissing the woman, Jesus contrasts her insight and devotion with the blindness and insensitivity of her accusers. He defends her right to touch him, he speaks with her openly, and he commits an additional breach of propriety: he tells her that she is forgiven and sends her on her way in *shalom*—peace and wholeness. In so doing, he does not deny the obligation of caring for the poor. What he denounces is "the speciousness of using generosity toward the poor as a club to brutalize a good deed sprung from a good heart."[12]

❖ ❖

"Simons" still surround us; they are those members of political and commercial and religious establishments who continue to judge women's contributions as untraditional and inappropriate. They are those who still react to women with automatic disapproval, regarding them as uninvited, unwelcome guests. For Jesus, however, neither maleness nor sinlessness was a prerequisite for service. He accepted people as they were; he was pleased even by service rendered so emotionally that it disturbed the politically correct.

For women in every walk of life, both Jesus and the woman who anointed him can stand as models. He demonstrates extraordinary inner wholeness and freedom from prejudice; she demonstrates the integrity and courage women still need in order to penetrate the glass ceilings of the business world and the custom-encrusted walls of church precincts.

The story of the woman who anointed Jesus demonstrates another point as well. While lack of concern for the poor is suspect, so is refusal to celebrate a beautiful deed that stirs the heart. Art and music and poetry are not

11. Wahlberg, *Jesus According to a Woman*, 51.
12. Denise Lardner Carmody, *Biblical Woman* (1989), 93.

luxuries; they, too, are necessary to full human life. In memory of the anointer, women of today might pray:

Prayer

Gracious God, you anoint our heads with oil
and wrap us in your mantle of justice:
you make us vessels of your Spirit.
Grant that these bodies you have consecrated
may respond to you always.
May we hear you in the cries of the needy
and touch you in the lives of the broken-hearted.
As you have anointed us,
so may we anoint you wherever we find you—
on barren city streets, in hospices for the outcast,
in the sanctuaries of our houses of worship.
Grant us the courage
to return in service what you have given us.
Grant us the courage to pour out our gifts
of service and beauty and compassion
even when the indignant protest our very presence.
Grant us the courage to go so far as to be shattered,
if that is what is required
for the fragrance of your realm to penetrate our world.
For you, O God, are the potter; we are the clay.
We are the earthen vessels of your Spirit.
We are the alabaster jars you have made.[13]

Connections

1. Like the woman's jar, hearts, bodies and spirits can be broken. Sometimes, this kind of brokenness leads to an insight that changes the direction of a person's life. When has brokenness developed into a source of change or growth for you? *Change*

2. Jesus praises the woman; the evangelists forget her name. Who are the anonymous anointers of your world—people who work tirelessly for change, yet never become known to the powerful?

3. Simon is blind to the woman's courage and love. He dismisses her because of her bad reputation. What courageous acts have caused women you know to be scorned, dismissed, or assigned the reputation of troublemaker? *Rachel Carson*

13. Based on the stories, on 2 Cor 4:7, and on Isa 50:4, 61:1–3,10, and 64:7.

[handwritten marginalia: Note this story is more meaningful]

For Further Reading

Carmody, Denise Lardner, *Biblical Woman* (1989), 91–95.

Fisher, Neal F., *The Parables of Jesus* (1990), 76–77.

Moloney, Francis J., *Woman First Among the Faithful* (1984), 28–30, 67–68.

Moltmann-Wendel, Elisabeth, *The Women Around Jesus* (1982), 94–104.

Nunnally-Cox, Janice, *Foremothers* (1981), 104–5.

Schüssler Fiorenza, Elisabeth, *In Memory of Her* (1983), xiii–xiv, 128–29, 152–54.

Sleevi, Mary Lou, *Women of the Word* (1985), 63–66.

Tetlow, Elizabeth M., *Women and Ministry in the New Testament* (1980), 96–97, 105, 113.

Wahlberg, Rachel Conrad, *Jesus According to a Woman* (1975), 50–60.

Winter, Miriam Therese, *WomanWord* (1990), 66–74.

Yamasaki, April, *Remember Lot's Wife* (1991), 75–76, 81–82.

32 Mary Magdalene: Apostle to the Apostles

Mark 15:40–47, 16:1–14; Luke 8:1–3, 23:50–55, 24:1–11;
Matthew 28:1–10; John 19:25, 38–42, 20:1–18

"Mary Magdalene went and said to the disciples . . ."

Background

The presence of Mary Magdalene pervades all four of the Gospels. Luke reports that she is healed by Jesus and then serves him throughout his ministry. Matthew, Mark, and John present her as a foremost witness of the crucifixion. All four evangelists place her at Jesus' tomb, and Mark and John report special appearances of the risen Jesus to Magdalene alone. She is mentioned first in all but one listing of the women disciples. Overall, the Gospels thus depict her as a leader among the women comparable only to Peter among the men.

Some writings from the first centuries of Christianity (such as *The Gospel of Philip* and *The Gospel of Mary*) go even further. They characterize her as an apostle who *more* than rivals Peter in importance, because when the phrase "go and tell" (*apostellein* in Greek) recurs in the Easter accounts, it is always Magdalene—not Peter—who is commissioned. At the dawn of the third century, Hippolytus of Rome and other church fathers still spoke of Mary Magdalene as apostle and evangelist, and as late as the ninth century, Rabanus Maurus repeatedly called her "apostle" in a biography about her. To this day Eastern Catholic churches honor her as "apostle to the apostles."

Why, then, do dictionaries list "magdalene" as a synonym for "reformed prostitute"? The surname "Magdalene" simply refers to Mary's home town, Magdala—a lively, flourishing center of the fishing industry located on the west shore of the Sea of Galilee. Yet the prostitute tradition arose because a story in which Jesus forgives an anonymous female sinner who lavishes oil upon him (Lk 7:36–50) is immediately followed by the introduction of Mary Magdalene as a woman out of whom seven demons are driven (Lk 8:1–3). Readers of post-New Testament times began to equate demons with sin, a meaning demon only sometimes carried in the first century CE. At that time, demonic possession was also the customary explanation for any baffling physical or emotional condition. Since the seriousness or frequency of an affliction was suggested by the number of demons, "seven demons" might denote a severe or recurrent malady. Nevertheless, the image of Mary Magdalene as a penitent but flamboyant sinner caught the imagination of Western Christians, and it is in that role that Western artists have immortalized her. She is often shown clinging in excessive emotion to the feet of the risen Jesus, or flying to report the resurrection, a tangle of bright red hair floating behind her.

The Gospels themselves paint a different portrait—that of an articulate, generous woman of ability, courage, and faith. The earliest Gospel, Mark's, makes her steadfast devotion during the passion, death, and resurrection of Jesus especially clear. It is she alone, no male disciple, who provides the principle of continuity: she witnesses the crucifixion (15:40), she witnesses the burial (15:47), and she is commissioned to report the resurrection, first by an angel and then by Jesus himself (16:7, 9). Thus she pre-eminently fulfills the criteria that Luke and Paul, between them, set for apostleship: recognition of Jesus as Messiah, belief in him, and having served as eye witness to his life, death, and resurrection.[1]

The Story section that follows acknowledges that the Easter stories differ in detail. The very fact of discrepancies leads scholars to believe that they report authentic experiences: eye witnesses are notorious for recalling details differently. Yet amid the variations, two factors never change: Mary Magdalene is first to discover that the tomb is empty; Mary Magdalene is first (or among the first) to "go and tell" that Jesus is risen.

The Story of Mary Magdalene as Told in the Gospels

Freed from Demons, Mary Serves Jesus: *A Paraphrase of Lk 8:1–3*

As Jesus journeys from one town to another in Galilee, preaching and proclaiming the good news of God's reign, he is accompanied by the Twelve and by several women whom he cured of evil spirits and infirmities. They include Mary Magdalene, from whom seven demons had gone out; Joanna, wife of Chuza, estate manager to Herod Antipas; Susanna; and many others. These women provide for Jesus out of their own resources.

Mary Magdalene Witnesses Jesus' Death and Burial: *A Summary of Mt 27:56–61, Mk 15:40–47, Lk 23:50–54, and Jn 19:25*

As Jesus breathes his last, his mother and the women who have followed him from Galilee and cared for him look on. They include Mary Magdalene; Mary, the mother of James and Joseph [or Joses]; Salome, the mother of the sons of Zebedee; and many others. A distinguished member of the council and secret disciple of Jesus, Joseph of Arimathea, gains Pilate's permission to bury Jesus. He takes the body, wraps it in linen, and lays it in a new, rock-hewn tomb. Mary Magdalene and the other Mary remain seated there, facing the tomb.

---

1. Elizabeth M. Tetlow, *Women and Ministry in the New Testament* (1980), 119.

On Easter Sunday, Magdalene Is Commissioned to 'Go and Tell'

(Note: Because the role of Mary Magdalene varies in the resurrection stories, they are not collated into a single summary, but presented below, one by one. Only John's Gospel relates the "do not touch me" story.)

A Paraphrase of Mt 28:1–10

As Sunday is dawning, Mary Magdalene and the other Mary come to the tomb. A great earthquake occurs as an angel dressed in dazzling white descends from heaven, rolls back the stone, and sits upon it. Shaken with fear, the guards become like dead men. The angel tells the women not to fear, for Jesus, whom they seek, has been raised as he predicted. The angel invites the women to look at the empty tomb and then to go and report to the others that Jesus has risen and goes before them into Galilee, where they will see him. Fearful yet overjoyed, Magdalene and the other Mary run to announce this news. Jesus himself greets them on their way. They approach, embrace his feet, and pay him homage. Jesus says, "Do not be afraid. Go and take word to my brothers that they are to leave for Galilee. They will see me there."

A Paraphrase of Mk 16:1–8 (the Shorter Ending of Mark)

Early on the first day of the week, when the sabbath is over, Mary Magdalene, Mary the mother of James, and Salome take spices to the tomb to anoint the body of Jesus. They wonder who will roll back the large stone. But it is already rolled back, and a young man clothed in white sits upon it. He tells them not to be amazed; they seek Jesus, the crucified, who has been raised. They must go and tell Peter and the others that Jesus goes before them to Galilee, where they will see him. Seized with bewilderment and trembling, they flee from the tomb. In their great fear, they say nothing to anyone.

A Paraphrase of Mk 16:9–14 (from the Longer Ending of Mark)[2]

Early on the first day of the week, Jesus appears first to Mary Magdalene, out of whom he had driven seven demons. She goes and tells his companions, who are mourning and weeping. When she says that he is alive and that she has seen him, they do not believe her. They persist in their unbelief until later in the week when Jesus himself appears to them at table and rebukes them for their hardness of heart.

---

2. Scholars believe that the Christian community came to find the original ending of Mark unsatisfying in light of the more fully developed traditions reported in John and Luke. Every detail in Mark 6:9–14 is derived from the Gospel of Luke (8:1–3; 24:1–49). Scholars believe that the second, longer ending (Mk 16:9–20), which concludes with the Ascension of Jesus, was added in about the second century CE.

A Paraphrase of Lk 24:1–11

At daybreak on the first day of the week, the women who had followed Jesus from Galilee take spices to the tomb. They include Mary Magdalene; Joanna; Mary, the mother of James; and several others. They find the stone rolled back, but when they enter the tomb, they do not find the body of Jesus. While they puzzle over this, two young men dressed in dazzling white appear to them. Terrified, they bow to the ground. The men ask the women, "Why search among the dead for one who is alive?" When the angels remind them that Jesus said he must die at the hands of sinful men and rise again, the women remember his words. They go and proclaim "everything to the eleven and all the others." But their story seems like nonsense, and the men do not believe it.

A Paraphrase of Jn 20:1–18

On the first day of the week, Mary Magdalene arrives at the tomb while it is still dark. Seeing the stone removed, she runs to tell Peter and the disciple whom Jesus loved that the body has been stolen, and that she and the other women do not know where it has been taken. Peter and the beloved disciple run to the tomb. They, too, see only the burial clothes inside, and return home. Mary stays there, weeping. Then she bends to peer into the tomb, and sees angels sitting at the head and foot of the place where Jesus was laid.[3] They ask, "Woman, why are you weeping?" She responds, "They have taken my Lord, and I don't know where they laid him." Turning, she sees someone behind her.Taking him for the gardener she says, "Sir, if you carried him away, tell me where you laid him, and I will take him." It is Jesus; he says, "Mary!" She turns fully to him, reaches out and says "Rabboni"—"my Teacher." Jesus responds, "Do not cling to me, for I have not yet ascended to the Father." He directs her to tell his brothers that he is going to God. She rushes to the disciples, announces "I have seen the Lord!", and reports all that he told her.

Reflection

Judging from her position among Jesus' followers, the historical Mary of Magdala must have been a prominent woman. Some think she was a widow; others have speculated that she possessed wealth amassed by trade or inheritance. The seventh century *Golden Legend* (which confuses Mary of Magdala with Mary of Bethany) goes so far as to make her the proprietor of the entire town of Magdala, while Lazarus owns a large part of Jerusalem and Martha owns Bethany.[4] But whatever the financial resources Mary Magdalene might

---

3. In tombs of this time, bodies were placed on a shelf and allowed to decompose for a year. Then the bones were gathered and placed in an ossuary, literally a "bone box."

4. Marina Warner, *Alone of All Her Sex* (1976), 230.

have contributed to the care of Jesus and his followers, she must also have contributed charm and leadership ability, for all of the Gospels imply that she held together an entire troupe of women.

Writers and artists have suggested that Mary went on to become Jesus' lover, or perhaps—since it was culturally unheard of for a Jewish rabbi not to marry—his wife. Christian tradition has shied away from the idea of passionate love between Jesus and Mary, preferring instead to render her as a composite of the worst interpretations of Rahab the harlot; Gomer, the unfaithful wife of the prophet Hosea; and the "painted" Queen Jezebel, wife of Ahab (Judg 1, 6; Hos 1–3; 1 and 2 Kings). The image of Mary as a prostitute transformed by impassioned love of Jesus has been renewed in the twentieth century in the rock opera, *Jesus Christ Superstar*. The baser her origins, it seems, the better she demonstrates that no one is beyond the reach of grace.

Two elements of even this negative stereotype do, however, intersect with the Easter gospel stories—Mary's passionate nature and her closeness to Jesus. Denise Lardner Carmody, chair of the religion faculty at the University of Tulsa, notes that by favoring Mary on Easter morning, Jesus continues

> the maddening intimacy with women that had distinguished his rabbinate from the beginning. If there was a single . . . lesson implied for the future work of the apostles, it was the primacy of passionate love—that which took Jesus through death, that which reached into death and drew Jesus out, and that which made Jesus most moved by the Magdalene.[5]

The scene that unveils the depths of Mary Magdalene's feelings most dramatically is the one in which a weeping Mary mistakes Jesus for a gardener. The scene also reveals that she is one of Jesus' "own"—a gender-neutral, technical term the author of John applies to male and female disciples alike, for Jesus' disciples are like the sheep of whom he says, "my own" know me by my voice (Jn 10:14–16). At the tomb, Mary Magdalene proves herself pre-eminently Jesus' own when she recognizes him in the voicing of a single word—"Mary!" Yet if Jesus and Mary Magdalene hold each other in such love, how does one explain the "Do not touch me" verse (Jn 20:17)? The rejection of Mary the phrase implies has bothered theologians for centuries. More recent translations—"Stop holding on to me" (NAB), "Do not cling to me" (REB)—suggest a possible psychological symbolism. The implication is that the naivete of childlike faith must end; the pain of letting go must begin. Clinging cannot capture the essence of post-resurrection faith. Theologian Elisabeth Moltmann-Wendel thus offers her own rendering of "Noli me tangere": "Grow up, be mature! Accept the grief of parting."[6]

5. *Biblical Woman* (1990), 117.
6. *The Women Around Jesus* (1982), 72.

Interpretations like these help demonstrate that the story of Mary at the tomb can encapsulate anyone's journey of faith. Arriving in disorienting darkness, Mary sees no angel, only an empty tomb. We, too, often experience the emptiness of a dark and ambiguous world where no angels appear and God seems absent. Just as reason fails to provide Mary with an explanation for Jesus' absence, so reason cannot always provide us with answers. But when Jesus speaks, Mary recognizes him and goes forth transformed. In the same way, when we recognize the presence of God, even empty realities become charged with life.

❖ ❖

In the churches of today, imagine the richness that could result if the stereotype of Magdalene as a great sinner were abandoned, and her role as fiery proclaimer of the good news were celebrated. Carmody, quoted earlier, writes in the same passage,

> If the church believed its own [scriptures] enough to act on them, would it not make passionate love of God the central concern and so relegate other ethical, spiritual, and practical virtues to subordinate roles? Similarly, would it not [stop respecting] persons and stations [and] seek first to honor the great lovers of God?

Society at large can also benefit from the example of Mary Magdalene. Although our world allows women some power, it still imposes restrictions. The story of Magdalene demonstrates that God calls women to use whatever power they do possess, up to and beyond the limits recognized by society. Magdalene teaches us "that we must name and claim our power. We must grasp it, nuzzle it, nurture it, speak it, celebrate it, run with it, fly with it . . . use it in the best way we know how"—and "trust in God for the rest."[7]

In her own transformation from illness to wholeness, Mary Magdalene must have experienced a kind of resurrection that contributed to her understanding of the mystery of Jesus' life, death, and resurrection. After Easter, she must often have pondered afresh words she had heard spoken earlier:

Prayer

You are my own, whom I have chosen.
I did not tell you everything from the beginning,
for I was still with you.
But now I am going to the One who sent me,
and grief fills your hearts.

7. Mary Cartledge-Hayes, *To Love Delilah* (1990), 86.

I tell you truly, it is better for you that I go.
I have much more to tell you, but you cannot bear it now.
If I go, I can send you the Advocate who will guide you to all truth
and declare to you all that comes from the Creator and from me.
Yes, you will weep, you will mourn;
but your grief will turn into joy.
When a woman is in labor, she is in anguish
because her hour has arrived.
But when she has brought a child into the world,
she no longer dwells on the pain.
So are you in anguish now, but I will see you again
and your hearts will rejoice;
and no one will be able to take that joy from you.
Behold, the hour is coming—indeed, it is here—
when you will scatter to your homes and leave me alone,
though I am never really alone, for I AM is with me.
But take courage! Remember, and do not fear:
I have conquered the world, and I am with you.[8]

Connections

1. Before Jesus healed her, what kind of life do you think Mary Magdalene lived? Could her "demons" have been so simple as a level of ambition or articulateness considered unwomanly by her society? Once Jesus had driven out her demons, what kind of relationship do you think developed between them?

2. The Easter stories present Mary Magdalene as a model of faith. How do they also present her as a model of action?

3. Why do you think the stereotype of Magdalene as repentant sinner has endured so long? Is it because a flawed Mary is more like us, and thus easier to approach? Or do you perceive other reasons for the resilience of the image?

4. Joseph Campbell, famed teacher of comparative mythology, offered a formula for pursuit of "the soul's high adventure": "Follow your bliss," he urged his students.[9] Mary Magdalene did that. How do you pursue your bliss?

8. Based on Isa 43:5, 10 and 45:4, and verses from Jn 16:4–33.

9. Joseph Campbell with Bill Moyers, *The Power of Myth* (New York: Doubleday, 1988), 148.

For Further Reading

Carmody, Denise Lardner, *Biblical Woman* (1989), 114–19.

Cartledge-Hayes, Mary, *To Love Delilah* (1990), 76–87.

Deen, Edith, *All of the Women of the Bible* (1955), 200–5.

Moloney, Francis J., *Woman: First Among the Faithful* (1986), 90–92.

Moltmann-Wendel, Elisabeth, *The Women Around Jesus* (1982), 68–77.

Moltmann-Wendel, Elisabeth, *A Land Flowing with Milk and Honey* (1988), 84–85.

Nunnally-Cox, Janice, *Foremothers* (1981), 113–15.

Schüssler Fiorenza, Elisabeth, *In Memory of Her* (1983), 50–51.

Sleevi, Mary Lou, *Women of the Word* (1985), 69–72, 99–102.

Tetlow, Elizabeth M., *Women and Ministry in the New Testament* (1980), 113–15, 118–19.

Warner, Marina, *Alone of All Her Sex* (1976), 224–35.

Weaver, Mary Jo, *New Catholic Women* (Harper & Row, 1985), 208–9.

Weems, Renita J., *Just a Sister Away* (1988), 84–97.

Winter, Miriam Therese, *WomanWord* (1990), 156–62.

33 Women on the Road, at the Cross, at the Tomb: True Disciples

Mark 15:40–47, 16:1–9; Matthew 27:19, 56–61; 28:1–10;
Luke 8:1–3; 23:27–31, 50–55; 24:1–10; John 19:25, 38,
40–41

"With him were . . . a number of women . . ."

Nov. 2

Background

When the Gospels are read closely, women emerge everywhere. The presence of some women is implied, or mentioned only as an aside. These are the wives and sisters who urge ailing men to approach Jesus for a cure; they are the mothers who pack loaves and fishes so the entire family can spend a day listening to Jesus on a grassy hillside. They are the women who stand upright at Jesus' touch; they are the serving girl in the courtyard and the procurator's wife in the palace. But the presence of other women—a cohesive group known simply and familiarly as "the women"—comes in for repeated mention. These are the women who support Jesus' ministry from its earliest days in Galilee, the women who travel in Jesus' entourage. They are courageous enough to stand at Jesus' cross, and they are the first disciples to know that Christ is risen.

For women of Roman Palestine of the first century CE, unconventional behavior of these kinds demonstrated rare courage. While wealthy Jewish women sometimes supported traveling rabbis, a woman risked scandal if she attempted actually to travel or study with a rabbi.[1] Further, it was downright dangerous for women to brave a bloodthirsty crowd in order to lament the execution of a condemned criminal. An apt symbol of the courage shown by all of these women is one who did not actually travel with them—the wife of Pilate. According to Matthew, she somehow became so impressed with the person or reputation of Jesus that she dared to interrupt a public trial in order to beg the highest local official, her husband Pilate, not to condemn an innocent man.

---

1. The title "rabbi" came into widespread use to designate a teacher of Jewish law about the time the Gospels were being written. The writers retroactively called Jesus a rabbi because he used rabbinic methods such as teaching through parables and proverbial sayings, and forming a company of disciples whom he instructed orally.

What explains women's devotion to Jesus? A clue about some women lies in Luke, who says that Jesus healed them (8:2). Touched to the core from such an encounter, they seem immediately to have recognized him as a man of God, and never to have wavered from that faith. Even after the shock of Jesus' death, they were the first to "remember" his words—a powerful term meaning not mere recall, but bringing previously spoken words into the present with increased power and insight.

All four Gospels report that the women who followed Jesus from Galilee and tended to his needs also mourned him at the cross (Mk 15:40–41; Mt 27:55–56; Lk 23:49; Jn 19:25). In Luke, even as Jesus struggles toward Golgotha, he speaks with a group he addresses as "Daughters of Jerusalem" (23:7–31). While these women may have been professional mourners from Jerusalem, it seems more likely that a Jesus in pain stopped to address women who had been dear to him since Galilee, granting them a metaphoric title to suggest their representation of all Israel.

Altogether, the Gospel passages mentioning women healed and women present at the cross and the tomb imply a good-sized group—a dozen or more. Only a few are named: Mary Magdalene; Mary, the mother of Jesus; Susanna; Joanna; Salome; and "the other Mary." Mary Magdalene and Mary, the mother of Jesus, are discussed in other chapters. Collating of passages from Matthew, Mark, and Luke makes it clear that "the other Mary" is the mother of grown sons named James and Joses (or Joseph). She may also be the Mary called "wife of Clopas" in Jn 19:25. Of the others named, Luke reports that Susanna came from Galilee, was healed by Jesus, followed him, and helped support him out of her own resources (Lk 8:2–3). Joanna, who is also described as healed, is further identified as wife of a high official in the court of Herod Antipas, and as one of the women who visit the tomb on Easter morning (Lk 8:2, 24:10). By combining passages from Matthew and Mark, tradition has identified Salome as the same person as the wife of the fisherman Zebedee and the mother of James and John. On one occasion this mother seeks positions of power for her sons; "Salome" later stands on her own at the cross and assists in the burial of Jesus (Mt 20:20; Mk 15:40, 16:1).

The various Gospel lists make several points abundantly clear. Women are the first (or among the first) to dedicate themselves to Jesus; they come from backgrounds as disparate as fishing village and royal palace; and they surpass men in the totality of their commitment. Male disciples seek to protect themselves by betraying, denying, or abandoning Jesus, but female disciples follow him all the way from Galilee to Jerusalem, risking their reputations and resources; and even to the cross, risking their lives.

The stress on women's presence at the cross and then on their commission to spread the good news of Jesus' resurrection takes on added significance when one recalls that Jewish tradition ordinarily granted little or no credibility to the testimony of women. Among New Testament writers, only

Paul ignores the tradition that the risen Jesus appeared first to the women; he asserts that Jesus appeared first to Peter and then to the other men (1 Cor 15:5). But Paul's version of events is counterbalanced by the sheer weight of the traditions that fed the gospel writers. Given the writers' preference for placing men in starring roles, it seems unlikely that so heavily emphasized a "women first" tradition could reflect anything but what actually occurred.

The Story of "The Women" as Told in the Gospels

Women on the Road: *A Summary of Lk 8:1–3 and Mt 20:17–28*

As Jesus journeys from one town to another in Galilee, preaching and proclaiming the good news of the kingdom of God, he is accompanied by the Twelve and by several women whom he cured of evil spirits and infirmities. They include Mary Magdalene, from whom seven demons had gone out; Joanna, wife of Chuza, steward to Herod Antipas; Susanna; and many others. These women provide for Jesus out of their own resources.

Eventually Jesus leaves Galilee to go up to Jerusalem. He has told his followers it is there that he must be handed over, die, and rise. On the way, the mother of the sons of Zebedee approaches him with her sons. Jesus asks what she wants. She replies, "Give orders that in your kingdom these two sons of mine may sit next to you, one at your right hand and the other at your left." Turning to James and John [apparently the instigators of the request], Jesus tells them they do not understand what they ask. They insist they *can* drink the cup Jesus will drink, and he responds that they shall. But the handing out of places of honor is reserved to the Creator alone. Those who truly wish to be great must imitate Jesus himself, becoming servants to all.

Women at the Cross: *A Summary of Mt 27:19, 56–61; Mk 15:40–47; Lk 23:50–55; and Jn 19:25,38–40*

While Pilate, the Roman procurator, is seated in his chair of judgment, his wife sends him a message: "Have nothing to do with that innocent man; I was much troubled on his account in my dreams last night." Pilate nevertheless permits Jesus to be condemned to death, and he is led to Skull Place [Golgotha] to be crucified. A large crowd follows him, including many women who mourn and lament. Jesus says to them, "Daughters of Jerusalem, do not weep for me; weep for yourselves and your children." He warns them that destruction is coming, a time when people will call upon the hills to cover them and will acclaim the childless as blessed.

When Jesus breathes his last on the cross, the women who have followed him from Galilee and cared for him look on from a distance.[2] They include

---

2. The Romans cordoned off places of execution from the general public.

Mary Magdalene; Mary, the mother of James and Joseph [Joses]; the mother of the sons of Zebedee; and many others. A distinguished member of the council and secret disciple of Jesus, Joseph from Arimathea, gains Pilate's permission to bury Jesus. Taking the body, he wraps it in clean linen, and lays it in a new, rock-hewn tomb. Joseph then rolls a huge stone across the entrance, and departs.[3] The women who have followed Jesus from Galilee watch as Jesus is laid in the tomb.

Women at the Tomb: *A Summary of Mk 16:1–7 and Lk 24:1–10*

At daybreak on the first day of the week, when the sabbath is over, the women who had followed Jesus from Galilee take spices to the tomb. They include Mary Magdalene; Joanna; Mary, the mother of James; Salome; and several others. Because the stone across the tomb is very large, they wonder who will roll it back for them. But the stone is already rolled back, and the body of Jesus is not in the tomb. While they puzzle over this, young men dressed in dazzling white appear to them. Terrified, they bow to the ground. The men remind the women that Jesus said he must die at the hands of sinful men and rise again, and the women remember Jesus' words. They go and tell Peter and the others that Jesus goes before them to Galilee, where they will see him. But their story seems like nonsense, and the men do not believe it.

Reflection

The sight of their master dangling from a cross sends Jesus' male disciples scurrying into hiding; some run all the way back to the security of their fishing nets on the Sea of Galilee. But the women remain and the women remember—women whose identities the Gospel writers only half recall. These women seem to have constituted so established a part of the scenery that they could be taken for granted, while the writers had to scramble for the names of twelve men who could symbolize the twelve tribes of the renewed Israel of Jesus.

Most of these women, like the first men to follow Jesus, probably came from the villages and towns surrounding the Sea of Galilee. Had Jesus not appeared, their days would have been consumed by traditional tasks—drawing water, grinding grain, baking bread, spinning yarn, making cloth, selling produce. Women like these may have felt they had little to lose by devoting their talent, time, and substance to Jesus—a Jesus who, at first, mainly needs their material help. (One can imagine them paying the bills, cooking, and mending clothes along the way.) Later on, however, Jesus needs them for the

---

3. Anyone executed as a criminal had to be buried the same day (Deut 21:22–23). Graves outside Jerusalem were cut into the limestone. A large, round, flat slab of rock was fitted into a groove in front of each grave and rolled across the entrance.

urgent mission of spreading the good news of his resurrection. Either way, the women "serve" or "minister to" Jesus, in Greek the same verb that lies at the root of the word (and office), "deacon." The Gospels never depict women as less able or less worthy than men to be called into service; if anything, it is some of the men who are characterized as overly emotional. (Recall, for example, the mad dash of Peter and the beloved disciple to check the tomb for themselves.)

Of the women briefly described by the Gospel writers, the mother of the sons of Zebedee may have been the most fiery. She seems to have shared the personality of her boys, nicknamed "the sons of thunder." Although she once tries to live through her sons, asking Jesus to honor them, in the end it is *she* who stands next to the cross. Joanna may have been the wealthiest, most cosmopolitan member of the group. Previous to her encounter with Jesus, she was a political wife: in Herod's court, her husband, Chuza, served as the equivalent of a modern finance minister or cabinet official. (Chuza is not known ever to have followed Joanna to Jesus.) Tradition credits Joanna with bringing a degree of comfort and elegance to Jesus' entourage. It is said that she wove him a fine one-piece garment, provided oils for his anointing, paid the rental on the upper room, and covered the cost of many a meal.[4] Like Nicodemus among the men, she comes from society's upper crust. But unlike Nicodemus, who comes to Jesus by night, Joanna stands at cross and tomb in the bright light of day.

In a way, it is no real surprise that women were quick to grasp Jesus' ministry and message. Like the Yahweh of Exodus and Deuteronomy, Jesus repeatedly reached out to the weakest and least respected members of society. For women, he offered an attractive realm in which divisions between men and women were canceled. He never treated women as objects or stereotypes; in fact, he was so good a friend to women that his male disciples marveled at his openness with them. It remains true, however, that the women who followed Jesus risked reputation and social standing in a way men did not, even in Galilee where restrictions on women were looser than in Jerusalem.

Jesus himself invited not only scandal but even danger: male authorities perceived his behavior as subversive to the social order. Although the phrase did not make it into the version officially adopted by the church, an early manuscript of Luke's Gospel cites Jesus' effect on women (and children) as one of the specific reasons his enemies wanted him dead: "We found this man inciting our people to a revolt, opposing payment of the tribute to Caesar, *leading astray the women and the children*, and claiming to be Christ, a King. . . ."[5] The phrase is as current as today in a

---

4. Elisabeth Moltmann-Wendell, *The Women Around Jesus* (1982), 136.

5. The Marcion variant of Lk 23:2, quoted in Swidler, *Biblical Affirmations of Woman* (1979), 276–277.

world where many people, male and female alike, still find it unnatural for even the most gifted of women to pursue public, "masculine" roles to the height of their abilities.

Nor are other parallels between women of today and the named and unnamed women who followed Jesus difficult to find. Women still support suspect causes; women still weep at the waste of innocent lives; women still mourn the crucifixion of people of talent. Sometimes they still try to live through their children, only to learn with greater maturity to pay heed to their own needs. Above all, women continue to serve as Jesus served, even when their stories, their work, their giftedness, and their very names are ignored or forgotten. Looking to God, women continue to be amazed that others fail to see what they see:

Prayer

> O God, our God, how glorious is your name over all the earth!
> The heavens proclaim your glory;
> the mouths of women and children pour forth your praise.
> When we study the heavens, the work of your hands,
> we marvel that you should care for us creatures of clay.
> Yet you tell us, "It is I who have begotten you."
> You make us little less than gods;
> you crown every one of us with glory and honor.
> Why, then, this tumult among the nations,
> these useless contentions among the powerful?
> You place all things in human care—
> the beasts of the field, the birds of the air,
> whatever swims the paths of the seas—
> everything you have made or enabled us to make.
> O God, our God, how glorious is your name!
> Would that, with us,
> all might come to you, united in joy and awe.[6]

Connections

1. "The women" apparently abandoned their homes to follow Jesus. How did they know it was time? How can you tell when it is time to make a change in your life?

2. Some women stood at the cross; others watched from a distance. When do you "keep your distance," living up to your principles only to a point?

6. Based on Ps 2:1–11 and Ps 8:1–9.

3. In what sense does "remember" still mean "do"? What does it really mean, for example, to remember the poor or the homeless or the hungry?

4. How do anonymous women still serve as the backbone of churches, businesses, and other organizations, even if the official leadership remains predominantly male? In what ways can you identify with the anonymous women who traveled with Jesus?

For Further Reading

Carmody, Denise Lardner, *Biblical Woman* (1989), 96–101.

Deen, Edith, *All of the Women of the Bible* (1955), 205–8,

Moloney, Francis J., *Woman: First Among the Faithful* (1986), 30–35, 69–71.

Moltmann-Wendel, Elisabeth, *The Women Around Jesus* (1982), 108–17, 130–42.

Nunnally-Cox, Janice, *Foremothers* (1981), 116–117.

Swidler, Leonard, *Biblical Affirmations of Woman* (1979), 276–81.

Tetlow, Elizabeth M., *Women and Ministry in the New Testament* (1980), 99–106.

Wahlberg, Rachel Conrad, *Jesus According to a Woman* (1975), 61–72, 93–97.

Weems, Renita J., *Just a Sister Away* (1988), 84–97.

Winter, Miriam Therese, *WomanWord* (1990), 143–71.

Yamasaki, April, *Remember Lot's Wife* (1991), 61–64, 77–78, 83–84, 93–96.

Women Leaders of Acts and Epistles:
Presiders and Prophets, Deacons
and Apostles

Nov. 9

From Acts, 1 Corinthians, Romans, and 2 Timothy

"They were all filled with the Holy Spirit." (Acts 2:4)

Background

Just as the Gospels credit women like Mary of Magdala and Martha of
Bethany with leadership in the Jesus movement, so do the Acts of the
Apostles and several Epistles. In a single passage, Paul lists twenty-nine
prominent people, ten of them women (Rom 16:1–16). Overall, in fact, the
Epistles and Acts suggest that New Testament categories of leadership were
far more diverse, far more complex, and far more loosely defined than even
scholars once supposed. Far from being limited to Paul and the Twelve, leadership roles were held by Jews and Gentiles of diverse backgrounds in every
region evangelized. Women and men alike presided over house churches,
spoke and taught as prophets and teachers, served as deacons, and worked as
apostles to establish new churches.

Women appear in the record wherever Christianity spreads. Texts that
mention women of Judea begin with the story of Pentecost, which sets the
theme of an outpouring of Spirit on women and men alike (Acts 1–2). The
texts go on to speak of *Mary of Jerusalem*, mother of John Mark, and her
servant *Rhoda* (Acts 12); an *order of widows* (Acts 6:1–3; 1 Tim 5:3–16);
Dorcas, who acts as benefactor to the widows of Joppa (Acts 9:36–42); and
the four *daughters of Philip*, all of whom act as prophets (Acts 21:8–9).

In the cities of Asia Minor (today's Turkey), prominent women include
Nympha of Colossae, presider over a house church (Col 4:15); *Apphia of
Colossae*, who hosts a house church with her husband Philemon (Col 4:9
and Philem 1–2); and *Prisca*, a mobile missionary who, with her husband
Aquila, works mainly in Ephesus (Acts 18–19, 1 Cor 16:19; Rom 16:3–5; 2
Tim 4:19).

From the European cities of Macedonia and Greece, we read about the
businesswoman *Lydia* and a *girl of Philippi* possessed with a prophetic spirit
(Acts 16:13–40). *Euodia and Syntyche* of Philippi serve as co-workers with
Paul "in the cause of the gospel" (Phil 4:2–3). *Chloe* speaks for some members
of the church of Corinth (1 Cor 1:11), and *Phoebe* is deacon of the nearby

church of Cenchreae[1] (Romans 16:1–2). From Rome, capital of the empire, *Claudia* sends greetings to Timothy (2 Tim 4:20). Prominent women of the Roman community include an otherwise unknown *Mary*; the apostle *Junia*; the "hard workers" *Tryphaena, Tryphosa*, and "dear *Persis*"; the *mother of Rufus*; *Julia*; and the *sister of Nereus* (Rom 16:1–16). Additionally, Paul says that the *wives* of Peter and other apostles travel with their husbands throughout the region (1 Cor 9:5). (Paul does not specify whether the wives serve as supportive companions or as co-evangelizers, but it seems likely that they participated in apostolic ministry. Indeed, all or many of them may have belonged to that eye-witness band of women who followed Jesus from Galilee to the cross.)

The overwhelming impression created by even a partial list like the one given in the three paragraphs above is that first-generation Christians put into effect the gender equality practiced by Jesus. Enormous sociocultural pressures militated against such equality, however, and by the end of the first century CE the letters to Timothy already imply a trend toward re-establishment of male dominance in public ministry. In the early decades of the second century, the major Christian offices crystallized as bishop, deacon, and presbyter (priest). During subsequent centuries, social and political changes worked to transform Christianity from radical heresy to state religion. Institutional structures within the church solidified along the lines of Roman government, and the limiting of leadership offices to men gradually became the norm. By the third century, women were usually barred from the priesthood. By the fourth century, the female deacon (*diakonos*) had been demoted from service of the entire community to service primarily of women, and the word "deaconess" (*diakonissa*, which never occurs in the New Testament) had been coined to denote this lesser position.

Archaeological and literary evidence reveals, however, that elimination of women from church office was resisted. Frescoes, mosaics, and inscriptions designate women as priests, and a catacomb fresco in Rome that dates to the fourth century identifies a woman as a bishop.[2] The language of an edict of the Council of Orange in 441 indicates that as late as the fifth century, even deaconesses were still considered clerics: "Let no one proceed to the ordination of deaconesses anymore."[3] Indeed, abbesses of monasteries retained many of the powers of bishops—at least their more secular powers—until the Council of Trent abrogated them in the *sixteenth* century.[4]

---

1. Cenchreae (*sen' • krē̄ • uh*) was a harbor community a few miles east of Corinth.

2. Janice Nunnally Cox, *Foremothers* (1981), 129; Karen Jo Torjesen, "Reconstruction of Women's Early Church History" in *Searching the Scriptures* (1993), ed. Elisabeth Schüssler Fiorenza, 293–94.

3. Leonard Swidler, *Biblical Affirmations of Woman* (1976), 314.

4. Abbesses ruled both nuns and monks of their orders, acted as feudal lords in the management of monastery lands and dependents, and appointed village clergy,

As a broad generalization, however, it can be said that from the fourth century onward, power within the church became a male preserve.

Once male dominance became the norm, men found it necessary to explain away the roles of women indicated by early Christian art work, inscriptions, and scriptural texts. For example, finding women identified on tombstones and in frescoes by feminine forms of the Greek words for bishop and priests, men concluded that these women must have been the *wives* of bishops and priests. The word "deacon" presented greater difficulty, because the New Testament applies the identical form of the word—*diakonos*—to women and men alike. Additionally, a New Testament passage on the qualifications for deacons specifically mentions "*Women* in this office" (1 Tim 3:11). Blinded, however, by knowledge of the later, lesser office of deaconess, male interpreters concluded that when applied to a woman, even *diakonos* meant only "helper" or "deacon's wife."

Similar interpretations were developed regarding passages suggesting that women acted as eucharistic presiders in house churches. Male interpreters decided that they must have performed simple hostessing duties while male leaders actually officiated. For centuries, however, since commentators realized that no male form of the name "Junia" existed in the Hellenistic world, no one found it possible to deny that Paul applied the word "apostle" to a woman of that name (Rom 16:6–7). It was left to medieval commentators, distant from the Hellenized world, to perform an outright sex change: they simply renamed Junia *Junias*. Martin Luther popularized the change in his translation of the Bible, and translators after him followed suit until well into the twentieth century.[5]

As recently as the Summer of 1994, Pope John Paul II attempted to close all discussion of the ordination of Catholic women, even though two decades ago—in 1976—a majority vote of the Pontifical Biblical Commission affirmed that no scriptural basis exists for denying women ordination to the ministerial priesthood.[6] What the New Testament does support is an array of ministries, open to women and men alike.

The Story of Some of the Women of Acts and Epistles

Mary, Mother of John Mark; and Rhoda: *A Summary of Acts 12:1–16*

King Herod launches an attack on certain members of the church.[7] When certain prominent Jews show approval, he imprisons Peter as well.

according to Bonnie S. Anderson and Judith P. Zinsser, *A History of Their Own*, I (1988), 184.

5. Elizabeth M. Tetlow, *Women and Ministry in the New Testament* (1980), 120; Cullen Murphy, "Women and the Bible," *The Atlantic Monthly*, August 1993, 62.

6. Tetlow, *Women and Ministry in the New Testament*, 140–41.

7. Herod Agrippa, who ruled Judea 41–44 CE. He is grandson of Herod the Great (king when Jesus was born) and nephew of Herod Antipas (king when Jesus died).

Meanwhile the church prays fervently for Peter at the house of Mary, mother of John Mark.[8] One night an angel visits the jail. Peter's chains fall from his wrists and he is led past the guards, into the street. Only then does he realize he is not dreaming. He hurries to Mary's house and knocks at the gate. A serving girl named Rhoda responds. She is so overjoyed to hear his voice that she leaves him standing outside while she runs to announce his arrival. The community at first believes she is out of her mind. But Peter goes on knocking until the astounded community admits him.

Dorcas and the Widows of Joppa: *A Paraphrase of Acts 9:36–42*

In Joppa there lives a disciple named Tabitha—in Greek Dorcas. She fills her days with kindness and charity. She falls ill and dies, and they wash her body and lay it in an upstairs room. Knowing that Peter is nearby, the disciples urgently summon him. Peter comes at once, and all the widows stand around him in tears, showing him the shirts and coats Dorcas used to make for them. Peter sends everyone out and prays beside Dorcas. When he says, "Tabitha, get up," she opens her eyes and sits up. He helps her to her feet, calls together the widows and the entire community, and shows her to them alive. News of this event spreads throughout Joppa, and many come to believe in Jesus.

Lydia of Philippi and the Possessed Girl: *A Summary of Acts 16:13–40*

On the sabbath, Paul and Silas visit the riverbank outside Philippi, where they have heard a synagogue exists. They find Jewish women gathered in prayer. Among them is Lydia, a dealer in purple fabric, from the city of Thyatira. Earlier, she had converted to Judaism. Now God opens her heart to Paul's message. She is baptized, and her entire household with her. She insists that Paul and Silas use her house as a headquarters. On their way to the riverbank one day, Paul and Silas are followed by a girl whose divining spirit earns large profits for her owners. She keeps shouting, "These are servants of the Most High God, and are declaring to you a way of salvation." After several days of this, Paul commands the spirit to leave the girl in Jesus' name. It comes out instantly. Seeing their profits disappearing, the girl's owners seize Paul and Silas and drag them to the city authorities. The authorities beat and imprison them, but release them the next day. They return to Lydia's house, where they meet with their fellow Christians and speak words of encouragement to them.

Prisca and Aquila: *A Summary of Acts 18:1–20:1; 1 Cor 16:19; and Rom 16:3–5*

In Corinth Paul meets Aquila, a native of Pontus,[9] and his wife Priscilla (Prisca). They have recently emigrated from Italy because of an edict of Emperor Claudius, evicting Jews from Rome. Like Paul they are tentmakers,

---

8. Sometimes identified with Mark, author of the earliest-written Gospel.

9. A province of Asia Minor stretching along the south shore of the Black Sea.

so he makes his home with them and works with them. Sabbath after sabbath, Paul holds discussions in the synagogue, speaking both to Jews and to Gentiles. After some time, Prisca and Aquila sail with Paul for Asia Minor. When they land at Ephesus, Prisca and Aquila settle there and resume their missionary work. Paul writes back to Corinth, "Many greetings in the Lord from Aquila and Prisca and the church that meets in their house."

Later on, a Jew named Apollos arrives from Alexandria, Egypt. He is eloquent in his use of scripture, but knows the preaching of John the Baptist better than that of Jesus. He begins to speak boldly in the synagogue, where Prisca and Aquila hear him. They take him in hand and expound to him in the greater detail the way of Jesus. Paul, meanwhile, travels around the countryside. Over the next two years he makes converts among "the whole population of the province of Asia, both Jews and Gentiles" (19:10). He returns to Ephesus, where Christian denunciation of goddess images crafted by local silversmiths leads to a riot. Paul wants to speak to the mob, but his fellow Christians prevent him from doing so. When the disturbance is over, Paul leaves Ephesus.

Some time later, Prisca and Aquila revisit Rome, and Paul writes to the church there, "Give my greetings to Prisca and Aquila, my fellow workers in Christ Jesus. They risked their necks to save my life, and not I alone but all the gentile churches are grateful to them. Greet also the church that meets at their house."

The Daughters of Philip; Phoebe; and Junia: *Acts 21:8–9; Rom 16:1–2, 6–7*

In Caesarea, Paul and his companion visit the home of Philip the evangelist. He is one of the Seven [deacons of Acts 6:1–6] and has four unmarried daughters, all of whom possess the gift of prophecy. Later, from Corinth, Paul writes to the Roman community, commending to them Phoebe, a fellow Christian who is a deacon in the church at Cenchreae. "Give her . . . a welcome worthy of God's people, and support her in any business in which she may need your help, for she has herself been a good friend to many, including myself." He also directs the community to greet Andronicus and Junia, his compatriots and comrades in captivity, "who are eminent among the apostles and were Christians before I was."

Reflection

Even John Chrysostom (c. 347–407), who usually speaks acidly of womankind, praises the women of epistles and Acts:

> [It is] an honor we have, in that there are such women among us, but we are put to shame, in that we men are left so far behind by them. . . . For the women of those days were more spirited than lions.[10]

10. From a sermon on the women of Rom 16:1–16. Migne, *Patrologia Graeca*, vol. 51, cols. 668f, quoted in Swidler, *Biblical Affirmations of Woman*, 295.

Even this praise, however, implies that women of Chrysostom's own day are lesser beings. Similarly, readers of today may find it difficult to overcome cultural conditioning. At a subconscious level, they may believe that men like Paul *permitted* women to help, the women acting as a sort of ladies' auxiliary. Actually, New Testament texts often suggest the reverse. Many Jewish women come to faith while Paul is still persecuting Christians (Acts 8:3, 9:1–2, 22:4–5); Paul specifically acknowledges that Junia preceded him in faith; and he lists as equal ("fellow") workers with himself Tryphaena, Tryphosa, and Persis of Rome. He implies that Chloe of Corinth is a person of considerable influence, and that the opinions of Euodia and Syntyche of Philippi (two more "fellow workers") carry such weight that a dispute involving them could destroy the community. Further, the stories about Lydia of Philippi, Prisca of Ephesus, and Phoebe of Cenchreae suggest that some women held such established positions in their communities that the visiting Paul needed *their* patronage. Even so, most of the women who sprinkle the pages of Acts and Epistles remain only names to us. A larger impression can be gained of only a few.

❖ ❖

Mary of Jerusalem, the mother of John Mark, is a kinswoman of the missionary Barnabas (Col 4:10). She governs a household large enough to employ servants, and it is no small thing for her to open this residence to other believers. Such gatherings angered an empire that labeled the Jesus movement "subversive," making clandestine meetings necessary. The basic unit of the early church became the house church, and except for cases where a house is identified as belonging to a married couple, these were usually residences owned by women of means. Since women like Mary of Jerusalem and Nympha of Colossae evidently headed their own households, scholars consider it unlikely that anyone but those women broke the bread and passed the cup of fellowship—a eucharistic ritual that quickly became as essential to Christian worship as the sharing of Jewish scriptures and listening to stories of Jesus.[11]

Dorcas is the only New Testament woman to whom a feminine form of the word "disciple" is applied, like a title. The account about her in Acts suggests that she is a leader in her community, perhaps patron and head of the widows—a woman so deserving of honor that Peter must be summoned. Though no miracle appears to have been expected, the account goes on to identify her as the only believer restored to life by one of the Twelve. *Lydia of Philippi* is a prominent businesswoman, able and intelligent enough to succeed in an arena dominated by men. She is often called the first European convert to Christianity. She contrasts with *the slave girl,* whose owners probably discard her when she can no longer utter prophecies or oracles.

---

11. In 1 Cor 11:23-26, an Epistle predating the writing of the Gospels, the eucharistic sharing has already achieved ritual language.

Perhaps Lydia welcomed her into her own household, or at least into the riverside synagogue. From Paul's later letter to Philippi and his concern about a dispute there between *Euodia and Syntyche*, we know that a Christian community continued to flourish in Philippi, and that women retained prominence.

Prisca and Aquila are a Jewish missionary couple who support their ministry by working as tentmakers. Marriage was the norm among early Christians (both Jewish and non-Jewish), and even though the Jesus movement accepted the single and the widowed as leaders, it was celibacy—not marriage—that required justification. Prisca and Aquila are well-traveled cosmopolites who know Rome, Corinth, and Ephesus. Their mobility and the time they possess to develop scriptural expertise suggest that they are childless. So well versed are they in the Jewish scriptures and the teachings of Jesus that they can take another gifted speaker in hand and instruct him more fully. Of the six mentions of Prisca and Aquila in Acts and Epistles, Prisca is listed first four times—a construction so unusual in her world as to suggest that she was the more prominent of the two.

Phoebe, deacon (*diakonos*) of Cenchreae, appears to have been the leading minister of her community. Early deacons seem both to have served (presided over) the eucharistic meal and preached the way of Jesus. In Romans 16, Paul demonstrates his esteem for Phoebe by introducing her even before he greets his friends. Paul also calls Phoebe *prostatis,* translated in the REB as "*good friend* to many, including myself." In Phoebe's world, *prostatis* variously denoted leader, ruler, or protector. As Paul uses it, it implies that she gave him her personal endorsement and backed him financially. Taken together, *diakonos* and *prostatis* suggest that her local rank and influence compare with those we would associate with a bishop.

Junia and Andronicus are assumed to have been another married couple, or at least brother and sister, since those are the two acceptable ways in which male and female names were linked. As Paul's compatriots ("relatives" in some translations), they were born outside Judea, as reflected in their names: Junia is a Hellenistic (Greek) name and Andronicus is Roman. For Paul, suffering and fruitfulness placed a stamp of authenticity on anyone's call to apostleship. By identifying Junia and Andronicus as apostles, he therefore implies not only that they have suffered for their beliefs, but that their work has borne fruit.

The four daughters of Philip appear only in Acts 21, but references to their burial place in documents of the second century suggest that their influence was long-lasting. We can deduce something of their role from other passages of Acts and Epistles. Paul lists prophecy as second only to apostleship among ministries, and second only to love among gifts of the Spirit. In his time prophecy was a ministry distinguished from speaking in tongues and associated, rather, with proclamation and teaching. According to 1 Cor 14:1–6 and Acts 13:1–3, prophets and teachers presided at worship, made official decisions, and commissioned others for special missions.

❖ ❖

Stories of people like these lead scripture scholar Elizabeth M. Tetlow to conclude that, in their day,

> There were only ministries of Jesus in which both men and women . . . served the people of God, each with his or her own gifts, for the building up of the Christian community. . . . According to the New Testament, the exclusion of women from ecclesiastical ministry is neither in accord with the teaching or practice of Jesus nor with that of the first century Church.[12]

Christian churches of our time—even those that ordain women—have yet to achieve a comparable atmosphere of welcome for the talented, capable Phoebes and Priscas and Junias who are able and ready to serve.

As women work to open up male bastions of religion, they need to remember, however, that Jesus defined ministry as service performed in love. If the good news is to unfold under our tents as it unfolded under that of Prisca, we need less to dwell on injustices of the past than to stress the positives of Judaeo-Christian tradition. One such positive is, of course, New Testament evidence of equality in early Christian ministry. Another is the portrait of Lady Wisdom contained in the Jewish books of Proverbs and Wisdom, the latter written about a century before Christ.[13] The author, a Jew of Alexandria, sought to encourage his (or her) people during a time of suffering and oppression. Women and men of today might pray as this writer did, both in praise of Lady Wisdom and in petition for her gifts:

Prayer

> In Wisdom, the artificer of all, is a spirit
> intelligent, holy, manifold, and subtle;
> not baneful, but loving the good;
> tranquil, and pervading all spirits.
> Wisdom is mobile beyond imagining:
> she penetrates and permeates all things cleanly.
> She is an aura of God, a pure effusion of the Almighty,
> a spotless mirror reflecting God's goodness.
> She renews everything and everyone.

12. Tetlow, *Women and Ministry in the New Testament*, 131.

13. The book of Wisdom appears in Roman Catholic Bibles, but because of the late date of its composition, it was not accepted into the Jewish canon or, later, the Protestant canon.

Passing into holy souls from age to age,
she produces prophets and friends of God.
God loves nothing so much as one who dwells with Wisdom.
She surpasses the stars and takes precedence
over the light of the sun.
As day supplants night,
so Wisdom prevails over prejudice and darkness.
As she reaches mightily from end to end of the cosmos,
may she enter us unhampered and, through us,
govern all things well.[14]

Connections

1. How has this chapter influenced your mental picture of the early Church? Did you come upon any surprises?

2. Of the many women mentioned in this chapter, which one appeals to you the most? Why?

3. How could Prisca and Aquila serve as role models for modern couples, especially when the wife is the more prominent of the two? From the length of their partnership, what do you deduce about Aquila's self concept and attitudes toward his wife?

4. Interpreters of the Bible have read the job as "deacon" if performed by a man, "assistant" if performed by a woman. Consider the work done by leading women in your church community. How well do their titles match their work?

For Further Reading

Anderson, Bonnie S., and Judith P. Zinsser, *A History of Their Own*, I (1988), 67–84, 183–93.

Carmody, Denise Lardner, *Biblical Woman* (1989), 120–25.

Cartledge-Hayes, Mary, *To Love Delilah* (1990),

Deen, Edith, *All of the Women of the Bible* (1955), 212–13.

Gillman, Florence Morgan, "The Ministry of Women in the Early Church," *New Theology Review* (May 1993), 89–94.

Harkness, Georgia, *Women in Church and Society* (1972), 62–67.

Moltmann-Wendel, Elisabeth, *A Land Flowing with Milk and Honey* (1988), 87–89.

Murphy, Cullen, "Women and the Bible," *The Atlantic Monthly* (August 1993), 39–45, 48, 50–55, 58, 60.

---

14. Based on Wis 7:22–8:1.

Nunnally-Cox, Janice, *Foremothers* (1981), 123–36.

Schüssler Fiorenza, Elisabeth, *In Memory of Her* (1983), 47–48, 50, 52–55, 60–65, 160–99.

Sleevi, Mary Lou, *Women of the Word* (1985), 81–84, 87–90, 93–96.

Swidler, Leonard, *Biblical Affirmations of Woman* (1979), 291–320.

Tetlow, Elizabeth M., *Women and Ministry in the New Testament* (1980), 106–7, 116–53.

Torjesen, Karen Jo. "Reconstruction of Women's Early Church History" in *Searching the Scriptures* (1993), ed. Elisabeth Schüssler Fiorenza, 290–310.

Winter, Miriam Therese, *WomanWord* (1990), 187–292.

Yamasaki, April, *Remember Lot's Wife* (1991), 107–8.

35 Woman in the Epistles of Paul: Bound or Free?

Disputed whether Paul wrote this or not

From Galatians, 1 Corinthians, Colossians, Ephesians, 1 Timothy, and Titus

"It is for freedom that Christ set us free. Stand firm, therefore . . ." (*Gal 5:1*)

Background

Paul has been acclaimed by some as a feminist and dismissed by others as the worst male chauvinist of the Bible—sometimes on the basis of the same passages. What stance on Paul can be justified? Through examination of eight passages attributed to Paul, this chapter seeks a tentative answer. The passages start with Gal 3:28, Paul's ringing declaration of equality in Christ, and move on to controversial texts from 1 Corinthians, Colossians, Ephesians, 1 Timothy, and Titus. In this chapter, a "Texts and Commentary" section replaces the usual Story section. "Texts and Commentary" takes the passages one at a time, presenting a passage and then commenting on it before going on to the next.

Before examining the texts, however, it is only fair to Paul to note that he did not write all of the Epistles attributed to him. On the basis of language, style, theology, and the issues and events mentioned in the letters, scholars conclude that Paul is the author of Romans, 1 and 2 Corinthians, Galatians, Philippians, 1 Thessalonians, and Philemon. Debate continues, however, on the authorship of Colossians, Ephesians, and 2 Thessalonians. Most scholars agree that Paul did not write 1 and 2 Timothy or Titus, a set of letters considered the work of a later writer. That writer is called "Pseudo-Paul," from his having adopted the custom of attaching a famous man's name to his work. A note on the probable authorship of each text appears next to it in this form: <u>PAUL</u>, <u>DISPUTED</u>, or <u>PSEUDO-PAUL</u>.

Texts and Commentaries

Equality in Christ: *A Paraphrase of Gal 3:28*   <u>PAUL</u>

Baptized into union with Christ, you have all put on Christ like a garment. There is no longer any such thing as Jew or Greek, slave or free, male and female; you are all one person in Christ.

Commentary. Gal 3:28 proclaims an ancient baptismal formula. It seems to represent not any one man's breakthrough, but the broad and usual belief of early Christians. As Elisabeth Schüssler Fiorenza points out, the "male and female" phrase specifically evokes Gen 1:27, where humanity is created "male and female." The phrase thus does not assert that gender is abolished in Christ, but that a patriarchal understanding of social roles is inappropriate within the Christian movement.[1] And since it is baptism of all rather than circumcision of males that inititates people into Christ, every Christian shares the same rights and duties: "in Christ" denotes a sphere of existence in which persons of all kinds are welcomed as full members.

Sex in Marriage: *A Paraphrase of 1 Cor 7:1–4, 7* PAUL

Now for the matters you wrote about. You say, "It is a good thing for a man not to have intercourse with a woman." I say, in such immoral times let each man have his own wife and each woman her own husband. He must give her what is due to her, and she must give him what is due to him. The wife cannot claim her body as her own; it is her husband's. Equally, the husband cannot claim his body as his own; it is his wife's. To the married I give this ruling from the Lord Jesus: wives and husbands must not divorce each other. I would like everyone to be [celibate] as I am, but each person has the gift God has assigned, one this gift and another one that gift.

Commentary. Corinth, located on the isthmus between mainland Greece and its southern peninsula, was a cosmopolitan port also known as a "sin city." The notoriety arose in part from the presence of the cults of Dionysus and Cybele, which involved ritual sex, and also from the presence of well-educated, high-class courtesans called *hetaerae*. That the city boasted other articulate women as well is demonstrated by references to Prisca, Phoebe, and Chloe in Acts, Romans, and 1 Corinthians. But ordinary women were confined to their homes and received no formal education; and the men of Corinth assumed as a right their use of wives for legitimate children, slave women for instant sexual gratification, and *hetaerae* for professional entertainment and literate conversation.

The passage from 1 Corinthians 7 may nevertheless arise out of a different context. From other parts of Paul's letters, it can be deduced that a pattern of withdrawing from long-term sexual relationships had arisen in the church of Corinth. Many women, especially those called to the prophetic ministry, seem to have asserted authority over their own bodies and violated social custom by withdrawing from sexual relations. In this passage, Paul acknowledges that his heart is with the women who wish to abstain. But

---

1. *In Memory of Her* (1983), 211.

because he also fears that lack of sexual self-control could powerfully disrupt a community (as other parts of his letters demonstrate), he urges—but does not command—the resumption of conjugal relations within marriage.[2] The question to which Paul responds is couched in terms of men, but he phrases every part of his response in terms of woman as well as man. He stresses the mutual obligation of married people to meet each other's sexual needs, and he commands mutual fidelity as Jesus' own ruling. Only as his own personal preference does he mention celibacy, but he is careful not to identify it as superior to marriage. Instead he offers what may be his clearest word on the issue of marriage and celibacy: gifts differ.

Hair Styles and Head Coverings: *A Paraphrase of 1 Cor 11:3–16*   <u>PAUL</u>

I want you to understand that man has Christ as his head, while woman's head is man, as Christ's head is God. A man who covers his head while he prays or prophesies brings shame on his head; a woman who prays or prophesies bareheaded brings shame on her head; it's as bad as if her head were shaved.[3] A man must not cover his head because he is the image of God and the mirror of God's glory, whereas a woman reflects the glory of man. For man did not originally spring from woman, but woman from man. And man was not created for woman's sake, but woman for the sake of man. Therefore a woman should have a sign of authority on her head, because of the angels.[4] In our community, woman is as essential to man as man to woman. Woman was made out of man originally, but man now comes to be through woman, and God is source of all. Judge for yourself. Doesn't nature teach you that long hair disgraces a man but is a woman's glory? Her hair was given her as a covering. If anyone still wants to argue, I tell you no such custom exists among us or in any congregation of God's people.

Commentary. In 1 Corinthians Paul's thought is often difficult to follow, because he is responding to questions put to him by the community—questions we do not possess for reference. In this passage, Paul's overall intention can be understood: Lest Christians be mistaken for prostitutes or members of ecstatic cults, they should style their hair in a manner everyone considers respectable. The arguments Paul advances in support of this thesis are more difficult to sort out.

2. For a full discussion of the women of Corinth, see Antoinette Clark Wire's *The Corinthian Women Prophets* (1990). On this passage, see especially 72, 81, and 82–84.

3. At the end of the passage hair itself—not a veil—seems to be defined as the appropriate head covering.

4. The dangling phrase may denote angels thought to watch over liturgical services, envoys from other churches, or a thought that Paul failed to complete.

The "head" passage has been taken to mean that man is superior to woman, but Paul avoids the Greek word for head that denotes "ruler"—*archē,* as in "archduke." He chooses instead *kephalē,* here meaning "source," as in "headwaters." In all of these sentences based on the story of the creation of Adam and Eve (Gen 2), Paul takes pains *not* to conclude that prior creation makes man superior to woman. If that were the case, he implies, all men living would have to consider women their superiors, for every man is born of woman. Paul finally attempts to extricate himself from his own clumsy use of the Adam and Eve story by reminding his hearers that God is the ultimate Source. (And belatedly recalling that Greek Christians might not know Hebrew scriptures, Paul then adds for them a weak argument from "nature"— that is, custom.) Regarding head coverings, one line from this text—woman's wearing a sign of authority on her head—has been read as requiring women to wear a veil as a sign of submission to authority. More recent commentators interpret the line as meaning the opposite: that a woman's respectable hair style serves as a sign of her own claim to Christian authority.

Overall, Paul's convoluted presentation seems not to satisfy even himself, and he ends by resorting to authoritarian pronouncement: Adopt my ideas about proper hair styles because I say so and because they represent standard practice. As further background for this passage, it may nevertheless be helpful to compare his words with some of the hair styles he would have been envisioning: Respectable Greek women bound up their hair, and Greek men wore theirs relatively short. The *hetaerae* wore elaborate, jeweled coiffures, and regular prostitutes often clipped their hair extremely short. In the cult of Isis, male initiates shaved their heads. In the cults of Isis, Dionysus, and Cybele, female initiates wore their hair long and loose. Among Jews, respectable women wore their hair braided and veiled.

Woman's Voice in Worship: *A Paraphrase of 1 Cor 14:33-35*   DISPUTED

As in all congregations of God's people, women should keep silent at the meeting, keeping their place as the law directs. It is a shocking thing for them to talk at the meeting. If they want to know something, they can ask their husbands at home.

Commentary. Since total silence would bar women from saying so much as "Amen," even fundamentalist readers take this passage as a ban only on women's leading services or preaching. However, the text contradicts other passages by Paul which take for granted woman's equal role in worship; no Pauline "law" of Christian worship is known; the verses interrupt the flow of the chapter; and the passage sounds suspiciously like Pseudo-Paul's exhortations in 1 Tim 2:8–15 (discussed below). For all of these reasons, many scholars conclude that a scribe inserted the verses into a copy of Paul's letter at a time when opposition to women's exercise of leadership was growing.

It is also possible, however, to imagine Paul writing such a paragraph. Scripture scholar Antoinette Clark Wire demonstrates that the manuscript evidence for considering this passage an insertion is quite poor. No manuscript exists, for example, that omits these words. She goes on to discuss the sentences in context. They follow Paul's regulation banning disruptive speaking in tongues, and they hark back to his urging in 1 Corinthians 7 that married women should return to a more conventional role. Wire finds it difficult to perceive this passage as anything less than an attempt to silence outspoken women prophets—an attempt in which Paul employs everything from written law to social convention to shame such women. For Paul to put his authority on the line in this way, Wire concludes, the stakes must have been high indeed. The women he opposed must have been some of the most respected members of the Corinthian community.[5]

"Household Codes": *A Paraphrase of Col 3:18–22, 4:1*   DISPUTED

Wives, be subject to your husbands, as your Christian duty. Husbands, love your wives and do not be harsh with them. Children, obey your parents in all things. Slaves, give entire obedience to your earthly masters. Masters, be just and fair to your slaves, knowing that you also have a master in heaven.

A Paraphrase of Ephesians 5:21–25, 28, 33   DISPUTED

Be subject to one another out of reverence for Christ. Wives, be subject to your husbands as though to the Lord, for the man is the head of the woman just as Christ is the head of the church.[6] As the church is subject to Christ, women must be subject to their husbands in everything. Husbands, love your wives as Christ loved the church and gave himself up for it. You should love your wives as you love your own bodies. You must love your wife as your very self. Wives, show reverence for your husbands.

Commentary. Domestic or Household Codes were standard treatises both within Jewish-Hellenistic and within Greco-Roman society at Paul's time. Comprised of class divisions and lists of the duties proper to each category, they were devised to promote the good order of household and State. By welcoming slaves and married women from conservative Greco-Roman households, early Christian communities violated the class distinctions of these codes. By the end of the first century, however, some Christians had grown anxious for acceptance; they wished to avoid even the appearance of disrupting State order. Some teachers therefore adopted the secular codes of conduct verbatim, adding only minor modifications: Col 3, above, inserts the words "Christian duty"; a parallel passage from 1 Pet 2:13–3:7 adds only the opening phrase, "For Jesus' sake."

5. *The Corinthian Women Prophets* (1990), 149–58.
6. See the previous discussion of "head" under 1 Cor 11:3–16.

Eph 5, in contrast, interweaves Christian motivation throughout, and establishes a degree of male-female mutuality even in the sentences after the first one. The Greek verb in *"be subject* to your husbands" means voluntarily to place oneself at the disposition of another. The Greek verb in *"love* your wives" means to act in a way that shows a caring attitude. Both terms connote giving up self-interest in order to respond to the needs of another. Bristow therefore prefers to translate the commands, "Wives, be supportive of your husbands" and "Husbands, be responsive to the needs of your wives."[7]

Woman's Place in Worship: *A Paraphrase of 1 Tim 2:8–15*   PSEUDO-PAUL

It is my desire that in every place men should pray. Women must dress in a becoming, sober manner, not with elaborate hair styles, lavish jewels, and expensive clothes, but adorned with good deeds, as befits women who claim to be religious. Their role is to learn, listening quietly and with due submission. I do not let women teach or dictate to the men. They should keep quiet, because Adam was created first, and Eve afterwards. Adam was not deceived, but the woman was deceived and became a transgressor. Salvation for the woman lies in the bearing of children, provided they[8] persevere in faith, love, holiness, and modesty.

Commentary. Pseudo-Paul's directives about clothing and hair styles appear similar in intent to the pragmatic advice Paul addressed to the people of Corinth, though Pseudo-Paul addresses women only. Basically he tells women to avoid the clothing and hair styles associated with high class prostitutes like the *hetaerae* of Corinth. The prohibition against women's teaching men may also arise partly out of fear of giving scandal. Among strictly observant Jews, a man could divorce his wife for speaking with other men in public. Among Greeks, only cult priestesses or courtesans like the *hetaerae* debated ideas with men outside the home. The directive that women should "learn" seems to reflect the writer's biased belief that women are stupid and weak-minded, especially since his final lines advocate outright discrimination against women. Unlike Paul, who uses Adam and Eve stories with the utmost care, this writer argues that woman is inferior because Eve was created after Adam. Is man then inferior to the whale, having been created after the whale? The author is not interested in logic, however. Wishing only to support his own negative attitude toward women, he goes so far as to imply that Adam never sinned at all, and that only woman "transgressed."

In the process, Pseudo-Paul approaches heresy. It is remotely possible that his statement about childbearing is intended, in part, to oppose the Gnostic belief that sexual intimacy is evil. But he comes close to making

---

7. Bristow, *What Paul Really Said About Women,* 39–45.

8. The unreferenced "they" is variously read as meaning husband and wife, women in general, or a woman's children. Some translators simply opt for "she."

childbearing sound more important than faith or baptism, and he endorses that view consistently. In 2 Tim 1:5 he makes it sound as though faith was handed on to Timothy from Lois and Eunice, his grandmother and mother, through the actual physical process of childbirth.

Standards for Gender Roles: *A Paraphrase of Titus 2:2–6*   PSEUDO-PAUL

The older men should be sober, dignified, temperate, and sound in faith, love and fortitude. The older women should be reverent in demeanor, not scandalmongers or slaves to drinking. Older women must set a high standard and teach the younger women to be loving wives and mothers, to be temperate, chaste, busy at home, and kind, respecting their husbands' authority. Urge the younger men also to be temperate in all things, and set them a good example yourself.

Commentary. Writing late in the first century, Pseudo-Paul here adopts the Domestic or Household Codes of his time outright. There is nothing specifically Christian about this passage. Although the writer mentions men, he makes his bias clear by devoting much more space to keeping women homebound, occupied, and submissive. The very fact that he feels compelled to offer these directives suggests, however, that women still were, in fact, adopting other roles outside the home.

Reflection

Was Paul a consummate male chauvinist, a feminist who championed the equality of all human beings, or something else? Of this chapter's eight passages, the five that are of disputed or Pseudo-Pauline authorship bind woman far more than they free her. The three attributable with certainty to Paul include Gal 3:28 ("no male and female") and the two from First Corinthians on sex in marriage and the significance of hair styles. In those two passages, Paul works hard to address women and men evenhandedly. Add, as well, the passages from Romans, 1 Corinthians, and Philippians cited in the previous chapter—passages in which Paul hails women leaders as his equals—and authentic-Paul seems to emerge, overall, as friend to woman.

Still, his culture prevented him from grasping the full implications of human equality. Thus while I cannot call him a male chauvinist, I cannot call him a feminist, either. He seems, rather, a man who sometimes flounders as he works to interpret the word of Jesus to a church beset by external menace and internal bickering. He is a good leader who seeks to reconcile differences within the communities he has founded. He is a good negotiator who can accept a degree of compromise for the sake of order. I doubt that this rabbinically trained Jew ever imagined his *ad hoc* advice—still in draft mode in terms of the Christian principles he was attempting to apply—would one day become enshrined as dogma. All things considered, I find a harried pastor more than anything else—a pastor whose own interpretations of Jesus' message sometimes faltered, even as he engaged in putting out one brush fire after another.

Pseudo-Paul and later interpreters, however, seem deliberately to have closed their eyes to the vision of Jesus. Reasonably, one might expect a religious movement to place greater emphasis on the words and deeds of its founder than on letters designed to bring the movement into conformity with secular society. Unfortunately, however, church history is no more logical than any other kind. As early as the second century CE and certainly by the fifth, writers known as the Latin Fathers had actually reversed some elements of the gospel of Jesus. On the basis of passages such as those drawn from Household Codes, they had substituted authority for service. They had also come to promote life-denying forms of asceticism over Jesus' life-affirming celebrations of eating and drinking and marrying. And they had ground woman down from full human estate to sub-human status.

The Greek philosophical systems which then and later permeated the structure of society taught (among other things) that woman was a malformed man and a source of filth. Far more influenced by such views than by the Jewish roots of Christianity or the actions and attitudes of Jesus, the Fathers browbeat woman, doing incalculable harm both to women themselves and to the spirit of Christianity. Tertullian (160–225), for example, scorned woman as "the devil's gateway"; Jerome (342–420) implored, "What do these wretched sin-laden hussies want!"[9]

Most shameful of all is the story of Cyril and Hypatia. Cyril (376–444) was Bishop of Alexandria, Egypt; Hypatia (c. 370–415) was a celebrated mathematician and philosopher of the Alexandrian Neoplatonic School. The bigoted, violent Cyril drove thousands of Alexandrian Jews from their homes and synagogues; and in a country that boasted a centuries-long tradition of educated women, he persisted in teaching that women could not, and must not be allowed to, deal with weighty matters. The very existence of the beautiful, multi-talented Hypatia proved him wrong on a daily basis. She attracted scores of students; she invented scientific instruments; she wrote treatises on mathematics and astronomy. The tensions climaxed one day in 415 when a mob of Christian monks—directly or indirectly incited by Cyril—dragged Hypatia from her chariot, stripped her, cut her throat, and burned her body and her books.[10] As Episcopal priest Janice Nunnally-Cox writes in her book *Foremothers*,

9. Quoted both in Janice Nunnally-Cox, *Foremothers* (1981), 153–54; and in Leonard Swidler, *Biblical Affirmations of Woman* (1976), 346, 348.

10. Bonnie S. Anderson and Judith P. Zinsser, *A History of Their Own*, I (1988), 62–63; Nunnally-Cox, *Foremothers*, 155; and Swidler, *Biblical Affirmations of Woman*, 344–45.

Stories like this should make us weep. For what happened to Hypatia was symbolically happening to women of the church: woman was stripped, naked; she was humiliated, scorned, and condemned. She alone carried the burden of sin; she alone bore a tarnished image.[11]

❖ ❖

Some might argue that mitigating circumstances existed during the early centuries of Christianity; that women could surely endure a few backward regulations about silence and hair styles if the rules would help Christianity ride out a storm of Greco-Roman outrage. But that particular storm had passed by Cyril's time. If today's Western church no longer enforces total submission upon women, the reason is not that the church has recovered the principles of its founder, but that secular society has led the way. Nor is the change complete. Women exist in a twilight zone, half bound and half free, waiting for their officials to open their eyes to the daylight of human equality, a daylight rich in potential for humankind.

As one small step in the right direction, women might immediately urge church authorities to end public proclamation of all of the texts presented in this chapter, with the exception of Galatians 3:28. The other texts—even those by authentic-Paul—remain so enmeshed in first-century cultural details as to defy immediate understanding; and no matter how well the texts are explained *after* proclamation, they have already renewed the force of centuries of baneful interpretation. Further, while listeners may manage no longer even to hear the condoning of slavery implied in the text from Colossians 3, many still accept as natural the subordination of woman to man—especially when they hear the words proclaimed from the sanctuary. Enshrining such texts in our liturgies is no way to help people understand that sexism is just as unchristian as slavery. In place of such readings, let us proclaim passages like these, which do echo the spirit of Jesus:

Prayer

In one Spirit we were baptized,
and we, though many, form one body in Christ.
There no longer exists among us
Jew or Greek, bound or free, male and female:
we are all one person in Christ.
Stand firm, therefore, and refuse to submit again
to yokes that dominate and divide.

As members of Christ,
you have been richly blessed with gifts from God.

11. Nunnally-Cox, *Foremothers,* 155.

Some are apostles or teachers; some perform noble works.
Others are gifted in healing or administration.
There are different gifts, but one Spirit;
different forms of service, but one Lord.
One God works in all, giving each person
a different manifestation of the Spirit
for the good of all.
Share your gifts, therefore,
in compassion, humility, and gentleness.
Bear with one another. If you have any grievances,
forgive one another as God has forgiven you.

Over everything, put on love,
for love is the bond of perfection.
Love is patient, love is kind.
Love neither seeks its own interests nor broods over injury,
but bears all things, believes all things,
hopes all things, endures all things.
Love never fails.
Knowledge will be brought to nothing, tongues will cease,
great works will be forgotten.
But faith, hope, and love remain;
and the greatest of these is love.[12]

Connections

Check out Galatians Ephesians

1. How do you assess Paul? Has your opinion varied over the years? To what extent can you agree with the views expressed in the Reflection of this chapter?

2. Imagine a service at your church in which women do not preach, sing, pray aloud, or even say "Amen." What effect would women's *total* silence have on the quality of worship? On your sense of community? On your image of yourself?

3. Some passages from Paul and Pseudo-Paul dwell on styles of hair and clothing. Does one's appearance make that important a statement? What might a visitor to your church deduce from the way members of your congregation dress?

4. In what ways (if any) do you think the life style of a church member should differ from the life style of any other member of society?

12. Based on Gal 3:27–28 and 5:1; Col 3:12–17; and 1 Cor 12:2–13, 27–31; 13:1–13; and 14:39–40.

For Further Reading

Bristow, John Temple, *What Paul Really Said About Women* (1988), 1–129 (entire book).

Carmody, Denise Lardner, *Biblical Woman* (1989), 126–31.

Eisler, Riane, *The Chalice and the Blade* (1987), 115.

Gundry, Patricia, *Neither Slave Nor Free* (San Francisco: Harper & Row, 1987), 47.

Harkness, Georgia, *Women in Church and Society* (1972), 53.

Marrow, Stanley P., *Paul: His Letters and His Theology* (1986), 18–19, 50–55.

Mollenkott, Virginia Ramey, *Women, Men, and the Bible* (1988), 12–13, 78–79.

Moloney, Francis J., *Woman: First Among the Faithful* (1986), 36–42.

Nunnally-Cox, Janice, *Foremothers* (1981), 137–19.

Schüssler Fiorenza, Elisabeth, "Continuing Our Critical Work," in *Feminist Interpretation of the Bible*, ed. Letty M. Russell (1985), 134.

Schüssler Fiorenza, Elisabeth, *In Memory of Her* (1983), 52–55, 60, 208–37, 251–79.

Stanton, Elizabeth Cady, *The Woman's Bible*, Part II (1898), 164–65.

Swidler, Leonard, *Biblical Affirmations of Woman* (1979), 162–63, 321–38, 354–55.

Wire, Antoinette Clark, *The Corinthian Women Prophets* (1990), 72–81, 82–84, 149–58.

Woodward, Kenneth, "How to Read Paul, 2,000 Years Later," *Newsweek*, 29 February 1988, 65.

Epilogue:
Biblical Traditions Affirming Woman

"Do not be afraid; you are worth more than any
number of sparrows." (*Matthew 10:31*)

The history of Christianity is rife with misuse of the Bible to oppress, even per-secute women, and most Christian and Jewish women can tell their own horror stories in relation to the preaching of specific passages. Yet just as arguments rooted in the Old Testament are no longer advanced to require circumcision of Christian men, so the use of texts that restrict women can no longer be justified on theological (or any other) grounds. Feminist biblical theologians have been of enormous help to all believers through their work to distinguish between passages that offer divinely inspired themes and passages that reflect culturally imposed bias.

On the large scale, the feminist approach highlights themes and images that are liberating to all believers: God is one who creates, liberates, and comforts; God is one who holds especially dear the most vulnerable members of human society; God is one who carries us all from birth to death. On the small scale, feminist analysis illuminates passages previously translated poorly or taken as expressing God's will when, in fact, they merely reflect the unconscious bias of the male author or interpreter. Some citations actually become affirmative of woman when their nuances are explored, such as "I will make a suitable partner for the man" (Gen 2:18, chapter 1). Others, such as "I do not permit a woman to teach" (1 Tim 2:12, chapter 35), must be balanced against the weight of scripture as a whole—including such pas-sages as "Honor your father and your mother" (Ex 20:12); "Your sons and your daughters shall prophesy" (Joel 2:28); "In Christ there is no longer Jew or Greek, slave or free, male and female" (Gal 3:28).

Additionally, many biblical images indirectly affirm woman by portray-ing God as feminine. In addition to the presentations of Lady Wisdom cited in the Prologue, other such passages from the Old Testament include Ps 91 and 131 (God as mother eagle and as mother holding a child), Isa 46:3–4 and 49:14–16 (God as experiencing labor and pregnancy), and Job 38:8–11, 29–30 (God as cosmic mother). In the New Testament, Jesus' images of God include those of a homemaker who loses a silver coin (Lk 15:8–10) and a baker woman who understands the properties of yeast (Lk 13:20–21, Mt 13:33). An image common to both Testaments is that of God as nursing mother: "Taste and see that [God] is good" (Ps 34:8); "Like the newborn infants you are, you should be craving for pure spiritual milk so that you may thrive on it and be saved; for surely you have tasted that [God] is good" (1 Pet 2:2–3).

According to theologian Phyllis Trible, another powerful image of God as feminine lies hidden in a recurrent Old Testament phrase limited to no single author or historical period—*Yahweh rahûm,* "Yahweh merciful [and gracious]." Trible contends that both the adjective *rahûm* ("merciful" or "compassionate") and the noun *rahamîm* ("mercy" or "compassion") derive from the same root as *rehem,* "womb." The literal meaning of *rahamîm,* mercy or compassion, thus becomes "trembling from the inner parts" or "yearning from the womb." The Old Testament applies the words *rahûm* and *rahamîm* not only to the saving actions of Yahweh on behalf of Israel, but also to God's response to individuals in distress:

> Is Ephraim my dear son? my darling child? For the more I speak of him, the more do I remember him. Therefore, *my womb trembles* for him; I will truly show *motherly-compassion* upon him.
>
> —Jer 31:20[1]

> But you . . . are God, *compassionate* and gracious. . . . Turn toward me and show me your favor. . . .
>
> —Ps 86:15–16

Even if one rejects Trible's linguistic analysis, she provides a service by drawing attention to the image of a God filled with mercy and compassion. Like the portrait of the father in Jesus' parable of the Prodigal Son, the qualities of such a God transcend gender limitations. Such a God is more parental than patriarchal; such a God models the finest of human—not merely male—attributes.

The more obvious biblical images of God as feminine were known and celebrated until fairly recent historical times. Church Fathers who expanded upon feminine images of God include Clement of Alexandria (c. 150–211), John Chrysostom (347–407), Origen (c. 185–c. 254), Irenaeus (c. 120–c. 200), and Augustine (354–430). Later writers and mystics who explored such images include Bede (673–735), Bernard of Clairvaux (1090–1153), Peter Lombard (1110–1164), Thomas Aquinas (1225–1274), Catherine of Siena (1347–1380), Bridget of Sweden (c. 1303–1373), Margery Kempe (c. 1373–c. 1440), Julian of Norwich (1342–after 1416), Teresa of Avila (1515–1582), and John Donne (1572–1631).

Yet throughout this history of viewing God as feminine as well as masculine, patriarchal attitudes still dominated church and society. Some of the same Fathers who waxed eloquent on God as mother despised the mothers in

---

1. Presented in Trible's translation, from "Journey of a Metaphor" in *God and the Rhetoric of Spirituality* (1978), 31–45.

their own congregations. In other words, inclusive language and imagery have coexisted and can coexist with injustice toward living women. By itself, use of images inclusive of the feminine cannot reverse the injustices of centuries. Nonetheless, recognizing the feminine within God can help us to demonstrate our own commitment to human equality, and it can show that we recognize the mystery of God as transcending any single set of images.

❖ ❖

Returning to the large scale, we can find in the Bible an additional overarching theme of particular relevance to our world: a unified vision of humankind. The Bible may assume a society that follows patriarchal rules, yet it never divides human traits into the feminine and the masculine. No innate differences preclude women from adopting "male" roles, should the situation warrant it, or men's adopting "female" roles. Judith can execute a dreaded foe; David can take to his bed in grief on the death of a child. In their thoughts and emotions, strategies and gifts, biblical women and men show no appreciable differences. Rebekah and Laban both employ deception to achieve their ends; Prisca and Aquila expound the scriptures side by side; psalmists cry out not in male joy or despair, but in human emotion. Economic, educational, and sociological changes of recent centuries have made possible for us a less gender-divided world, and waves of feminism have given us a vision of a world organized according to a cooperative model. The biblical concept of an essential humanity shared equally by woman and by man speaks far more directly to such a world than gender divisions derived from Greek philosophy ever did.

Remaining on the large scale, we can also note that whole chunks of the Bible affirm woman. One such chunk is the Book of Ruth, discussed in chapter 15. Another is the Song of Songs. This earthy poem celebrates an erotic love so devoid of patriarchal overtones that scholars cannot always distinguish between the voices of the woman and the man. The lovers' mutual delight in and total love of one another—a love in no way predicated upon a need or desire to produce children—bursts from the pages of the Bible as a celebration of human mutuality. Both the woman and the man work as shepherds (1:7–8, 2:16); each seeks and calls out to the other (3:1–5, 5:2–8); either may initiate the lovemaking (2:10–15); each delights in and praises the other's body (4:1–15, 5:10–16). Together they rejoice in the intimacy and mutuality of a love "strong as death," a love that "many waters cannot quench" (8:6–7).

The Gospels as a whole also affirm woman. In contrast with the many passages that portray male disciples as lacking faith, the Gospels contain only positive images of woman.[2] Even though the Gospel writers had themselves been inculcated from birth with patriarchal attitudes, they could not prevent

---

2. The single exception is the portrait of Herodias, who appears in a story of John the Baptist rather than in a story of Jesus.

themselves from reporting the gender blindness of a Jesus who saw *people*—not valuable males and valueless females. Jesus' attitude is summarized in an essay by English writer Dorothy L. Sayers (1893–1957):

> Perhaps it is no wonder that the women were first at the Cradle and last at the Cross. They had never known a man like this Man—there never has been such another. A prophet and teacher who never nagged at them, never flattered or coaxed or patronized; who never made arch pokes about them, never treated them either as "The women, God help us!" or "The ladies, God bless them!"; who rebuked without querulousness and praised without condescension; who took their questions and arguments seriously; who never mapped out their sphere for them, never urged them to be feminine or jeered at them for being female; who had no axe to grind and no uneasy male dignity to defend; who took them as he found them and was completely unselfconscious. There is no act, no sermon, no parable in the whole Gospel that borrows its pungency from female perversity; nobody could possibly guess from the words and deeds of Jesus that there was anything "funny" about women's nature.[3]

Finally, of course, stories of individual biblical women affirm the value of woman. In retrospect, it is remarkable that the patriarchal writers of the Bible should have named or shown respect for even one woman. That they mention well over three hundred and develop the stories of more than forty is extraordinary. Despite themselves, the writers repeatedly demonstrate that God is no respecter of gender, but selects and involves women and men alike in the divine activities of giving, preserving, and redeeming life.

God's own chosen people are defined not as all descendants of Abraham, but only as those who can call Sarah mother. God confides not to Isaac but to Rebekah the fact that Jacob is to be favored over Esau. Moses, the great liberator, is himself saved by an entire group of women. Deborah, Jael, Judith, and Esther serve as direct instruments of liberation. God blesses many whom society considered outsiders, among them Tamar (daughter-in-law of Judah), Rahab, Ruth, the Canaanite woman, and women whom society dismissed as ritually unclean. God fills Mary, mother of Jesus, with a Spirit bent on freeing people from bondage of every sort. On a par with male disciples, Martha and Mary, Mary Magdalene, the Samaritan woman, Prisca, Phoebe, Junia, and many other women spread the good news of Jesus Christ. Given such women to celebrate, it no longer seems so strange that women of today continue to say "yes" to the biblical tradition in which they find their roots:

3. Dorothy L. Sayers, "The Human—Not-Quite Human," *Unpopular Opinions* (London: Victor Gollancz, 1946), 121–122. Quoted in Carolyn G. Heilbrun, *Toward a Recognition of Androgyny* (New York: W. W. Norton & Company, 1973), 19.

We Remember

When our world crumbles,
we remember Eve
and persevere.

When we are uprooted,
we remember Sarah
and celebrate God's surprises.

When we enter the arid desert,
we remember Hagar
and trust in the God of Vision.

When we become mired in old behaviors,
we remember the wife of Lot
and move forward.

When our clever plans turn out badly,
we remember Rebekah and Leah and Rachel
and seek to know God's will.

When authorities fail to act justly,
we remember the women who rescued Moses
and rouse ourselves to action.

When disaster threatens,
we remember Rahab and Deborah and Jael
and act to protect our own.

When friends suffer rape or abuse,
we remember the daughters of Leah and Jephthah and Maacah
and work to build a world where assault is unthinkable.

When our situation seems unendurable,
we remember Hannah and the widows of the Bible
and turn to the God who rescues the lowly.

When we feel alone,
we remember Ruth and Orpah and Naomi
and nurture our friendships.

When others are maligned for their loyalties or actions,
we remember Delilah, Bathsheba, and Jezebel
and acknowledge how little we know.

When heroes seem lacking,
we remember Judith and Esther
and rally behind people of vision.

When God's ways seem dark and mysterious,
we remember Mary, the Mother of Jesus,
and ponder the Word in our hearts.

When the wisdom of the world fails us,
we remember seers from Huldah to Elizabeth
and listen to the prophets of our lives.

When we are condemned or ostracized,
we remember the women Jesus healed
and turn to the God who restores us.

When our church denies us a voice,
we remember the Samaritan woman,
Magdalene, Prisca, and Junia
and know that God nevertheless calls us.

When our world seems lost to violence and rage,
we remember the women of the Bible
and work for God's reign of peace and justice.[4]

For Further Reading

Carmody, Denise Lardner, *Biblical Woman* (1989), 29–30, 60–65, 72–76, 157–62.

Frymer-Kensky, Tikva, *In the Wake of the Goddesses* (1992), 108–17, 121, 127–28, 213–17.

Greeley, Andrew M., and Jacob Neusner, *The Bible and Us* (1990), 144.

Mollenkott, Virginia Ramey, *Women, Men, and the Bible* (1988), 69–73.

Mollenkott, Virginia Ramey, *The Divine Feminine* (1989), 8–14.

Okure, Teresa, "Women in the Bible" in *With Passion and Compassion* (1988), ed. Virginia Fabella and Mercy Amba Oduyoye, 47–57.

Schneiders, Sandra M., *Women and the Word* (1986), 22–53.

Swidler, Leonard, *Biblical Affirmations of Woman* (1979), 21–50, 72–95, 161–205.

Trible, Phyllis, *God and the Rhetoric of Sexuality* (1978), 31–45, 144–65.

Warner, Marina, *Alone of All Her Sex* (1976), 123–27.

Yamasaki, April, *Remember Lot's Wife* (1991), 51–52.

4. "We Remember" Copyright © 1993 Rose Sallberg Kam

Bibliography

Basic References

Achtemeier, Paul J., general ed. *Harper's Bible Dictionary*. San Francisco: Harper & Row, 1985.

Bergant, Dianne, and Robert J. Karris, general eds. *The Collegeville Bible Commentary*. 2 vols. Collegeville, Minn.: The Liturgical Press, 1992.

Biederman, Hans. *Dictionary of Symbolism: Cultural Icons and the Meanings Behind Them*. New York: Facts on File, Inc., 1992.

Brown, Raymond E. *The Community of the Beloved Disciple*. New York: Paulist Press, 1979.

Brown, Raymond E., Joseph A. Fitzmyer, and Roland E. Murphy, eds. *The New Jerome Biblical Commentary*. Englewood Cliffs, NJ: Prentice-Hall, 1990.

Cirlot, J. E. *A Dictionary of Symbols*. 2d ed. New York: Philosophical Library, 1971.

Freyne, Sean. *The World of the New Testament*. Wilmington, Del: Michael Glazier, Inc., 1982.

Jeremias, Joachim. *Jerusalem in the Time of Jesus*. Philadelphia: Fortress Press, 1969.

McKenzie, John L. *Dictionary of the Bible*. Milwaukee: The Bruce Publishing Company, 1965.

Marrow, Stanley B. *Paul: His Letters and His Theology*. Mahwah, N.J.: Paulist Press, 1986.

Mays, James L., general ed. *Harper's Bible Commentary*. San Francisco: Harper & Row, 1988.

Miller, Robert J., ed. *The Complete Gospels: Annotated Scholars Version*. Sonoma Calif.: Polebridge Press, 1992.

Pritchard, James B., ed. *The Harper Concise Atlas of the Bible*. Harper Collins Publishers, 1991.

Von Rad, Gerhard. *Genesis*. Rev. ed. Philadelphia: Westminster Press, 1972.

Walker, Barbara G. *The Woman's Dictionary of Symbols and Sacred Objects*. San Francisco: Harper & Row, 1988.

Works on Women and the Bible

Bristow, John Temple. *What Paul Really Said About Women*. San Francisco: Harper & Row, 1988.

Carmody, Denise Lardner. *Biblical Woman: Contemporary Reflections on Scriptural Texts*. New York: Crossroad, 1989.

Cartledge-Hayes, Mary. *To Love Delilah: Claiming the Women of the Bible*. San Diego: LuraMedia, 1990.

Crouch, James E. "How Early Christians Viewed the Birth of Jesus." *Bible Review* 7, no. 5 (October 1991): 34–38.

Deen, Edith. *All of the Women of the Bible*. San Francisco: Harper & Row, 1955.

Dunning, James B. "Scrutinizing the Samaritan Woman." *Catechumenate* (January 1993): 27–30.

Fabella, Virginia, and Mercy Amba Oduyoye, eds. *With Passion and Compassion: Third World Women Doing Theology*. Maryknoll, N.Y.: Orbis Books, 1988.

Frymer-Kensky, Tikva. *In the Wake of the Goddesses: Women, Culture, and the Biblical Transformation of Pagan Myth*. New York: Fawcett Columbine, 1992.

Gillman, Florence Morgan. "The Ministry of Women in the Early Church." *New Theology Review* 6, no. 2 (May 1993): 89–94.

Heltzmer, Michael. "The Book of Esther—Where Does Fiction Start and History End?" *Bible Review* 8, no. 1 (February 1992): 24–30, 41.

Johnson, Ann. *Miryam of Nazareth: Woman of Strength and Wisdom*. Notre Dame, Ind.: Ave Maria Press, 1984.

Kirk, Martha Ann. *God of Our Mothers: Seven Biblical Women Tell Their Stories*. Cincinnati, Ohio: St. Anthony Messenger Press, 1985. Audiocassette, 90 min.

Mollenkott, Virginia Ramey. *The Divine Feminine: The Biblical Image of God as Female*. New York: Crossroad, 1983.

Mollenkott, Virginia Ramey. *Women, Men, and the Bible*. Rev. ed. with study guide. New York: Crossroad, 1988.

Moloney, Francis J. *Woman: First Among the Faithful*. Notre Dame, Ind: Ave Maria Press, 1986.

Moltmann-Wendel, Elisabeth. *The Women Around Jesus*. New York: Crossroad, 1982.

Moltmann-Wendel, Elisabeth. *A Land Flowing with Milk and Honey: Perspectives on Feminist Theology*. New York: Crossroad, 1988.

Murphy, Cullen. "Women and the Bible." *The Atlantic Monthly* (August 1993): 39–45, 48, 50–53, 55, 58, 60, 62–64.

Nunnally-Cox, Janice [J. Ellen Nunnally]. *Foremothers: Women of the Bible*. San Francisco: Harper & Row, 1981.

Ostling, Richard N. "Handmaid or Feminist?" *Time* 138, no. 26 (cover story, "The Search for Mary," 30 December 1991): 62–66.

Russell, Letty M., ed. *Feminist Interpretation of the Bible*. Philadelphia: Westminster, 1985.

Sabua, Rachel. "The Hidden Hand of God [in Esther]." *Bible Review* 8, no. 1 (February 1992): 31–33.

Schaberg, Jane. *The Illegitimacy of Jesus: A Feminist Theological Interpretation of the Infancy Narratives*. New York: Crossroad, 1990.

Schneiders, Sandra M. "God is More Than Two Men and a Bird." *U.S. Catholic* (May 1990): 20–27.

Schneiders, Sandra M. *Women and the Word: The Gender of God in the New Testament and the Spirituality of Women*. New York: Paulist Press, 1986.

Schüssler Fiorenza, Elisabeth. *In Memory of Her: A Feminist Theological Reconstruction of Christian Origins*. New York: Crossroad, 1983.

Schüssler Fiorenza, Elisabeth. "Lk 13:10–17: Interpretation for Liberation and Transformation." *Theology Digest* 36, 4 (Winter 1989): 303–19.

Schüssler Fiorenza, Elisabeth, ed., with Shelly Matthews. *Searching the Scriptures: A Feminist Introduction*. New York: Crossroad, 1993.

Sleevi, Mary Lou. *Women of the Word*. Notre Dame, Ind: Ave Maria Press, 1989.

Stanton, Elizabeth Cady. *The Woman's Bible*. New York: Arno Press, 1972. [Originally, New York: European Publishing Company, Part I, 1895; Part II, 1898.]

Swidler, Leonard. *Biblical Affirmations of Woman*. Philadelphia: Westminster Press, 1979.

Tetlow, Elizabeth M. *Women and Ministry in the New Testament*. New York: Paulist Press, 1980.

Thurston, Bonnie Bowman. *The Widows: A Women's Ministry in the Early Church*. Minneapolis: Fortress Press, 1989.

Trible, Phyllis. "Bringing Miriam out of the Shadows." *Bible Review* 5 (February 1989), 14–25, 34.

Trible, Phyllis. *God and the Rhetoric of Sexuality*. Philadelphia: Fortress Press, 1978.

Trible, Phyllis. *Texts of Terror*. Philadelphia: Fortress Press, 1978.

Wahlberg, Rachel Conrad. *Jesus According to a Woman*. Rev. ed. New York: Paulist Press, 1986.

Warner, Marina. *Alone of All Her Sex: The Myth and the Cult of the Virgin Mary*. New York: Alfred A. Knopf, 1976.

Weems, Renita J. *Just a Sister Away: A Womanist Vision of Women's Relationships in the Bible*. San Diego: LuraMedia, 1988.

Winter, Miriam Therese. *WomanWisdom: A Feminist Lectionary and Psalter. Women of the Hebrew Scriptures*, Part One. New York: Crossroad, 1991.

Winter, Miriam Therese. *WomanWord: A Feminist Lectionary and Psalter*. New York: Crossroad, 1990.

Wire, Antoinette Clark. *The Corinthian Women Prophets: A Reconstruction Through Paul's Rhetoric*. Minneapolis: Fortress press, 1990.

Yamasaki, April. *Remember Lot's Wife and Other Unnamed Women of the Bible*. Elgin, Ill.: faithQuest, 1991.

Other Works Cited

Aburdene, Patricia, and John Naisbitt. *Megatrends for Women*. New York: Villard Books, 1992.

Alter, Robert. *The World of Biblical Literature*. BasicBooks, A Division of Harper Collins Publishers, 1992.

Anderson, Bonnie S., and Judith P. Zinsser. *A History of Their Own: Women in Europe from Prehistory to the Present*. 2 vols. New York: Harper & Row, 1988.

Brooten, Bernadette J. *Women Leaders in the Ancient Synagogue: Inscriptional Evidence and Background Issues*. Brown Judaic Studies 36. Chico, Calif.: Scholars Press, 1982.

Campbell, Joseph, with Bill Moyers. *The Power of Myth*. New York: Doubleday, 1988.

Castro, Janice. "Caution: Hazardous Work." *Time* (Fall 1990 Special Issue, "Women: The Road Ahead"), 79.

Crown, Alan D., "The Abisha Scroll—3,000 Years Old?" *Bible Review* 7, no. 5 (October 1991): 13–21, 39.

Countryman, L. William. *Dirt, Greed, and Sex: Sexual Ethics in the New Testament and Their Implications Today*. Minneapolis: Fortress Press, 1988.

"Data vastly understate rape, new report says." *The Sacramento Bee* (24 April 1992), A30.

Drury, John. *The Parables in the Gospels: History and Allegory*. New York: Crossroad, 1985.

Eisler, Riane. *The Chalice and the Blade*. HarperSanFrancisco, 1987.

Eskey, Kenneth. "Women's Paychecks Growing, but Men's Income Still Higher." *The Sacramento Union* (27 September 1990), A1, A11.

Fisher, Neal F. *The Parables of Jesus: Glimpses of God's Reign*. New York: Crossroad, 1990.

Friedman, Richard Elliott. *Who Wrote the Bible?* New York: Summit Books, 1987.

Gadon, Elinor W. *The Once and Future Goddess: A Symbol for Our Times*. San Francisco: Harper & Row, 1989.

Gelman, David, and others. "The Mind of the Rapist." *Newsweek*, 23 July 1990, 50.

Gibbs, Nancy. "When Is It Rape?" *Time*, 3 June 1991, 48–54.

Gimbutas, Marija. *The Civilization of the Goddess*, ed. Joan Marler. HarperSanFrancisco, 1991.

Great People of the Bible and How They Lived. New York: Reader's Digest Association, Inc., 1974.

Greeley, Andrew M. *Myths of Religion*. New York: Warner Books, 1989.

Greeley, Andrew M., and Jacob Neusner. *The Bible and Us: A Priest and a Rabbi Read Scripture Together*. New York: Warner Books, 1990.

Gundry, Patricia. *Neither Slave Nor Free*. San Francisco: Harper & Row, 1987.

Harkness, Georgia. *Women in Church and Society: A Historical and Theological Inquiry*. Nashville, Tenn.: Abingdon Press, 1972.

LaCugna, Catherine Mowry. "Catholic Women as Ministers and Theologians." *America* 167, no. 10, (10 October 1992): 238–48.

Lefebure, Leo. *Life Transformed*. Chicago: ACTA Publications, 1989.

Matthews, Victor H. and Don C. Benjamin. *Social World of Ancient Israel 1250–587 BCE*. Peabody, Mass.: Hendrickson Publishers, 1993.

Pummer, Reinhard, "The Samaritans—A Jewish Offshoot or a Pagan Cult?" *Bible Review* 7, no. 5 (October 1991): 22–29, 40.

Salholz, Eloise, and others. "Women Under Assault." *Newsweek*, 16 July 1990, 23–24.

Schneiders, Sandra M. *The Revelatory Text: Interpreting the New Testament as Sacred Scripture*. HarperSan Francisco, 1991.

Shanks, Hershel, ed. *Understanding the Dead Sea Scrolls*. New York: Random House, 1992.

Smith, Joan. *Misogynies: Reflections on Myth and Malice*. New York: Fawcett Columbine, 1989.

Smolowe, Jill. "What the Doctor Should Do." *Time*, 29 June 1992, 57.

Stone, Merlin. *When God Was a Woman*. New York: Dorset Press, 1976.

Telushkin, Joseph. *Jewish Literacy: The Most Important Things to Know About the Jewish Religion, Its People, and Its History*. New York: William Morrow and Company, Inc., 1991.

Weaver, Mary Jo. *New Catholic Women: A Contemporary Challenge to Traditional Religious Authority*. San Francisco: Harper & Row, Publishers, 1985.

Woodward, Kenneth. "How to Read Paul, 2,000 Years Later." *Newsweek*, 29 February 1988, 65.

Index